The Translation of Children's Literature

TOPICS IN TRANSLATION
Series Editors: Susan Bassnett, *University of Warwick, UK*
Edwin Gentzler, *University of Massachusetts, Amherst, USA*
Editor for Translation in the Commercial Environment:
Geoffrey Samuelsson-Brown, University of Surrey, UK

For more details of these or any other of our publications, please contact:
Multilingual Matters, Frankfurt Lodge, Clevedon Hall,
Victoria Road, Clevedon, BS21 7HH, England
http://www.multilingual-matters.com

TOPICS IN TRANSLATION 31
Series Editors: Susan Bassnett, *University of Warwick* and
Edwin Gentzler, *University of Massachusetts, Amherst*

The Translation of Children's Literature
A Reader

Edited by
Gillian Lathey

MULTILINGUAL MATTERS LTD
Clevedon • Buffalo • Toronto

Library of Congress Cataloging in Publication Data
The Translation of Children' s Literature: A Reader/Edited by Gillian Lathey.
Topics in Translation: 31
Includes bibliographical references and index.
1. Children' s literature–Translations–History and criticism. 2. Intercultural
communication. I. Lathey, Gillian. II. Series.
PN1009.5.T75T73 2006
809' .89282–dc22   2006010924

British Library Cataloguing in Publication Data
A catalogue entry for this book is available from the British Library.

ISBN 1-85359-906-9/ EAN 978-1-85359-906-4 (hbk)
ISBN 1-85359-905-0/ EAN 978-1-85359-905-7 (pbk)

Multilingual Matters Ltd
UK: Frankfurt Lodge, Clevedon Hall, Victoria Road, Clevedon BS21 7HH.
USA: UTP, 2250 Military Road, Tonawanda, NY 14150, USA.
Canada: UTP, 5201 Dufferin Street, North York, Ontario M3H 5T8, Canada.

Typeset by Wordworks Ltd.
Printed and bound in Great Britain by the Cromwell Press Ltd.

Contents

Acknowledgements

Anthea Bell (1987) Translator's notebook: Delicate matters. *Signal* 49, 17–26. Reprinted by permission of the author and the publisher, Nancy Chambers.

David Blamires (1989) The early reception of the Grimms' *Kinder- und Hausmärchen* in England. *Bulletin John Rylands Library* 3, 63–77. Reprinted by permission of the author and the John Rylands Library.

Mieke Desmet (2001) Intertextuality/intervisuality in translation: The Jolly Postman's intercultural journey from Britain to the Netherlands. *Children's Literature in Education* 32 (1), 31–42. Reprinted by permission of the author and Kluwer Academic/Plenum Publishers.

Cathy Hirano (1999) Eight ways to say you: The challenges of translation. *The Horn Book Magazine* 75 (1), 34–41. Reprinted by permission of the author and *The Horn Book Magazine*, Inc, Boston, MA (www.hbook.com).

Nancy K. Jentsch (2002) Harry Potter and the Tower of Babel: Translating the magic. In L. Whited (ed.) *The Ivory Tower and Harry Potter* (pp. 285–301). Missouri: University of Missouri Press. Reprinted by permission of the author and publisher.

Gillian Lathey (2003) Time, narrative intimacy and the child: Implications of tense switching in the translation of picture books into English. *Meta* 48 (1/2), 233–240. Reprinted by permission of the author and publisher.

Marisa Fernández López (2000) Translation studies in contemporary children's literature: A comparison of intercultural ideological factors. *Children's Literature Association Quarterly* 25 (1), 29–37. Reprinted by permission of the author and the Children's Literature Association.

Eithne O'Connell (1999) Translating for children. In G. Anderman and M. Rogers (eds) *Word, Text, Translation* (pp. 208–216). Clevedon: Multilingual Matters. Reprinted by permission of the author and the publisher.

Riitta Oittinen (1995) The verbal and the visual: On the carnivalism and dialogics of translating for children. *Compar(a)ison* 2, 49–65. Reprinted by permission of the author and the editors of *Compar(a)ison*.

Emer O'Sullivan (2003) Narratology meets translation studies, or The voice of the translator in children's literature. *Meta* 48 (1–2), 197–207. Reprinted by permission of the author and the publisher.

Emer O'Sullivan (1998) Translating pictures. *Signal* 90, 167–175. Reprinted by permission of the author and the publisher, Nancy Chambers. This piece was originally presented as a conference paper at the European Children's Literature symposium in Stadtschlaining, Austria, in May 1998. It was subsequently published as 'Translating pictures: The interaction of pictures and words in the translation of picture books' in P. Cotton (ed.) *European Children's Literature II* (pp. 109–120). Kingston University.

Emer O'Sullivan (1992) Does Pinocchio have an Italian passport? What is specifically national and what is international about classics of children's literature. *The World of Children in Children's Books – Children's Books in the World of Children* IBBY 23rd World Congress (pp. 79–99). Munich: Arbeitskreis für Jugendliteratur. Reprinted by permission of the author and the publisher.

Tiina Puurtinen (1994) Translating children's literature: Theoretical approaches and emprical studies. In C. Robyns (ed.) *Translation and the (Re) production of Culture* (pp. 273–283) Leuven: The CERA Chair for Translation, Communication and Cultures. Reprinted by permission of the author.

Karen Seago (1995) Nursery Politics: *Sleeping Beauty*, or the acculturation of a tale. *New Comparison* 20, 14–29. Reprinted by permission of the author and the publisher.

Zohar Shavit (1986) Translation of children's literature. *Poetics of Children's Literature* (Chapter 5: pp. 111–130). Athens: University of Georgia Press. Reprinted by permission of the author.

J.D. S tahl (1996) Mark Twain's 'Slovenly Peter' in the context of Twain and German culture. *The Lion and the Unicorn* 20 (2), 166–180. © The Johns Hopkins University Press. Reprinted by permission of the author and The Johns Hopkins University Press.

Birgit Stolt (1978) How Emil becomes Michel: On the translation of children's books. In G. Klingberg (ed.) *Children's Books in Translation* (pp. 130–146). Stockholm: Almqvist and Wiksell. Reprinted by permission of the author.

With thanks to Mieke Desmet, who first alerted me to the existence of two of the articles reprinted in this Reader.

Introduction

Critical interest in the translation of children's literature has developed at
an accelerating pace over the last 30 years. The third symposium of the
International Research Society for Children's Literature (IRSCL) in 1976
represented a turning point: it was the first, and for many years the only,
children's literature conference devoted to translation and the international exchange of children's books. At a time when the study of children's
literature – whether national or international – was only just beginning to
gain academic credibility, Austrian scholar Richard Bamberger (1978: 19)
claimed at the symposium that the role of translation had 'hardly been
touched upon ... in spite of the fact that translations, as a rule, are of even
greater importance in children's than in adult literature'. Bamberger
supported his comment on the primacy of translations for children by
referring to the apparent universality of 'classics' such as Grimms' tales,
Pinocchio, Pippi Longstocking, or *Alice in Wonderland*. Moreover, he argued,
children are not interested in a book *because* it is a translation, as may be the
case for adults, but in the power of narratives as 'adventure story, fantasies
and so on, just as if the books were originally written in their own language'
(Bamberger, 1978: 19). Yet Bamberger's list of international classics demonstrates the dominance of north European texts that has subsequently been
interrogated by O'Sullivan (2005). His second point about children's
unawareness of the foreign is also open to question, since there are times
when it is those very qualities of the unfamiliar that attract and captivate
young readers. Nonetheless, Bamberger's emphasis on differences between
the reception of translations for adults and children provided a long
overdue impetus for further research.

It has taken even longer for scholars in the field of Translation Studies to
examine the particular challenges of translating for children. Birgit Stolt
commented at the 1976 IRSCL symposium that 'In the theoretical works on
the subject [translation] one hardly finds anything relevant on this
subject.'(Stolt, 1978: 133; see Part 2 of this Reader for the full text of Stolt's
article). And, as recently as 1999, Eithne O'Connell expressed surprise that
within Translation Studies 'this area [the translation of children's litera-
ture] remains largely ignored by theorists, publishers and academic institutions' (1999: 208; see O'Connell, Part 1).

Yet the first signs of an interest in the broader issues of cross-cultural influence and the international dissemination of children's literature had emerged much earlier, from within the discipline of Comparative Literature – a branch of literary study defined by Susan Bassnett as 'concerned with patterns of connection in literatures across both time and space' (Bassnett, 1993: 1). Paul Hazard, the French comparatist, published in *Les Livres, les enfants et les hommes* (1932) his manifesto for a world republic of children's literature, proposing a romantic vision of the development of international understanding and the exchange of aesthetic appreciation through children's books. It was in the wake of Hazard's pioneering work that Bamberger devoted his attention in the 1960s and 70s to cross-cultural influences in children's literature. Bamberger suggested a number of lines of enquiry – amongst them the investigation of the international impact and transfer to the children's canon of Defoe's *Robinson Crusoe* or the travels of Collodi's *Pinocchio* – that have since been vigorously pursued (see Zohar Shavit in Part 1 and Emer O'Sullivan in Part 4 of this Reader). Bamberger's speech at the IRSCL symposium echoed Hazard's position by claiming that: 'we can now rightly speak of a genuine world literature for children that can do much to further international understanding. Children all over the world are now growing up enjoying the same pleasures in reading, and cherishing similar ideals, aims and hopes' (Bamberger, 1978: 21).

One of the first academics to move beyond general, idealistic statements and pay serious attention to the linguistic processes, ideology and economics of translating children's books was Göte Klingberg, the Swedish co-founder of the IRSCL and co-editor with Mary Ørvig of the proceedings of its third symposium, *Children's Books in Translation* (Klingberg & Ørvig, 1978). Klingberg's own contribution to that volume listed a number of potential avenues for research into the translation of children's books, from empirical statistical studies of translation streams to economic and technical factors, and from the selection of books for translation to the reception and influence of translations. Ten years after the symposium, Klingberg published the first results of an investigation into the adaptation of children's books to meet the norms and customs of the target culture in *Children's Fiction in the Hands of the Translators* (1986). This volume and the IRSCL proceedings were for a number of years the only two substantial publications on translation for children.

As scholars and critics have come to appreciate children's literature as an aesthetically and ideologically dynamic medium, the study of translation has come into its own. When viewed through the finely ground lens of the act of translation, the transposition of a children's text from one language and culture to another reflects differing expectations and interpretations of childhood. In the last 20 years, scholars across the world – Reinbert Tabbert (for an overview of critical studies on translation for children see Tabbert (2002)) and Emer O'Sullivan in Germany, Jean Perrot in France, Marisa Fernández López in Spain and Riitta Oittinen in Finland – have been working towards an understanding of the international progress and influence of children's texts through the medium of translation.

Children's literature journals, too, have addressed this dimension, from the internationalism that is the natural subject of *Bookbird, A Journal of International Children's Literature*, published by the International Board of Books for Young People, to special issues of children's literature journals on cross-cultural and translation issues. The *Lion and Unicorn* of December 1996, for example, was dedicated to *Struwwelpeter and Classical Children's Literature* (see J.D. Stahl's article on Mark Twain's translation of *Struwwelpeter* in Part 5 of this volume), with subsequent issues dedicated to Irish (September 1997), French (January 1998), and Italian (April 2002) children's literatures. Nancy Chambers, editor of the irreplaceable *Signal: Approaches to Children's Books*, made a point during the journal's 33 year lifespan of including articles on translation and translators, two of which are reprinted here. And, as a mark of the growing interest in children's literature amongst comparatists and translation scholars, entire issues of comparative literature and translation journals have been devoted to children's literature in the last ten years (*New Comparison*, 1995, no. 20; *Meta*, 2003 nos 1 and 2). Finally, successful international conferences on translation for children too place recently: Traducción y Literatura Infantil at the University of Las Palmas in March 2002, with a follow-up conference in 2005, and Writing through the Looking-Glass: International Conference on the Translation of Children's Literature' at VLEKHO in Brussels in March 2004.

The new millennium marked a second turning point in the field, with the publication of two outstanding contributions to knowledge and debates on the translation of children's books. In *Kinderliterarische Komparatistik* (O'Sullivan, 2000; English translation, *Comparative Children's Literature*, 2005), Emer O'Sullivan applies the insights of a comparatist to books written for the young. In addition to a scholarly overview of the field, she offers a number of case histories that inspire a fresh look at the international history of children's literature. By questioning Zohar Shavit's view that the development of all children's literatures follows a similar trajectory 'from instruction to delight', O'Sullivan suggests that research into the diversity of children's literatures, particularly non-European literature, will help to redress the balance in the field of children's literature at an international level. Riitta Oittinen pursues an entirely different line of enquiry in *Translating for Children* (2000). Oittinen, herself a translator, author and illustrator of children's books, turns to the child reader, viewer and listener to investigate children's potential responses to translated texts, and to argue in favour of a child-centred approach to translation. Both O'Sullivan and Oittinen have made fruitful links to other disciplines and areas of research: O'Sullivan applies models of narrative communication to the process of translating for children (see Part 2 of this volume), and Oittinen draws on the work of Mikhail Bakhtin in identifying the dialogic nature of translation (see Oittinen in Part 2).

The publication of this Reader, then, is timely. Its purpose is to bring together, and make readily available to students and scholars, English-language journal articles and chapters from published books that reflect the development and range of writing on the translation and international exchange of children's books over the last 30 years. Although the Reader is, like its editor, based in the field of Children's Literature rather than Translation Studies, all contributors draw on relevant aspects of translation theory when identifying issues specific to the translation of children's literature. Whatever their starting point, writers challenge the still commonly held perception that the internationalism of children's literature is unproblematic, and that figures such as Pinocchio, Alice and Babar have crossed national and linguistic boundaries with ease. They alert readers to the halting and uneven travels of children's texts, to the mediation that takes place during translation, to the effects of differing views of childhood across history and across the globe, and, not least, to the significance of developmental factors. Translating a nonsense rhyme for a three-year old is, after all, an utterly different task from working on a text for an adolescent reader.

The articles and chapters reprinted in this Reader demonstrate time and again that translating for children differs from translating for adults in two fundamental respects. Firstly, there is the social position of children and the resulting status of literature written for them, and, secondly, the developmental aspects of childhood that determine the unique qualities of successful writing for children and that make translating for them an imaginative, challenging and frequently underestimated task. The following introduction to both these dimensions of translating for children offers a context for the articles and chapters to follow.

Adult Perceptions of the Child Reader and the Status of Children's Literature

An unequal relationship

One inescapable factor that governs the process of writing and translating for children is the unequal relationship between the adult writer or translator and the child audience. It is adults who decide the very extent and boundaries of childhood. Currently in the UK, for example, the official end of childhood is reached at the age of 18 rather than 21 as was the case some years ago, and what is regarded as the permissible age for purchasing cigarettes, alcohol or engaging in sexual activity has changed a number of times in the latter half of the 20th century. Childhood, since it was first designated as a discrete phase of life, has always been a flexible period that is adjusted to meet economic necessity. In the global market of the early 21st century, concepts of childhood depend increasingly on the initiatives of the fashion, games and toy industries, and marketing strategies divide childhood into phases: the 'pre-schooler', the 'pre-teen', the 'adolescent', the 'young adult' and so on.

Adults, too, dictate what children read, in that they are the writers, publishers and arbiters of children's reading matter. Jacqueline Rose (1994) investigated this paradox from a psychoanalytic perspective by taking Peter Pan as a case study of what she calls 'the impossibility of children's fiction'. Rose argues that adult self-interest is at stake in writing for children, whether as part of a cathartic revisiting of childhood concerns or because the adult has retained certain childhood qualities. Yet even the adult writers who come closest to understanding the desires of childhood can never fully adopt a child's perspective, and this fundamental adult–child difference frequently expresses itself in the duality of the narrator's mode of address to the child reader. Translators have to take into account an adult presence within the text in a number of forms, from the spectre of the controlling adult presence looking over the child's shoulder, to a playful irony intended for the adult reading aloud to a child.

Children's authors, whatever their motivation, do on the whole make a clear decision to write for the young, whereas translators may take a different stance towards the 'asymmetry' (O'Sullivan, 2000) of the adult–child relationship. Translators for children range from the professional translator who occasionally takes on a commission to translate a children's book, to the experienced children's writer who turns his or her hand to translation. Inevitably, therefore, there is a variation in the translator's understanding of the child reader. In the work of translators who are neither children's writers nor steeped in the world of childhood, there may be a distinct uneasiness at the prospect of translating for children.

Ann Lawson Lucas, for example, treads an equivocal line in the preface to her retranslation into English of Collodi's *Pinocchio*, stating that her version is 'not specifically or exclusively for children' (Collodi, 1996: 1). Lawson Lucas's primary concern was to produce a scholarly edition of a classic text, favouring the adult in the form of the scholar and thereby losing some of

Collodi's facility as a storyteller. On the other hand, the translator of the first German edition of *Winnie-the-Pooh*, E.L. Schiffer, diminishes the adult's enjoyment of reading the book aloud to children by removing witticisms and irony intended for adults (O'Sullivan, 1993). Both Lawson Lucas and Schiffer are well aware of the potential adult audience for these two children's texts; the one shifts address towards the academic adult reader (and appreciator of Collodi's social satire), whereas the other removes the implied adult reader inscribed within the source text. Yet neither translator has taken account of the *duality* that characterises much of the best writing for children, and that makes in the original texts in these two instances a literary virtue of the unequal relationship between adult and child.

Ideological differences: Didacticism and censorship

Ever since a separate literature for children emerged, reading matter for the young has been a vehicle for educational, religious and moral instruction and the teaching of literacy. Children's literature, including translated texts, tells us whether children are regarded as innocent or sinful in any given historical period or location, what rights or duties they have, and how they are socially or intellectually educated. Translators and publishers have in the past eagerly seized upon morally instructive texts in other languages. In line with the 'civilising' approach to education of the late 18th century Mary Wollstonecraft (1989, first published 1790), for example, applauded the rationality and sober morality of Christian Gotthilf Salzmann's *Elements of Morality for the Use of Children* in the 'Advertisement' to her translation from the German. In this instance, as in many others throughout the history of British children's literature, the choice of text for translation is indicative of the instrumental role of the translator in disseminating social and cultural trends with respect to childhood.

Over 100 years later, another translator's preface offers a revealing glimpse of the distance between adult and child in the early 20th century. Emma Stelter Hopkins, translator of Johanna Spyri's *Homeless* into English in 1912, expresses in tight-lipped fashion in her preface the hope that Spyri's stories will teach children to appreciate home comforts 'to which they grow so accustomed as often to take them for granted, with little evidence of gratitude' (Spyri, 1912: iii). Stelter Hopkins' stern words smack of the righteous and punitive attitudes in child-rearing practices of the late Victorian and Edwardian eras in the UK.

Differing cultural expectations of child readers give rise to censorship in the process of translation, particularly in the representation of violence and the scatological references in which children take such delight. One of the better-known omissions is that of the toe and heel mutilation and the pecking out of the sisters' eyes in the Grimm Brothers' version of Cinderella, *Aschenputtel*, in many English-language versions for children (see David Blamires' article on the translation of Grimms' Tales in Part 5). In a more recent and perhaps surprising example, Birgit Stolt's account (in Part 2) of the censorship of a story by Astrid Lindgren for the American market – the replacement of a dung heap with a pile of leaves – is as telling as it is amusing.

Ideological differences between the contexts from which national children's literatures emerge, of which didacticism and censorship are just two aspects, are the subject of a number of articles in this Reader. In Part 1, Marisa Fernández Lopez considers the translation of children's literature as social history in her study of the Spanish translation of Richmal Crompton's 'William' stories and the work of Enid Blyton, while Emer O'Sullivan examines the differing literary and educational norms governing Pinocchio's Italian- and German-language incarnations in Part 4.

Cultural context adaptation

A developmental issue that concerns the translator of children's texts is the inevitable limitation to the young reader's world knowledge. Young readers cannot be expected to have acquired the breadth of understanding of other cultures, languages and geographies that are taken for granted in an adult readership. Since translators' footnotes are an unsatisfactory solution to this problem, localisation or 'domestication' (Venuti, 2000) is a frequently used but contentious tactic in children's texts. Göte Klingberg's phrase 'cultural context adaptation' has been adopted as an umbrella term for a variety of strategies for moving an original text towards the child reader in the target culture. Adaptation rests on assumptions that young readers will find it difficult to assimilate foreign names, coinage, foodstuffs or locations, and that they may reject a text reflecting a culture that is unfamiliar.

Göte Klingberg recommends that adaptation should be restricted to details and the source text manipulated as little as possible (Klingberg, 1986: 17). Award-winning English translator Anthea Bell, however, has advocated greater flexibility. In some instances, she argues, an 'impenetrable-looking set of foreign names' on the first pages of a book might alienate young readers, so that a translator has to 'gauge the precise degree of foreignness, and how far it is acceptable and can be preserved' (Bell, 1985: 7). There is certainly good reason to translate names if they have a meaning relevant to the story – Pippi Långstrump to Pippi Longstocking, for example – but children can and do take delight in the sound and shape of unfamiliar names. Once a narrative engages their interest, young readers will persevere with names and localities that are well beyond their ken in myths, legends and fantasy fiction written in their native languages, let alone in translations, and they will certainly never be intrigued and attracted by difference if it is kept from them.

One form of contextual adaptation that is particularly significant for child readers is that of dialect or slang, since children's texts include a high proportion of dialogue. The didactic impulse has in the past dictated, for example, that the stylized Berlin street slang of Erich Kästner's gang of children in *Emil and the Detectives* should be transposed to the language of the English boarding school story of the period, peppered with adjectives such as 'awfully' 'frightfully' and 'tophole' (translations into English by Margaret Goldsmith in 1931 and Eileen Hall in 1959). Here is clear evidence for Zohar Shavit's contention that there is a tendency for the translation of children's texts to follow existing models in the target culture (see Shavit, Part 1). But changes to Kästner's vernacular also reflect a concern that children should encounter only standard English in their reading matter. Despite the more natural representation of children's spoken language in recent children's literature, this concern that children's spoken language may in some way be contaminated by dialect or the vernacular still lingers, for example, in the change from non-standard English to standard French and German in translations of *Harry Potter and the Philosopher's Stone* (see Nancy Jentsch's article in Part 4).

The status of children's literature and of its translators

Finally, Zohar Shavit's work on polysystem theory locates translation practices for a child audience within a model of literary hierarchies. Translators have historically treated children's texts in cavalier fashion, and have made alterations that are far less likely to occur in translations for adults. Shavit indicates ways in which the low status of children's literature, indeed its ranking in many countries alongside popular literature, has led to radical alteration and abridgment, citing examples of classic texts that have migrated from the adult to the children's canon such as *Gulliver's Travels* and *Robinson Crusoe* (see Part 1). It is for similar reasons that translation for children is not a prestigious occupation and financial rewards are frequently even lower than for translating adult literature.

There are, however, exceptions to this pattern. During an era when the child was central to the socialist enterprise, translators for children in the former German Democratic Republic enjoyed favourable conditions in comparison with their colleagues in the West. Gaby Thomson-Wohlgemuth (2003) has, in the course of painstaking work in German archives and interviews with translators, uncovered evidence of the high social status of children's translators and children's literature in the period between the founding of the GDR and its demise in 1989. This is indeed a rare occurrence, but such privilege can be a poisoned chalice: Thomson-Wohlgemuth has also demonstrated the ideologically driven selection of texts and the censorship that constrained the work of translators.

Childhood and the 'Childness' of Children's Texts

In addition to questions of status, didacticism and adult considerations of what is good for the child, it is essential for a translator of children's literature to keep in mind the intrinsic qualities of successful writing for children and of childhood reading. One of the most demanding, and at the same time inspiring, aspects of translating for children is the potential for a creativity that characterises what Peter Hollindale (1997: 46) has called the 'childness' of children's texts: 'the quality of being a child – dynamic, imaginative, experimental, interactive and unstable'. This numinous quality of childhood reading originates in a writer's understanding of the freshness of language to the child's eye and ear, of the child's affective concerns and of the linguistic and dramatic play that are inherent in early childhood.

Translators for children, if they are not already children's writers themselves, have to make a transition to the child's mindset through the medium of the original writer's style. The best writing for children has a pregnant simplicity, a condensation of meaning that is extremely difficult to achieve and is caught in Jill Paton Walsh's analogy with a soap bubble, cited by Hollindale (1997: 40-41): 'all you can see is a surface – a lovely rainbow thing to attract the youngest onlooker – but the whole is shaped and sustained by the pressure of adult emotion'. Astrid Lindgren's prose in her two classic fairy tale fantasy novels *Mio min Mio* (*Mio my Mio*) and *Bröderna Lejonhjärta* (*The Brothers Lionheart*) has a breathless and emotionally intense quality that addresses a child's deepest concerns in the manner that Paton Walsh describes. Such a style presents a challenge to the translator, especially when, as so often in Lindgren's work, language and word play are essential to the narrative and constitute the 'inner rhythm' that Riitta Oittinen describes in Part 2. This is where translating prose for the child up to the age of twelve or thereabouts diverges most markedly from translation for adults, with two aspects (translating sound and translating the visual) demanding particular attention.

Translating sound

In writing for children, especially for younger children, authors like Lindgren pay attention to sound and rhythm in a manner that aligns their prose with poetry. Much writing for the young child is read aloud; indeed, Cay Dollerup (2003: 82) has argued that translating for reading aloud 'is an art requiring great competence of translators'. Quite apart from the necessity of reading aloud to the youngest children who cannot yet read stories for themselves, the aural texture of a translation is of paramount importance to a child still engaged in discovering the power of language. Young children are eager learners of whatever languages surround them; they learn naturally through practice, play and the repetition and encouragement of their fluent elders. Ruth Weir's (1962) classic account of her son Anthony's pre-sleep monologues, *Language in the Crib*, demonstrates the sheer joy of experimentation with sound patterns as a two-and-a-half-year-old child rehearses the phonology of his native language. Repetition, rhyme, onomatopoeia, wordplay and nonsense are all common features of children's texts and require a linguistic creativity that is a challenge to any translator.

Take, for instance, the representation of animal noises that is a common feature of children's rhymes and stories. As long ago as 1659 Charles Hoole grappled with this conundrum in his translation of the *Orbis Sensualium Pictus* by Czech philosopher and educationalist Johannes Amos Comenius. This text, originally published in German and Latin, includes a section designed to teach the sounds of letters of the alphabet; captions in Latin and (in Hoole's translation) in English accompany pictures of animals and birds. Hoole renders the alliteration and onomatopoeia as best he can, with some curiosities, for example the letter 'g': 'Anser gingrit, ga ga. The goose gagleth'. Translators of texts for young children across the world regularly transpose the barks, squeals, roars and neighs of a varied menagerie into the conventional equivalents of their own tongue.

An appreciation of nonsense also stems from children's enjoyment of the aural qualities of language. Children's authors and poets, from the anonymous collective composers of nursery rhymes to Edward Lear, Lewis Carroll and Christian Morgenstern, have recognized the sounds that appeal to the young. When translating literary effects dependent on aural qualities, translators have to switch from one phonological system to another, as though transposing a piece of music to a different key. Anthea Bell's translation of Christian Morgenstern's sound poem *Das grosse Lallula* ensures that at least some of the sounds uttered in English will replicate the aural quality of the German original. In the third line of the poem Bell renders the German '*Bifzi, bafzi*' as 'Biftsi, baftsi' (Morgenstern, 1995), thereby reproducing in English the 'ts' sound of the German 'z'. Bell does not always employ this strategy; indeed, the very freedom of translating pure sound without a semantic layer enables her to create a poem that replicates Morgenstern's, but is not identical with it. Wordplay that includes a semantic element taxes a translator's ingenuity in a different manner, demanding what translator Anthea Bell has called a 'crossword mentality'. Bell has given an account of translating puns and wordplay in the Astérix series from French into English in *Signal* (Bell, 1980), and in Part 4 of this Reader, Nancy K. Jentsch exposes some of the lost allusions in the translation of proper names in the Harry Potter books.

Translating the visual

The visual dimension to children's texts that is uncommon in adult fiction has been the subject of extensive critical attention (Nodelman, 1988; Lewis, 2001; Nikolajeva & Scott, 2001). Children's literature has been a visual medium from its inception, initially because younger children could not be expected to read printed text. Images play an essential role in the narrative enactment that takes place when an adult shares a picture book with a young child, or when line drawing interacts with written text in longer stories. Developments from the illustrated book to the modern picture book have meant that, to use Anthea Bell's words, translators of children's books frequently operate in a 'no-man's land' between source text, target text and image. Comments in this introduction will remain brief, since Part 3 of this Reader is devoted in its entirety to this essential aspect of the art of translating for children. Articles address the significance for the translator of the counterpoint between picture and text; the picture book as a catalyst for dramatic play, and questions of intertextuality and intervisuality.

These, then, are the stylistic, literary, developmental and ideological factors that distinguish translating for children from translating for adults, and have generated the discussion, speculation and research in these pages.

The Future

Now that research into and critical discussion of the translation of children's literature is well established, it is possible to look ahead to the potential impact on children's literature studies of more recent trends in Translation Studies and translation practice. Lawrence Venuti's recommendation that the reader should always be made aware that s/he is reading a translation (Venuti, 2000) is unlikely to be adopted by translators for children. His argument that easy readability renders the translator invisible and is exploitative in 'putting the foreign to domestic uses' (Venuti, 2000: 341) is a persuasive one in a number of historical instances, but it does not, of course, take account of the young inexperienced reader. This is an area where a greater emphasis on empirical research into reader response, into just how much 'foreignness' young readers can and do tolerate, would inform current speculation.

As regards the process of translation, research in the 1990s on translators' 'think-aloud protocols' (Venuti, 2000), and the computer analysis of large corpora of translated texts (Olohan, 2004), both have potential for investigating children's literature. It may in the future be possible to improve our understanding of the extent to which the child audience determines a translator's thought processes, and to pinpoint through large-scale corpus analysis cultural trends as well as linguistic patterns that occur in existing translations for the young reader. If either route raises awareness of the general underestimation of the child reader and of the range of skills and understanding required to translate for children, that can only be of benefit to the young and to the translating profession. Interviews with translators and historical research into translation strategies for a child audience, too, would not only reveal evidence of changing practices, but also of the nature and origins of the cross-cultural influences and exchanges that are a relatively neglected aspect of children's literature research.

The Reader: Organisation

In this general Reader on translation for children, five separate sections incorporate the variety of writing on the subject, beginning in Part 1 with an introduction to some of the theoretical approaches of the past 30 years. Articles in Part 2 address narrative communication between the translator and the child reader, both the real reader and the child implied in the source and target language texts. Following Part 3 on translating the visual element of children's books, Part 4 draws readers' attention to the cross-cultural travels, influences and transformation of children's books from the earliest translation of Grimms' tales to the international success of Harry Potter. In the final part, three translators, Anthea Bell, Mark Twain (in J.D Stahl's account) and Cathy Hirano, reveal the diversity and subtlety of the translator's purpose and art when addressing a children's text or a child audience.

As is always the case with such collections, the Reader will engage its audience as much by what had to be left out as by what is included. But if readers subsequently fill the gaps by pursuing the subject further, this publication will have served its purpose well.

Part 1

Translation for Children: Theoretical Approaches and Their Application

Translation Studies has its origins in the academic discipline of linguistics and, as far as the translation and comparison of literatures and international literary influence is concerned, that of Comparative Literature. Since its emergence as a discrete area of study in the mid-20th century, Translation Studies has oscillated between a linguistic approach to the analysis of the translation process, and an awareness of cultural and ideological factors that affect translation and the reception of translated texts. Jeremy Munday in *Introducing Translation Studies* (2001) and Lawrence Venuti in his *Translation Studies Reader* (2000) offer examples of this tension, and of the shift from prescriptive to descriptive approaches to translation in the 1980s. The earlier emphasis on 'equivalence' in the 1960s and 70s was one where 'translating is generally seen as a process of communicating the foreign text by establishing a relationship of identity or analogy with it' (Venuti, 2000: 121). In the 1980s, however, Gideon Toury (1980, 1985, 1995) began to advocate the study of translated texts and their position within the target literary system, adopting a descriptive rather than a prescriptive approach. Descriptive studies have subsequently developed in many directions, one of which is the 'cultural turn' in the work of Susan Bassnett and André Lefevere (1998). As indicated in the Introduction to this Reader, this trend in the 1970s and 80s towards description of the translated text in its socio-historical setting has proved to be particularly relevant to the study of translations for children.

Eithne O'Connell's overview of Translation Studies in relation to the translation of children's literature reflects these broad patterns of development. Writing for publication in 1999, she first addresses the essential question that taxes all who address the subject: the definition and parameters of children's literature. After lamenting the general critical neglect of the subject within the field of Translation Studies, O'Connell endorses the change of direction to a more descriptive approach that addresses the purposes and reception of the translated text for children in the target culture. She concludes with a plea for the inclusion of children's literature in translation courses, as well as a broadening of definitions to include not only the visual element in children's books, but also the audiovisual texts that are the subject of her publication *Minority Language Dubbing for Children: Screen Translation from German to Irish* (2003).

In her book *Poetics of Children's Literature* (1986), Zohar Shavit offers an explanation for the lack of attention paid to the translation of children's books by considering literature as a series of hierarchical systems and subsystems with two overarching categories: the canonical and non-canonical. In the chapter reprinted here, she argues that the peripheral position of children's literature within this polysystem has lead throughout the history of translated children's literature to the manipulation of original texts by both translators and editors. Taking as central case studies translations into Hebrew and the transition from the adult to the children's canon of texts such as Jonathan Swift's *Gulliver's Travels* and Daniel Defoe's *Robinson Crusoe,* Shavit demonstrates an affiliation to existing models within the target culture, as well as the effects of changing views of what is 'good for the child' and notions of 'comprehensibility' on translations of these 'classic' texts for children.

Marisa Fernández López examines a more recent interpretation of what is appropriate for a child audience in her discussion of intercultural ideological factors in the translation into Spanish of the work of Roald Dahl and Enid Blyton. Locating her analysis in a precise historical period, she illustrates the phenomenon of a delayed response in Spanish translations to the eradication of racist or sexist language in source texts during the 1970s and 80s. Fernández López regards this mismatch between 'purified' editions in the country of origin and a return to early versions for translation purposes as a seismograph of Spanish political and social history in the Franco and post-Franco eras. As a coda to this investigation, she sketches the radical influence of translations on Spanish children's literature post 1990.

In contrast to Shavit and López, Tiina Puurtinen (1994) adopts an empirical and linguistic approach to her study of two translations of *The Wizard of Oz* into Finnish. She sets out a methodology that rejects sociocultural issues as irrelevant to two translations that differ primarily in stylistic features, syntax, grammar and readability. Nonetheless, she evaluates a range of theoretical perspectives – including those of Klingberg and Shavit – in relation to her project. She acknowledges, for example, that both Reiss' emphasis on text types and Riitta Oittinen's concern for fluency, rhythm and read-aloud qualities are particularly relevant to a study that aims to gather evidence of children's responses to the written style of translated texts. Puurtinen's decision to examine in her research project the responses of both children and the adults who read texts aloud to them is a rare approach indeed, but one that could well become an exciting area for future development.

Eithne O'Connell

Translating for Children

... the translation, like the original, is written to delight as well as instruct.
Newmark, 1991: 44

Introduction

Children's literature has long been the site of tremendous translation activity and so it has come as something of a surprise to me to discover recently the extent to which this area remains largely ignored by theorists, publishers and academic institutions involved in translation research and training. I have also been struck by the fact that much of the recent material available in English on translating for children focuses on translations to and from lesser-used languages, in particular, Scandinavian languages or Hebrew.

It is now more than ten years since the Swedish educationalist, Göte Klingberg, listed in some detail five possible areas of research into the translation of children's books which he felt deserved urgent and detailed investigation. The potential areas for research activity he referred to were:

- statistical studies on which source languages yield translations in different target languages or countries;
- studies on economic and technical problems associated with the production of translations;
- studies on how books are selected for translation;
- studies of current translation practice and specific problems encountered by translations;
- and studies concerning the reception and influence of translations in the target language (TL). (Klingberg, 1986: 9)

Yet it is clear more than a decade later that many of these topics still have not been investigated thoroughly. This becomes easier to understand when one realises that the original subject matter, i.e. children's literature, is itself something of an undervalued or neglected area. According to Knowles and Malmkjaer (1996: ix) there is a 'curious discrepancy between the ubiquity and perceived importance of children's literature, and scholarly research in the field'. On the one hand, most parents and teachers must be aware of the importance of the genre and know that the development of good reading skills and a discerning attitude to one's reading materials are crucial for success in the education system and, indeed, in life in general. On the other hand, the public critical perception seems to be that works of children's literature, with a few notable and usually time-honoured exceptions, do not really deserve to be called 'literature' at all, and are generally somehow second-rate and functional rather than of high quality, creative and deserving of critical attention in the way that serious adult literature clearly is. Consequently, a frank acknowledgement of the fact that children's literature has long suffered from relative neglect is a useful starting point for any discussion of the general topic of books for young readers and, more specifically, the challenges posed by their translation.

What is Meant by 'Children's Literature'?

One of the primary difficulties in defining what is meant by 'children's literature' is the enormously inclusive scope and potentially vague nature of the semantic fields covered by the concepts referred to using the nouns 'children' and 'literature'. Some commentators such as Knowles and Malmkjaer (1996: 2) offer a very broad, pragmatic definition which seems to dodge the very difficult issues: 'For us children's literature is any narrative written or published for children and we include the "teen" novels aimed at the "young adult" or "late adolescent" reader.' The difficulty presented by the terms is addressed more frankly by Oittinen:

> There is little consensus on the definition of child, childhood and children's literature. The definition ... is always a question of point of view and situation: childhood can be considered a social or cultural issue; it can be seen from the child's or adult's angle ... I see children's literature as literature read silently by children and aloud to children. (Oittinen, 1993a:11)

As a result of the fact that the term 'children's literature' lacks specificity, many of those writing critically about books for children feel obliged to restrict their terms of reference in some way as above. Klingberg, quoted in Reiss (1982),[1] opts for this working definition:

> ... *Literatur für Kinder und Jugendliche (von hier an einfach Kinderliteratur genannt) wird definiert nicht als diejenigen Bücher, die Jugend gelesen hat (von Kindern und Jugendlichen wird und wurde eine umfangreiche Literatur gelesen), sondern als diejenige Literatur, die für oder hauptsächlich für Kinder und Jugendliche veröffentlicht worden ist.*
> (Literature for children and young people (referred to simply as children's literature from now on) is defined not as those books which they

read (children and young people read and always have read a wide range of literature), but as literature which has been published for – or mainly for – children and young people.) (Reiss, 1982: 7; editors' translation)

Adopting this as a functional definition, we can turn to address some of the most salient characteristics of children's literature as a genre. Firstly, books of this kind (while categorized by their primary target audience, i.e. young readers) in fact address two audiences: children, who want to be entertained and possibly informed, and adults, who have quite different tastes and literary expectations. The latter group, which comprises, in the first instance, editors and publishers, and, subsequently, parents, educators, academics and critics, is clearly much more influential than the former (Puurtinen, 1995: 19). It is adults, after all, who wield power and influence and it is they who decide what is written and, ultimately, more importantly, what is published, praised and purchased.

Secondly, while it is true that some works of children's literature appeal essentially only to the primary audience, many are what Shavit (1986: 63–91) calls ambivalent texts such as *Alice in Wonderland*, which can be read by a child on a conventional, literal level or interpreted by an adult on a more sophisticated or satirical level as well.

Thirdly, children's literature is written by people who do not belong to the target group:

> Children's books are written for a special readership but not, normally, by members of that readership; both the writing and quite often the buying of them are carried out by adult non-members on behalf of child members. (Briggs, 1989: 4)

An unfortunate consequence can be that writers of children's literature may be out of touch or not convincing, guilty at times of a measure of condescension in their work. Some adult writers do not know their primary audience sufficiently well and write as much to please the secondary audience of critics, parents and teachers as they do to please their young readers.

Finally, as Puurtinen (1995: 17) has pointed out, the genre is unusual because of:

> the numerous functions it fulfils and the diverse cultural constraints under which it operates. Children's literature belongs simultaneously to the literary system and the social-educational system, i.e. it is not only read for entertainment, recreation and literary experience but also used as a tool for education and socialisation. This dual character affects both

the writing and the translation of children's literature, whose relationships with literary, social and educational norms make it a fascinating
and fruitful field of research. (Puurtinen, 1995: 17)

Children's Literature and Prestige

Despite this important dual function, there are understandable reasons
for the tendency to regard children's literature as 'the Cinderella of literary
studies' (Shavit, 1992: 4) and these include the fact that children's literature
has tended to remain uncanonical and culturally marginalized. This may
be because books for young readers are written for a minority: the primary
target audience is children and they and their literature, like women and
women's literature, are treated in many cultural systems as, at worst,
peripheral, and, at best, not really central to the concerns of 'high art' and
culture.

According to Hunt:

an instructive parallel can be drawn between the emergence of children's literature and other 'new literatures' (national, ethnic, feminist,
post-colonial) that are becoming part of the institutional, cultural, critical map. Just as the literatures of colonial countries have had to fight
against a dominant culture, so children's literature (as a concept) has
had to fight against the academic hegemony of 'Eng. Lit.' to gain any
recognition. Just as colonized countries have adopted a paternalistic
stance towards the 'natives' and a patronising stance to their writings,
so, within what seems to be a single culture, the same attitude has been
taken to children's literature books. (Hunt, 1992: 2)

Hunt (1992: 2–3) maintains that the conventional literary system,
reflecting the values implicit in the traditional hierarchical family system,
tends to undervalue women's writing while children's literature fares even
worse as it concerns children primarily and is seen very much as the
domain of women – whether mothers or teachers.

The conventional literary system is, after all, very like the traditional
family: adult male literature predominates, women's literature is
secondary (and grudgingly recognized), while children's literature is
not only at the bottom of the heap, but (worse) it is very much the province of women. It was pointed out by the President of the Library and
Information Science Education in the USA in 1987 that in the field of children's and young adult's literature, 92% of the faculty were women, yet
fewer than 10% of those were full professors. (Hearne, 1991: 111)

Other factors have also contributed to the evaluation of children's literature as inferior. In the first instance, books for children often deviate from conventional literary norms and pose problems as regards conventional evaluation and classification.

Forced to describe themselves in terms of established norms, children's books do not shape up very well: their narratives are often novellas rather than novels; their verse is doggerel rather than poetry; their drama is improvisation rather than mediated text. As with other forms of literature, genre can degenerate rapidly into formula. (Hunt, 1992: 3)

As a consequence, critics often shun such writing because children's fiction 'thwarts would-be interpreters simply because so *few* children's novels move beyond the formulaic or stereotypical' (Nodelman, 1985: 5). In other words, the recurrent similarities in terms of structure, characters and language found in many works of children's literature are seen as contributing in a significant way to scholarly evaluation as 'inferior'.

But the fact that these works pose problems for those who would apply the tools of traditional literary criticism to them does not necessarily mean that it is the genre *per se* which is at fault. Perhaps, as Nodelman would have it, it is the means of interpretation which actually fail. 'Until we develop a new approach, we will not understand how a children's novel can in fact be unique even though its characters, its story, its "simple" language, and even its central core of patterns and ideas are not' (Nodelman, 1985: 20).

If the genre itself is not held in very high esteem by the world of scholarship, it is hardly surprising that the authors of books for children often suffer from problems of poor status and low pay. While in many countries there are awards for the writers of children's books, these same authors are not usually considered eligible for major literary awards under the general rubric of 'creative fiction'. Could someone like Astrid Lindgren, who was awarded the Hans Christian Andersen Award in 1958 and the International Book Award from UNESCO in 1993, ever be considered for the Nobel Prize for Literature? I think not, and yet Roald Dahl, who wrote for both adults and children, could at least in theory be a contender.

The Translation of Children's Literature

If children's literature has suffered from problems of low status, it is only to be expected that the translation of children's literature would have to endure a similar fate. For one thing, its very source material is considered of marginal interest and the professional activity, i.e. the translation carried out on this material, is, in itself, undervalued. This fact continues to find eloquent expression in the rates of pay and conditions offered to literary translators (Klingberg *et al.*, 1978: 88) and the minimal formal acknowledgement of the translator's contribution on the cover or elsewhere in a translated work.

Poor status, pay and working conditions can perpetuate a vicious circle in which publishers are often presented with what they deserve, namely, translated work which could be a good deal better. One development which could have far-reaching implications in terms of breaking this cycle would be to improve the skills (and thus the professional confidence) of those who translate children's fiction. Academics are as guilty as anyone of contributing to this problem of poor public perception and low prestige. How many undergraduate or for that matter postgraduate programmes in Translation Studies offer students the chance to develop skills in this field in either core or optional courses?

I must confess that my own institution, Dublin City University, has only recently developed an option in the very specific area of the translation of children's literature into Irish. If academic institutions involved in translator training were prepared to channel more resources in terms of research and teaching staff into investigations of the specific challenges of this field, it would surely make a difference, just as research into commercial and technical translation in the 1970s and 1980s enhanced the status and conditions of those engaged in that kind of work.

Of course, the full responsibility for the current state of children's literature translation cannot lie with the academic world alone. As already suggested, publishers are very active players in the field and, as a consequence, translators are not entirely free agents. Editors and publishers exert considerable influence over their output (Even-Zohar, 1992: 235), in a sense forcing an approach to the task of translation which has much more to do with conventions relating both to the target language (TL), in general, and children's literature in the TL, in particular, as well as target culture stereotypes relating to the source culture:

> Policy-makers in the publishing and marketing world play an important role not only in forming images, but also in strengthening the received images of other nations through translation, particularly in the case of minority cultures in their relation to dominant cultures. These images are often the result of historical development and cultural interchange, and they are frequently images the source culture itself wishes to convey to the outside world for conscious marketing strategies, or simply because it regards them as an intrinsic part of its national identity. (Rudvin, 1994: 209)

Rudvin's conclusions are based on a study carried out in relation to the translation of Norwegian children's books into English. She points out that, apart from the works of writers such as Henrik Ibsen and Knut Hamsun, Norwegian literature is generally not well known in English-speaking countries. The genre of children's literature is an exception, according to Brudevoll, who is quoted by Rudvin (1994: 203) as claiming that while just a few hundred copies of any translation for adults from Norwegian are usually published in English, several thousand copies of translated children's books are published.

These books tend to be selected on the basis that their content corresponds to the prevailing positive British image of Norway as a natural, unspoilt country of mountains, lakes and forests. Such a policy in relation to the selection of texts for translation leaves 'the classical canon unchallenged, boundaries unstretched, perpetuating stereotypes rather than giving room for innovative thinking and thereby introducing new literatures and authors' (Rudvin, 1994: 203).

Future Research Directions in Translating for Children

We now need more studies, like Rudvin's, of the translation of children's literature which address the topics suggested back in 1986 by Klingberg for research purposes. Furthermore, we need appropriate research tools and methodology. To this end, we must look beyond Klingberg who has been described as 'dogmatic and inflexible' in his approach to the translation of children's literature (Puurtinen, 1995: 59). His analyses of Swedish/English and English/Swedish translations of books for children were very much source language orientated in marked contrast to the polysystems TL approach developed by Israeli academics such as Even-Zohar and Toury and so successfully applied to investigations of the Scandinavian translation trends in the 1990s referred to in this chapter. Klingberg was highly critical of translators taking what he saw as unnecessary liberties with the text. This does not mean that he totally opposed any form of adaptation, for he conceded that this may be necessary, for example in the case of certain foreign, historical, geographical or cultural references. But his prescriptive approach advocated 'faithfulness' to the source text where at all possible.

A more descriptive approach to the translation of a particular literature, in this case children's literature, can, as Shavit (1986: 171) and Even-Zohar (1992: 231) illustrate, shed light on the norms which operate within a particular target system since 'none of the choices made by the translator or, for that matter, the author, are manifestations of individual whims or inspiration, but are made within the (poly-)system in which they operate'

(Even-Zohar, 1992: 231). Thus, contemporary target-orientated writers on these matters tend to shy away from Klingberg's tendency to apply some 'preconceived, fixed idea of the permissible extent of manipulation of the Source Text'. For the adherents of the polysystems approach, the focus is the TL and target culture and, as a result, 'the translator's decisions are likely to be based on prevalent norms and expectations, and the purpose of the translation' (Puurtinen, 1995: 60), rather than on some general code of good translator practice that could apply more or less equally to the translation of children's literature in different countries and eras.

Screen Translation for Children

In recent years minority language cultures, in particular, have started to show more interest in the important area of the translation of children's literature. However, it must be remembered that the major technological advances in the field of audiovisual communications over the last 20 years have had an important impact on the role of the printed word in the education and development of young people. Even highly literate children with extensive access to books, comics and magazines rely much more on oral/aural communication than the previous generation. The Swedish author of children's books, Lennart Hellsing, sees children's literature as a very broad field which encompasses everything that a child reads or hears (Oittinen, 1993b: 37). Viewed from this perspective, plays, puppet shows, computer and video games, radio and TV programmes, films, videos, etc. are just as important as books in terms of the education and entertainment of young people. Since, in the case of such texts, it is more accurate to speak of 'listeners' or 'viewers' rather than 'readers', Oittinen (1993b: 10) suggests the general term of 'receptor' is now more appropriate. In view of the long hours spent by most children in front of television screens, in particular, studies of translations produced for children must broaden their scope to include the analysis of screen translation for children as it is currently practised.

The two most prominent forms of screen translation are subtitling and dubbing. Although cost is usually an important factor in the production of children's programmes, and subtitling can prove up to ten times cheaper than dubbing, subtitling is rarely used because of anticipated problems relating to the variable reading abilities and speeds of young viewers. As a consequence, foreign language TV programmes, films and videos aimed at children and/or adolescents are invariably dubbed. When a film or video is to be dubbed, a script translator usually provides a complete draft translation that serves as a basis for the final, usually somewhat adapted, version that emerges when dubbing actors, producers and directors get together in the dubbing studio. The dubbing script translator usually faces many of the same linguistic challenges as those associated with the drafting of foreign language versions of other oral/aural material, for example radio and theatre plays. But the task is typically complicated by the constraints imposed by, for example, the need to achieve good quality lip synchrony whenever a close-up shot appears on screen and match, as closely as possible, syllable count and sentence length in the source and target versions. The problems and challenges associated with the translation of children's texts in general, and such scripts in particular, constitute an area well worth investigating and would include consideration of the particular difficulties associated with endeavouring to achieve satisfactory lip-synchrony while using the kind of constrained language and limited vocabulary that would be appropriate in view of the low mean age of the primary audience.

Major to Lesser-used Language Translation

As we have seen, translation, like all other cultural activity, is conducted according to certain norms. In the case of translation for children, these may be didactic, ideological, ethical, religious, etc. They determine what is translated when and where and they change continually. Furthermore, the norms may vary from language to language, culture to culture and genera-tion to generation. Thus, while specific norms exist in all cultures for the writing and translation of children's literature, it does not follow that the same approach is adopted in the case of any two languages. As Even-Zohar (1992) and Toury (1995) have pointed out, translations for children produced early in the century from German to Hebrew (a case of transla-tion from a major to a lesser-used language) were highly literary and intended to enrich the young readership's vocabulary. Now that the Hebrew language has established itself as a more stable, multifaceted contemporary language with distinct registers and oral and written styles, translated children's books are starting to reflect more colloquial varieties of the language tending more towards entertainment and less towards education.

My own particular research in this field has investigated the particular dynamic of the dubbing translation of animation programmes from a major language, German, into a lesser-used language, Irish. Children's stories by the German author, Janosch, were adapted in the 1990s for use as scripts for an animated children's TV series in Germany. The animation series was subsequently dubbed into Irish. Although the German scripts used a variety of registers and extensive vocabulary, the Irish versions tended to adopt a more colloquial style throughout and avoided the specialized terminology of the fairly sophisticated German scripts. One possible reason for the preferred use of a lower register in the Irish version relates to the norms of the TL, Irish, as it exists today. Although the classical scholarly tradition of the language continues at academic institutions and new poetry, prose, criticism, journalism, etc. is written and published every year, Irish is, at least for most native speakers, primarily a language for oral rather than written communication. This is fairly typical of the plight of lesser-used languages in decline or *in extremis* and is in stark contrast to the case of German which has many millions of native speakers, a large number of dialects, an extensive range of special languages and a highly developed range of registers to suit every oral and written situation.

Conclusion

Hebrew and Irish translations of German storybooks and TV animation aimed at children during different periods in this century are mentioned here only as illustrations of the wide range of factors (language pairs, text type, historical period, status, i.e. major/lesser-used language, primary target audience, literary, educational, translation, broadcasting and/or other norms, etc.) which all may play a part in determining the final shape of a particular translated text, whether written or aural. There is clearly wide scope for further detailed investigations of a descriptive kind which may add to the insights gained in recent years from preliminary research based on Scandinavian and German literature translated for children.

Notes
1. Reiss does not give a precise source for Klingberg's definition.

Zohar Shavit
Translation of Children's Literature

This chapter covers certain behavior patterns of children's literature. The discussion is based mainly on research into translations of children's books into Hebrew, though the described patterns of behavior are not necessarily typical only of Hebrew children's literature, but seem to be common to other national systems as well (mainly to dependent systems such as the Icelandic, the Arabic, the Swedish; see Klingberg *et al.*, 1978 and Even-Zohar, 1978). The act of translation is understood here not in the traditional normative sense, but rather as a semiotic concept. Thus, translation is understood as part of a transfer mechanism – that is, the process by which textual models of one system are transferred to another. In this process, certain products are produced within the target system, which relate in various and complex ways to products of the source system. Hence, the final product of the act of translation is the result of the relationship between a source system and a target system, a relationship that is itself determined by a certain hierarchy of semiotic constraints (see Jakobson, 1959, Toury, 1980, Even-Zohar, 1981). The texts that will be analysed here do not include only what have been traditionally discussed as translated texts, but abridgments and adaptations as well. The primary condition for their inclusion in this study is that they claim some sort of relationship between themselves and the original.

In viewing translation as part of a transfer process, it must be stressed that the subject at stake is not just translations of texts from one language to another, but also the translations of texts from one system to another – for example, translations from the adult system into the children's. Since the point of departure for this discussion is the understanding of children's literature not as an assemblage of elements existing in a vacuum but as an integral part of the literary polysystem, the transfer from one system to another is even more crucial for my discussion. Hence, I wish to examine the implications of the systemic status of children's literature to substantiate the claim that the behavior of translation of children's literature is largely determined by the position of children's literature within the literary polysystem.

Translated children's literature was chosen for discussion because it is believed to be a convenient methodological tool for studying norms of writing for children. In fact, the discussion of translated texts is even more fruitful than that of original texts because translational norms expose more clearly the constraints imposed on a text that enters the children's system. This is true because in transferring the text from the source into the target system translators are forced to take into account systemic constraints. I contend that this holds especially true for texts transferred from adult to children's literature, texts whose status in the literary polysystem has changed historically. This group of texts (such as *Robinson Crusoe* and *Gulliver's Travels*), considered classics for children, will be analysed as a sample for discussion of two issues: the norms of translating children's books (as opposed to those of adult literature) and the systemic constraints determining those norms.

Norms of Translating Children's Books

Unlike contemporary translators of adult books, the translator of children's literature can permit himself great liberties regarding the text, as a result of the peripheral position of children's literature within the literary polysystem. That is, the translator is permitted to manipulate the text in various ways by changing, enlarging, or abridging it or by deleting or adding to it. Nevertheless, all these translational procedures are permitted only if conditioned by the translator's adherence to the following two principles on which translation for children is based: an adjustment of the text to make it appropriate and useful to the child, in accordance with what society regards (at a certain point in time) as educationally 'good for the child'; and an adjustment of plot, characterization, and language to prevailing society's perceptions of the child's ability to read and comprehend.

These two principles, rooted in the self-image of children's literature, have had different hierarchal relations in different periods. Thus, for instance, as long as the concept of didactic children's literature prevailed, the first principle, based on the understanding of children's literature as a tool for education, was dominant. Nowadays, the emphasis differs; although to a certain degree the first principle still dictates the character of the translations, the second principle, that of adjusting the text to the child's level of comprehension, is more dominant. Yet it is possible that the two principles might not always be complementary: sometimes they might even contradict each other. For example, it might be assumed that a child is able to understand a text involved with death, and yet at the same time the text may be regarded as harmful to his mental welfare. In such a situation, the translated text might totally delete one aspect in favour of another, or perhaps even include contradictory features, because the translator hesitated between the two principles. In any case, these usually complementary principles determine each stage of the translation process. They dictate decisions concerned with the textual selection procedure (which texts will be chosen for translation), as well as with permissible manipulation. They also serve as the basis for the systemic affiliation of the text. But most important of all, in order to be accepted as a translated text for children, to be affiliated with the children's system, the final translated product must adhere to these two principles, or at least not violate them.

Systemic Affiliation

The systemic affiliation of a text entering the children's system is very similar to that of a text entering another peripheral system – the non-canonized system for adults. As noted in my discussion of the self-image of children's literature in Chapter 2 of *Poetics of Children's Literature* (Shavit, 1986), historically both systems use models prominent in the early stages of the canonized adult system. I have also noted that the models of both are frequently secondary models transformed from adult literature. For instance, in ambivalent texts the model of the fairy tale became acceptable in English children's literature only after the Romantic school had introduced and developed imagination and rejected realism – although realism did continue to prevail in children's literature. Gradually, imagination became acceptable in children's literature (mainly through translation of folktales and artistic fairy tales, such as Andersen's) until finally it became the prevailing norm.

Yet, it should be noted that in children's literature, the model transferred from adult literature does not function as a secondary model. Within the framework of children's literature, it functions initially as a primary model. Later it might be transformed into non-canonized children's literature, usually in a simplified and reduced form. The detective story in children's literature might illustrate this point. The model was transferred to children's literature only after it had been canonized[1] by adult literature (mainly through Dostoyevsky's *Crime and Punishment* and Doyle's *Sherlock Holmes*). It was first accepted by the canonized children's literature system where it functioned as a primary model, different in character from that of the adult model (see Erich Kästner's *Emil und die Detektive*, 1929, and R.J. McGregor's *The Young Detectives*, 1934). Only after it had been accepted and legitimized by the canonized children's system was the detective story transferred into non-canonized children's literature, though in a reduced and simplified form. Here it served as the basis for one of the most prominent models of children's literature over the last 50 years. Every Western children's literature has its own popular detective series, whether it be the American Nancy Drew and Hardy Boys or the English stories of Enid Blyton.

However, despite the great similarity between non-canonized adult literature and children's literature regarding their systemic affiliation, a big difference remains between them. As mentioned earlier, the primary difference lies in the fact that the children's system by itself is stratified into two main subsystems – canonized and non-canonized; an even more fundamental difference lies in the different source of constraints imposed on the text as a result of its affiliation. Though the constraints themselves may be similar (as is the case with the non-acceptability of primary models), their motivation and legitimation differ altogether. Whereas in the case of the non-canonized adult system the main constraint is commercial, the source of constraints in the canonized children's system is mainly educational.

These systemic constraints of the children's system are perhaps best manifested in the following aspects: the affiliation of the text to existing models; the integrality of the text's primary and secondary models, the degree of complexity and sophistication of the text; the adjustment of the text to ideological and didactic purposes; and the style of the text.

Affiliation to Existing Models

Translation of children's literature tends to relate the text to existing models in the target system. This phenomenon, known from general translational procedures (see Even-Zohar, 1978, Toury, 1980), is particularly prominent in the translation of children's literature because of the system's tendency to accept only the conventional and the well known. If the model of the original text does not exist in the target system, the text is changed by deleting or by adding such elements as will adjust it to the integrating model of the target system. This phenomenon also existed in the past in various adult literatures, although long after it ceased to be prevalent in the adult canonized system, it still remained prominent in children's literature.

Test Cases: *Gulliver's Travels* and *Robinson Crusoe*

The various adaptations and translations of *Gulliver's Travels* will serve as a good example. The abridged version of *Gulliver's Travels* was read by children in the form of a chapbook[2] soon after it was originally issued in 1726. As with another successful novel, *Robinson Crusoe, Gulliver's Travels* was quickly reissued in an unauthorized abridged version (and as a chapbook) soon after publishers realized its commercial potential. With

Robinson Crusoe the first part was published in April 1719, and already in August of that same year an abridged and unauthorized version of the text was published, followed by dozens of chapbook editions during the 18th century. The same was true of *Gulliver's Travels* (1726), whose first abridged and unauthorized versions were published by 1727 and contained only 'Lilliput' and 'Brobdingnag.' By the middle of the 18th century, quite a few editions of *Gulliver's Travels* were published in the form of chapbooks, containing only 'Lilliput.' Both abridged versions of *Robinson Crusoe* and *Gulliver's Travels* continued to appear even at the beginning of the 19th century, but by that time they were issued for children and young people only (see Perrin, 1969).

Originally, the lack of any other appealing reading material was the main reason for *Gulliver's Travels* being adopted by the children's system. Like all chapbooks, the book was enthusiastically read by children, in the absence of other literature written specifically for them, and in such a way filled a gap that still existed in the literary polysystem. Thus, the text was read by children even before the children's system actually existed; since then, over the last two centuries it has managed to occupy a prominent position in the children's system. This is the case not only because it quickly became a 'classic' for children, but mainly because *Gulliver's* Travels was continuously revised and adapted, in order to be affiliated with the target system. As the abridged text became a classic for children in the 19th century, it simultaneously lost its position in the adult system. This does not mean that the text disappeared altogether from the adult system. On the contrary, the text acquired the status of a 'canon,' as part of the literary heritage; that is, the text is read today by adults on the basis of its historical value, while in children's literature it is still a 'living' text.

What were the implications of the process by which the text was affiliated to the children's system? The first decision that translators had to make concerned the very selection of the text. This decision was in a way incidental because the text that already existed as a chapbook became later on a chapbook for children. However, what was common to the chapbooks and all other adaptations of Gulliver's *Travels* was their inclusion of only the first two books. In spite of the fact that *Gulliver's Travels* was frequently translated, not a single translation for children has included all four books. Most translations are of the first book only, and several others include the second book as well. The selection of the first two books is primarily connected with the decision to transfer the text from its original form as a satire into a fantasy or adventure story.

At first the text was transferred either into the model of fantasy or adventure just because they were such popular models in chapbooks. Later on, the same decision was the result of two additional factors: first, the over-whelming popularity of fantasy and adventure in children's literature as well; and second, the lack of satire as a genre in the target system (children's literature totally ignored the existence of such a genre). This was probably due to the fact that children were not supposed to be either acquainted with the subjects of the satire, nor with its meaning. Translators who wished to transform the text from a satire into either model (fantasy or adventure) of the target system had to omit the last two books for two reasons. Satire is built into *Gulliver's Travels* in sophisticated and complex ways, including the inter-relations of the four books. In wishing to avoid the satire, transla-tors into Hebrew had no further interest in retaining that now functionless relationship and could thus easily forego the other books entirely. Next, translators found it much easier to adjust elements of the first two books into models of the target system. For instance, the people of Lilliput could much more easily be transformed into dwarfs of a fantasy story than the people of the Country of Houyhnhnms, for whom it was almost impossible to find an equivalent in the models that already existed in the target system. Moreover, Gulliver's travels in unknown countries, as well as his battles and wars, could easily serve as the basis for an adventure story. However, when a translator decides upon one of the models, usually in accordance with the presumed age of the reader – fantasy for younger children, adven-ture story for older – the other model usually creeps into the text and thus both models can be discerned in almost all translations.

Those two models, contradictory by nature (fantasy tending to general-ization, while the adventure story tends to concretisation), dictate the very selection of the text and its manipulation. The transformation of the Lillipu-tian people into the dwarfs of the fantasy story exemplifies the model's manipulation of the text. While the original text emphasizes the similarity between the people of Lilliput and the people of Gulliver's country (who differ mainly in size but resemble each other in other respects – which then becomes the core of the satire), translators deliberately make every effort to blur the similarity and create an opposition that does not exist in the orig-inal, that is, an opposition between two worlds – the world of Gulliver and the fantasy world of the dwarfs. The fantasy world of the dwarfs has all the typical attributes of the fantasy model, especially as far as the fabula and characterization are concerned. Hence, in the adaptation for children, the dwarfs are part of an enchanted and strange world full of glory and magnif-icence. They are innocent little creatures forced to protect themselves against a negative force that has appeared in their world – a typical fabula of fairy tales. In such a way the Lilliputians are no more an object of criti-cism and satire but an object of identification and pity.

The opposition between Gulliver's original world and that of the Lilliputians is further revealed in adaptations for children by the description of both the emperor and his people in terms of the fantasy model. Thus, the creatures of the original text become *'strange* creatures' (p. 9), the inhabitants become *'dwarfs* inhabiting the country' (p. 9), and 'four of the inhabitants' become 'four men of the native *dwarfs'* (1976 Jizreel edition, my italics; all English translations of the Hebrew *Gulliver's* Travels are mine).

Moreover, unlike the original text, which uses several devices to emphasize the difference in size in order to hint at potential resemblance in other respects, translations always present the Lilliputians not as miniature human beings but as dwarfs, as creatures *different* from human beings. As a result, they emphasize their size by adding diminutive epithets. In the original text the description of the arrows fired by the Lilliputians compares them to needles: 'I felt above a hundred arrows discharged on my left hand, which prickled me like so many needles' (p. 18). The translations add to the description of the arrows the diminutive epithet 'tiny and minute' (1961 Massada version). In the same way translations add 'tiny as a fly' to the food Gulliver eats (Massada version), which is originally described as: 'shoulders, legs and loins shaped like those of mutton, and very well dressed, but smaller than the wings of a lark' (1960: 19). Furthermore, devices that are used by the original text to create the sense of the size of the Lilliputian world, such as accurate and detailed numbers, situations which create the sense of proportion (the children playing in his hair), are totally omitted because their original function was to emphasize the similarity between the two worlds, described originally as different only in size.

The same phenomenon of adaptation of the original text into the models of the target system can also be discerned in the characterization of the Lilliputians. Thus, while the original text presents complicated characterization of both Gulliver and the Lilliputians, translators tend to offer unequivocal presentations and hence to maintain the typical opposition between 'good' and 'bad' of both the fantasy and the adventure models. As a result, whereas in the original, the 'good' features of Lilliputians are only part of their characterization and are accompanied by harsh criticism, translators tend to include only the 'good' features, thus changing the characterization altogether. For instance, the criticism of the strange relations between parents and children and the absurd manners of burial of the original are totally omitted in translations, while good manners and high morality are indeed retained. An even more interesting example is the device for the manipulation of the threatening or tension-producing element, required for the model of the target system. Once a certain character is chosen to represent this element, the translation will ignore all other components, save the negative feature of the character, such as his mischievous use of power (see the description of the Chief Admiral in the El Hamaayan edition: 41, or in the 1976 Jizreel edition: 35).

This attempt to adjust the description of the Lilliputian world to the model of fantasy can be observed in the description of the emperor as well. In the original, the emperor's description is detailed and based on many aspects – his height, colour, voice, body, gestures: 'He is taller, by almost the breadth of my nail than any of his court, which alone is enough to strike an awe into the beholders. His features are strong and masculine, with an Austrian lip and arched nose, his complexion olive, his countenance erect, his body and limbs well proportioned, all his motions graceful, and his deportment majestic' (1960: 24). Translators tend to subordinate this type of description to that typical of the fantasy model – to emphasize only his height and impressive appearance as a metonym for his power, and omit all other features. Hence the original description is translated into: 'He was a handsome little man much taller than the rest of his court' (Ladybird: 17) or 'All his subjects dreaded his height' (Jizreel: 19). In such a way translators changed the original description of the emperor, which was based on popular travel books of the time, and transferred them to the stereotyped presentation common to fairy tales, in which descriptions of kings and rulers are aimed mainly at emphasizing the element of power.

The same phenomenon can be discerned in the description of the emperor's dress and sword. In the original text the description of the emperor's dress is as follows:

> I have had him since many times in my hand, and therefore cannot be deceived in the description. His dress was very plain and simple, and the fashion of it between the Asiatic and the European; but he had on his head a light helmet of gold, adorned with jewels, and a plume on the crest. He held his sword drawn in his hand, to defend himself, if I should happen to break loose; it was almost three inches long, the hilt and scabbard were gold enriched with diamonds. (1960: 24)

Various translators have omitted most of this detailed description, leaving only that which is typical of fairy tale emperors – glory and wealth – and frequently using the sword to symbolize the emperor's power: 'In his hand the King held his drawn sword whose handle was decorated with sparkling diamonds' (El Hamaayan: 16); 'He held in his hand a sceptre bigger than a match. Its handle and edges were decorated with jewels' (Massada: 26); and 'In his hand the Emperor held his drawn sword, a little shorter than a knitting needle. Its golden handle and scabbard sparkled with diamonds' (Zelkowitz: 21). It should be noted, however, that the process of adjusting the text to a certain model involves more than mere omissions of certain elements. One of the most interesting manifestations of text adjustment is those elements that translators find necessary to add to the original. These added elements are the best indicators of the force of constraints on the model, since adding new elements to an already short-ened text implies that the translator regards them as indispensable to the model. Additions are thus needed to reinforce the model, and their inclu-sion reveals even more than deletions do which elements are considered obligatory for the target model. As an example of such an addition, note that the 'plain and simple' dress of the original became in the translation 'magnificent and very special' (Sinai: 23). Another example of added elements to the text is that in which the original text describes the man who speaks with Gulliver as 'a person of quality.' The translator made him a typical character of the fantasy model, 'a man wearing a long and expen-sive cloak and a little boy holding it behind' (Sreberk).

In summary, the model's affiliation determined which texts would be included or excluded, which elements would be added or omitted, and which would remain, albeit with changed functions. In the translations for children, the satirical elements have either entirely vanished or remained minus their original function, usually acquiring a new function and in this way contributing to the model of the target system. In some cases they have even remained without any function at all. Thus, by leaving out some elements and by changing the functions of others, translators have managed to adjust the text to prevalent models of the target system.

The Text's Integrality

Today the norm of a complete, unabridged text is accepted in most trans-lations of the adult canonized system. Deletions, if at all, are incidental. But in the 19th century and even at the beginning of the 20th, such a norm was not obligatory, and translators were allowed to manipulate the integrality of the original text. In the adult system, this freedom to manipulate exists only in the non-canonized system. Here translators are free to add or delete in accordance with the demands of the target system, and more often than not they do not preserve the completeness of the original text (see, for instance, Hebrew translations of James Bond).

The same freedom of manipulation seems to exist in the children's system (even within the body of canonized literature) particularly when adult books are transferred into it. Within this body, the *raison d'être* for all abridged texts for children is based on the supposition that children are incapable of reading lengthy texts. Nevertheless, the actual decision as to what to omit is the result of the need to revise the text in accordance with two main criteria, in addition to the systemic affiliation: first, the norms of morality accepted and demanded by the children's system; second, the assumed level of the child's comprehension. Hence a translator's decision to adjust the text to children invariably means that he will have to shorten it and make it less complicated at the same time. These two procedures might, in reality, contradict one another because fewer elements are required to carry more functions. As a result, translators must carefully manipulate the text in order to maintain a workable balance, always keeping those two principles in focus.

The simplest manipulation of the text is done by deleting undesirable elements or whole paragraphs. However, this option is not always available to the translator. Sometimes the need to delete certain scenes turns out to be very problematical for the translator, especially when they are regarded as indispensable for the development of the plot. Such scenes are often altered to become suitable when the translator finds an acceptable formula or format for their inclusion. As an example, note the scene of Gulliver saving the palace from the fire by urinating on it. In the original text, the scene of extinguishing the fire is used to advance the plot as well as to integrate satire into the story. The Lilliputians reveal their ingratitude by not thanking Gulliver for saving the palace. On the contrary, they blame him for breaking the law of the kingdom and later use it as an excuse for sending him away. The whole scene is clearly used in order to satirize the arbitrariness of the laws and the ingratitude of the people. However, most translations could neither cope with Gulliver extinguishing the fire by urinating on it (an unacceptable scenario in a children's book) nor with the satire of the kingdom and its laws. On the other hand, some translations, especially those built on the adventure model, did not wish to leave out such a dramatic episode. In these versions, Gulliver does extinguish the fire either by throwing water on it (El Hamaayan) or by blowing it out (Zelkovitz). As a result, this episode is left in the text, even though it contradicts the entire characterization of Lilliputians as good and grateful people. Here it may be observed that in order to maintain the integrality of the plot, which is clearly the most important aspect in the adventure model, translators do not hesitate to contradict other components of the text such as characterization. Other translators, however, were happy to delete the entire scene, primarily because it constitutes a violation of the taboo in children's literature on excretions; moreover, it also violates the characterization of the dwarfs as victims. Another reason for its deletion in some translations is that it takes part in the build-up of the satire which translators so religiously try to avoid. Hence, the deletion of this unnecessary scene can be easily justified.

In fact, it can even be formulated as a rule that when it is possible to delete undesirable scenes without damaging the basic plot or characteriza- tions, translators will not hesitate to do so. Hence all translators of *Gulliver's Travels* happily give up the scene where Gulliver is suspected of having a love affair with the queen, for such a scene violates the taboo on sexual activity in children's literature. In the adult version, this scene plays an important role in the satire because it appears logistically impossible for the suspected lovers to have an affair owing to their vastly different dimen- sions. Seen as satire, this incident disappears altogether from translations for children; it is unnecessary and thus can be easily omitted.

The other major criterion that guides translators is their sensitivity to the level of reading comprehension of children. When a translator assumes that a certain paragraph will not be understood by the child, he will make either changes or deletions to adjust it to the 'appropriate' comprehension level. This is why translators of *Robinson Crusoe* delete the opening dialogue between Robinson and his father, in which the father presents the ethos of the bourgeoisie as opposed to that of the lower and upper classes.

The same phenomenon is also apparent in most translations of *Tom Sawyer*. In the original text, the familiar fence-whitewashing scene has two parts. The first describes Tom's ingenious device for making the children work for him and also pay for that pleasure. In the second, Twain throws out several sarcastic remarks about the 'sacred' values of work and plea- sure, aiming his irony not toward Tom and his treasures, but rather toward adults, whose values the text compares to those of the children. The result is a mocking and condescending attitude *vis-à-vis* adults. Most translators delete this part of the scene entirely, and thus the ironical level of the scene is completely expunged (Twain, 1911, 1940, 1960). There are quite a few reasons for this deletion. First, this passage does not contribute directly to the 'plot' in its narrowest sense. Translators, in spite of their endeavours to make longer texts shorter, are reluctant to omit a paragraph that has a substantive part in the 'plot.' This is because action and plot are considered the most important elements of children's books or in Nina Bawden's words: 'Writing for children is not easier than writing for adults; it is different. The *story-line*, clearly, has to be stronger ... The clue to what they really enjoy is what they reread, what they go back to, and this is almost always a book with a strong *narrative line*' (Bawden, 1974: 6; my italics). However, if a paragraph is considered non-essential to the plot, translators will happily exclude it. In addition, many translators feel uneasy in presenting ironical attitudes toward life and toward grown-ups that do not suit the values a child should be acquiring through literature. They justify their omission of irony by suggesting that such sophisticated attitudes, which demand a two-dimensional confrontation, cannot be understood by the child. Hence, whenever it is possible, the level of irony is totally excluded so as to make the text less complicated.

This tendency to avoid complex and/or unflattering characterizations of adults, and especially of parents, can be seen in other cases as well. As Wunderlich and Morrissey argue in their analysis of translations of *Pinocchio*, Geppetto's description is subject to the same procedure:

> Geppetto, the image of the parent, also undergoes change. The original Geppetto is a truly human figure. He displays anger, rage and frustration. ... The parent loves, but the parent also becomes angry and punishing. Raising a child, Collodi shows, is no easy matter. Parents, however, are no longer punishing. They display only love, warmth, support, and self-sacrifice towards the child. So, as with Pinocchio, Geppetto is weakened through the thirties; his punishing visage is eroded. (Wunderlich & Morrissey, 1982: 110)

The Level of Complexity of the Text

As stated earlier, the text's integrality is directly affected by the need to shorten the text and the demand for a less complicated text. When shortening a text, translators have to make sure that they also reduce the proportions between elements and functions and make fewer elements carry even fewer functions. In contrast to adult canonized literature, in which the norm of complexity is the most prevalent today, the norm of simple and simplified models is still prominent in most children's literature (canonized and non-canonized), as is also the case with the non-canonized adult system. This norm, rooted in the self-image of children's literature, tends to determine not only the thematics and characterization of the text, but also its options concerning permissible structures.

When dealing with the question of complexity, the text of *Alice in Wonderland* is most interesting. In Chapter 3 of *Poetics of Children's Literature* (Shavit, 1986), I asked how the text came to be accepted by adults and discovered that it was the result of the very characteristics later considered by adaptors and translators as unsuitable for children. Here I approach the problem briefly from the opposite direction – that is, to show how the text became acceptable for children, I ask which textual elements were changed in order to make the text, in the translator's opinion, acceptable for children. As a rule, all the elements that were considered too sophisticated were either changed or deleted. Hence, translators systematically deleted all the satire and parody of the original text. The paragraphs that contained those elements were not at all difficult to omit, because they did not contribute to the plot. Unlike them, the complicated presentation of the world in the text posed a more serious problem for the translators because they could not give it up altogether.

In the original *Alice in Wonderland*, Carroll intentionally made it impossible to determine whether things happen in a dream or in reality. Such a complicated presentation was not acceptable to the translators, who eventually solved the problem by motivating the whole story as a dream. Therefore, the transfer into children's literature resulted in a simplified presentation that insisted on a clear distinction between reality and fantasy. For instance, one adaptation opens in the following way: 'Once upon a time there was a little girl called Alice, *who had a very curious dream*' (Modern Promotions, my italics). Another adaptation ends in a phrase which leaves no doubt that it was anything but a dream: 'I am glad to be back where things are really what they seem,' said Alice, as she woke up from her strange Wonderful dream' (Disney, 1980). The procedure of transformation of a text into a less sophisticated one and its adjustment to a simplified model is always achieved either by deletions or by changing the relation between elements and functions. However, it may even happen that some elements will remain in the text, although they lose their original function without acquiring a new one. This occurs because the translator retains certain elements, assuming that they contribute to some level when they actually do not. For example, in the original *Tom Sawyer*, the aunt is ironically described by the funny way she uses her spectacles:

> The old lady pulled her spectacles down and looked over them about the room; then she put them up and looked out under them. She seldom or never looked *through* them for so small a thing as a boy; they were her state pair, the pride of her heart, and were built for 'style' not service – she could have seen through a piece of stove lid just as well. (Twain, 1935: 287)

The comment explains ironically why the aunt puts her spectacles up and down and does not look through them. In one of the translations (by Ben-Pinhas: Twain, 1964), the translator made her lift her spectacles up and down, but left out the writer's comment. The translator probably thought the spectacles contributed to the plot (because of the 'action') and did not pay attention to their function in the characterization of the old lady. Hence the spectacles in the translation remained functionless.

Ideological or Evaluative Adaptation

In earlier stages of adult literature, the concept of literature as a didactic instrument for unequivocal values or for a certain ideology was prominent. Long after it ceased to exist in adult literature, this concept was still so powerful in children's literature that translators were ready to completely change the source text in order to have the revised version serve ideological purposes. A typical example for such ideological revision is the translations of *Robinson Crusoe*. Perhaps the most prominent of these was the translation into the German by Joachim Campe (1746–1818) titled *Robinson der Jüngere* (1779–80), which served as a catalyst for further translations. Campe's adaptation was translated by himself into French and English (1781), although the most popular English translation was that of Stockdale, published in 1782 in four volumes. The text was further translated, and by 1800 translations also appeared in Dutch, Italian, Danish, Croatian, Czech, and Latin. Moreover, the text was translated into Hebrew no less than three times (1824, 1849, 1896?), and even into Yiddish (1784, 1840).

In such a way, *Robinson Crusoe* managed to be preserved in canonized children's literature for over a century, probably due to its ideological adjustment. Furthermore, the text was followed by various imitations that created one of the most prominent models in children's literature, that of the *Robinsonnade*. Yet, it should be emphasized that although Campe's adaptation was the main reason for *Robinson Crusoe's* becoming a classic for children, he practically made it into a totally different text, from the ideological point of view, retaining only some of the original setting.

Campe's motivations for translating *Robinson Crusoe* were primarily aimed at adapting it to Rousseau's pedagogical system, which served as the pedagogical system of his school in Dessau. Campe decided to translate *Robinson Crusoe*, because Rousseau himself suggested that it be the only book given to a child due to its portrayal of the individual's struggle with nature. When the book was examined with Rousseau's views in mind, however, it became clear to Campe that it demanded a thorough change – Defoe's views on the bourgeois ethos and colonialist values contradicted those of Rousseau. Thus, in the original text, *Robinson Crusoe* arrives at the island with all the symbols of Western culture (weapons, food, the Bible) and manages to cultivate nature. In Campe's translation, however, he reaches the island naked and possessionless (he even has to spark the fire by rubbing stones). Robinson has to learn to live within nature without building a quasi-European culture. Rather, he builds an anti-European culture and suggests it as an alternative to the European.

When Campe's adaptation was translated into Hebrew, the Hebrew translation needed further ideological revision in order to be adapted to the prevailing Enlightenment views of the 19th century. In one of the translations, that of Zamoshch (Defoes, 1824), the translator tried in a rather paradoxical manner to combine Campe's anti-rationalist views with the views of the Jewish Enlightenment; the latter, in fact, were similar to Defoe's ethos, the belief that a rationalist can overcome nature and even cultivate it. The translator tried to stress not only Rousseauian values, but also those of the Jewish Enlightenment movement such as productivization. Thus, the children listening to the story told by their father do not sit idle, but willingly busy themselves with some sort of work. In this example, it can be seen how a text is selected for adaptation on the basis of ideology, yet still requires ideological revision; paradoxically, the new version resulting from this revision included elements of both Defoe and Campe.

Stylistic Norms

Discussion in English of the stylistic norms governing translation of children's books into Hebrew is impossible; thus only the guiding principle will be presented here. The prominent stylistic norm in translation into Hebrew of both adult and children's literature is the preference for high literary style whenever possible. Despite the fact that both systems share a common stylistic norm, however, its motivation and legitimation is different in each system. While in adult literature high style is connected with the idea of 'literariness' per se, in children's literature it is connected with a didactic concept and the attempt to enrich the child's vocabulary. Again, as long as this didactic concept of children's literature prevails, as long as it is assumed that 'books can and do influence outlook, belief and conduct,' and that 'for this reason, the writer for children will weigh his words carefully' (Collinson, 1973: 37–38), then children's literature will not be able to liberate itself either from its didactic aims or from this specific norm of high style. Even if 'literariness' disappears from adult literature, it will still dominate children's literature, as long as it is regarded as educationally 'good' and until the didactic concept of children's literature declines or at least loses its sway.

This phenomenon reflects the strong grip that systematic constraints hold on the children's system. These constraints govern not only the selection of texts to be translated from the adult canonized system, but the presentation, characterization, and model affiliation as well.

Notes on primary texts

English editions
Carroll, Lewis (1865/1968) *Alice's Adventures in Wonderland*. New York: MacMillan.
Carroll, Lewis (1890/1966) *The Nursery Alice*. New York: Dover.
Defoe, Daniel (1719/1965) *Robinson Crusoe*. Harmondsworth: Penguin.
Swift, Jonathan (1726/1960) *Gulliver's Travels*. Cambridge, MA: Riverside.
Twain, Mark (1876/1935) *The Adventures of Tom Sawyer*. New York: Garden City.

Translations and adaptations

Lewis Carroll
Alisa be'eretz ha-plaot (1945) Translated by Avraham Aryeh Akavya. Tel Aviv: Sreberk.
Alisa be'eretz ha-plaot (1973) Translated by Bela Bar'am. Tel Aviv: Massada.
Disney, Walt (1976) *Alisa be'eretz ha-plaot*. Translated by Shulamit Lapid. Tel Aviv: Yavneh.
Disney, Walt (1980) *Alice in Wonderland*. Racine, WI: Golden Press.
Alice's Adventures in Wonderland (1980) Abridged by A.K. Herring. New York: Modern Promotions.

Daniel Defoe
Campe, Joachimm (1824) *Robinson der Yingere: Eyn Lezebukh für Kinder*. Eine Hebreische ibertragen fon David Zamoshch. Breslau: Sulzbach.
Robinson Crusoe (1936) Translated and abridged by Yehuda Grazovski. Tel Aviv: Massada.
Robinson Crusoe (1964),Translated and abridged by Ben-Pinhas. Tel Aviv: Niv.

Jonathan Swift
Massa Gulliver le-liliput, eretz ha-nanasim (1945) Translated by A. Cahana. Tel Aviv: Sinai.
Mas'ei Gulliver (1961) Translated and adapted by Yaacov Niv. Ramat Gan: Massada.
Gulliver be-eretz ha-gamadim (n.d.) Adapted by S. Skulski. Tel Aviv: El Hamaayan.
Gulliver be-artzot haplaot (1976) Translated by Avraham Aryeh Akavya. Tel Aviv: Jizreel.
Gulliver be-eretz ha-anaqim (n.d.) Tel Aviv: Zelkowitz.
Massa Lilliput (n.d.) Translated by Pesah Ginzburg. Tel Aviv: Sreberk.
Gulliver's Travels (1976) Loughborough: Ladybird.

Mark Twain
Meoraot Tom (1911) Translated by Israel Haim Tavyov. Odessa: Turgeman.
Tom Sawyer (1940) Translated and abridged by Avraham Aryeh. Akavya. Tel Aviv: Jizreel.
Meoraot Tom Sawyer (1960) Translated and abridged by Ben-Pinhas. Tel Aviv: Yesod.

Notes

1. 'Canonized' texts are those that are regarded as part of the literary heritage.
2. Chapbooks were cheaply produced pamphlets, usually illustrated with woodcuts and sold by itinerant traders.

Marisa Fernández López

Translation Studies in Contemporary Children's Literature: A Comparison of Intercultural Ideological Factors

In children's literature, and more particularly in mass-market literature, a formal instability of the text may be observed, manifested in its gradual modification over the years; the scant literary value assigned to this kind of writing probably makes it more susceptible to censorship and alteration. Original works are modified in subsequent editions to conform to the social standards prevailing at a given time and thus to satisfy the specific demands of the market. These modifications exist alongside a culturally imposed self-censorship by the author. In *American Childhood* (1994: 179), Anne Scott MacLeod lists a series of taboos that have traditionally been avoided in American children's literature. For example, violence may be present in a tale provided that the author does not allow more violence to breed from it; likewise, children rarely die except in the case of some martyrs and heroes.[1] If parents die, their death occurs prior to the commencement of the tale, and subjects such as divorce, mental illness, alcoholism and other addictions, suicide, and sex are all avoided; murderers do not usually appear, although thieves are permitted; racial conflicts do not arise or are merely referred to in passing; and the tale has a happy ending. This code has been applied systematically and on a worldwide basis, particularly where the theme of sex is concerned, as this subject was taboo in children's literature until the 1960s.

Sometimes the motivation for the modification of reprinted (and perhaps already self-censored) texts is commercial, for example updating in order to increase sales. A paradigmatic case is the treatment during the 20th century of the novels produced in the United States by the Stratemeyer Syndicate. Series such as the Bobbsey Twins, Nancy Drew, and the Happy Hollisters, which appeared in the first third of the century, were systematically changed in later editions in order to render them acceptable to consumers whose lifestyles and social customs were changing rapidly – especially, though not uniquely, with respect to food, fashion, and means of transport (Hildick, 1974: 191).

41

In addition, these textual modifications are attributable not only to strictly commercial motives, which habitually affect secondary aspects of the work. They are also due to profound ideological motivations and affect important passages of text, normally through a process of purification that involves textual elimination. In the last 60 years, numerous examples may be found of this kind of ideological purification of children's literature written in English, especially in the case of popular literature. The work of Enid Blyton, in particular that published during the 1940s, and the work of Roald Dahl in the 1960s and 1970s provide typical examples of the manipulation of texts. In these cases publishers themselves censored works in order to avoid problems.

But in recent years the criteria for censorship have changed. While the inclusion of sex, vulgar expressions, or liberal views no longer represents a problem in children's literature, censorship is applied to texts that are considered racist or sociopolitically incorrect. The fundamental rationale for this new censorship is today, as it was in the 18th century, didactic in nature. Those who defend censorship where children's literature is concerned do so not so much for political reasons but out of a romantic idea of the power of the printed word on impressionable young minds. They do not consider censorship an act of intolerance, but see it rather as a positive step in safeguarding childhood innocence and for maintaining the well-being of society in general (West, 1996: 507).

Children's literature translation studies are particularly interesting when they can highlight the differences between cultural behaviours by comparing contrasting treatments of a specific text. During the course of a systematic study of translations into Spanish of popular 20th-century novels for young people written in English, I observed a peculiar phenomenon: fragments of the source text that were purified of racist and xenophobic elements in subsequent English-language editions were published in Spanish in a translation that remained faithful to the original English versions (Fernández López, 1996). This characteristic even extended to illustrations. For example, take the pictures of the Oompa Loompas in Roald Dahl's *Charlie and the Chocolate Factory* (British edition 1985): after textual and graphic purification, they were represented as white, when in the original (and in Spanish editions) they are black. The discrepancy reveals ideological differences between the Spanish literary system on the one hand and that of Great Britain and the United States on the other. In other words, a society's patterns of behaviour and its moral values are not only reflected in the textual modifications introduced in translations of foreign works, which Göte Klingberg (1986: 18) defines as cultural context adaptations, in the case of Spain they are also reflected in the fidelity to the first editions of texts that have been modified in their countries of origin.

The translation of works for children has traditionally been mediated by pedagogical and didactic considerations that affect the so-called operational translation norms, such as what Gideon Toury (1980:128) terms stylistic elevation and stylistic homogeneity. Under these norms translators tend to use the standard literary language of the target system. Where Spanish is concerned, this practice implies eliminating repetitions and void pragmatic connectives and substituting lectic substandard forms or those that characterise an ethnic or social group for the standard variety. As Zohar Shavit writes,

> In contrast to adult canonized literature, in which the norm of complexity is the most prevalent today, the norm of simple and simplified models is still prominent in most children's literature (canonized and non-canonized), as is also the case with the non-canonized adult system. This norm, rooted in the self-image of children's literature, tends to determine not only the thematics and characterisation of the text, but also its options concerning permissible structures. (Shavit, 1986: 125)

As a result we find unmarked direct speech is substituted for marked speech and that clichés are stressed by expansion (Fernández López, 1996).

The Spanish system is not markedly different from those of other countries, although it evinces a greater respect for source texts, to the extent that it considers first editions in regard to translations as something of a preliminary norm. This fidelity does not mean that respect for the source text comes at the expense of problems of acceptability of the target text but rather that, in general, only those features of the text that could conflict with criteria considered canonical within the Spanish children's literature system undergo any kind of modification. Thus elimination is preferred to cultural context adaptations, while culturally linked elements – 'overt' in Juliane House's (1977: 246) terminology – are preserved untouched. Under the strong censorship that existed until the 1970s, the elements that were traditionally eliminated were those that related either to sex or to religion. Thus, in the Spanish version of 'Jumble' (a story in Richmal Crompton's 1922 *Just William*, translated in 1935 as *Travesuras de Guillermo*), the 15 lines referring to a kiss were eliminated. Similarly omitted was a paragraph in Crompton's story 'The Outlaws and the Missionary' in *William's Crowded Hours* (1931, translated as *Guillermo el atareado*, 1959), in which William complains, according to his own peculiar logic, of the behaviour of certain missionaries whom he compares to thieves. These omissions cannot be attributed to the translator, as otherwise there are no textual omissions that extend beyond a single sentence. Censoring by the publisher would appear to be the most probable reason. The elimination of the paragraph where William kisses his girlfriend must be assessed in the context of Franco's Spain. The long period of dictatorship in Spain (1939–1975) was characterized by a perfectly structured censorship that enforced general taboos concerning sex, politics, and religion. At the time the book was translated, taboos regarding sex included even the most innocent behaviours. Where religion was concerned, the reference was always to Catholicism, and the word Christian was always synonymous with Catholic. The Catholic Church supported Franco's government, and any negative references to priests were forbidden and always considered defamatory.

When the original contained material contrary to the Spanish system, especially with regard to unacceptable political references, publishers resolved the problem by simply ignoring its existence and not publishing it in Spain. Crompton's William series, although she has never been suspected of leftist tendencies, had some problems in Spain. The most obvious gap is the absence of any Spanish translation of the work *William the Dictator* (1938).[2] The problem stems from the cover illustration by Thomas Henry, whose drawings have become inseparable from Crompton's text in English and from most Spanish versions as well; the reader's idea of William is Henry's image of him. On the jacket, William is saluting in the fascist fashion wearing torn blue trousers, a brown shirt, and a greenish bracelet attached to his sleeve with a safety pin; he is standing in front of his guerrilla group, the Outlaws (*Proscritos* in Spanish). The satire on Nazism is confirmed by the title story, which is about William's attempt to obtain extra living space by invading his neighbors' gardens in a parody of the German call for *Lebensraum*.

Presumably Spanish censors remained ignorant of this volume; otherwise, it is inconceivable that so much of Crompton's work could have been published in Spain in the 1940s and 1950s, when Franco was most powerful and political censorship was at its height. It is probable, however, that the Spanish publisher, Molino, did know of the existence of *William the Dictator* but managed to keep it concealed during Franco's hegemony. Where the William books were concerned, the publisher had the advantage of being in a position to manipulate the texts with unusual ease, since the volumes were composed of short stories. Any of these could easily be omitted or replaced without the reader, or indeed the censor, having the slightest idea that the volume had been tampered with. Such tampering is probably what happened to the short story 'William and the Nasties,' written in 1934 and included in the volume *William the Detective* (1935). This tale was withdrawn by the British publisher for the second edition owing to the possibility of problems with the German embassy; the Nasties were, of course, a reference to the Nazis, William having invented the name for his gang when they decided to attack the village candy store, owned by a Jew, in order to take over his stock. The story reappeared in successive English-language editions only to be withdrawn again in the 1980s, when it was once more considered politically incorrect. The tale was never published in Spain, and it appears neither in *Guillermo Detective* nor in any other volume of the collection. Its absence suggests either censorship or that the source text was an English edition from which the tale had already been removed.

But if political climates change, a more prolonged tendency over the years has been toward stylistic homogeneity: the elimination of registers considered unacceptable for children and adolescents, which may be considered an authentic kind of purification (Klingberg, 1986: 58). For example, there have been numerous substitutions for insults in Blyton's work. In *Five Go off to Camp* (1948), translated as *Los Cinco van de camping* (1965/1985), 'You're perfect pigs over the tomatoes' (p. 48) becomes '*sois unos verdaderos glotones comiendo tomates*' (p. 43) ('you're absolute gluttons with the tomatoes'). The phrase 'The beast!' in *The O'Sullivan Twins* (1942: 62) is rendered as '*¡Qué insolente!*' ('How rude') in *Las Mellizas O'Sullivan* (1960: 78). And *Los Cinco frente a la aventura*, the 1966 translation of *Five Fall into Adventure* (1950), turns 'ass' (p. 21) into '*tonta*' (idiot) (p. 21). The use of the word 'pig' in the first example, for instance (and there are many synonyms for this word in Spanish), would be considered highly insulting in Spain. This general tendency to alter insults is more obvious when we are dealing with texts that were supposed to be appropriate for children, especially at a time in Spain when didactic considerations obliged the translators to purify even innocent insults.

The existence of an original text that over time undergoes modifications even in its native language because of the low status of children's literature and its perceived moral and didactic function causes difficulties when we seek to compare the translation with its source. Given this peculiarity, it often becomes necessary to perform what Toury calls a 'retrospective analysis,' the analysis of the target text to ascertain which of the possible source texts is its pair (1995: 102). In this way changes in the source text have been detected by means of a primary analysis of the Spanish translations that have remained unaltered.

In fact the fidelity apparent in Spanish editions to certain passages of text that have been profoundly altered in successive British editions is all the more noticeable in a social context that permits textual modifications of topics deemed taboo or of speech registers considered inappropriate for certain ages. This fidelity to original editions seems to be due not just to the fact that some Spanish translations were published in advance of the purification of the source text (as is the case with some of Blyton's works) but also to the Spanish tradition of adherence to the original version of a given text. This translation norm may in turn be due to the high regard shown by Spanish children's literature for its English-language analogue, a regard not demonstrated by other, less permeable children's literature systems. For example, the French have systematically adapted Blyton's works to suit their own national repertoire (see Bordet, 1985). Whereas in Great Britain and in other countries such as France with highly impermeable children's literature systems, Blyton's work has always been considered of scant literary worth, in Spain it has never received a word of negative criticism – at least during the author's 'golden age' in Spain (1960–1980) – inviting comparison with the work of canonized authors in English-speaking countries.

Thus while in Spain the translations of Blyton's adventure series retain the cultural traits of the source text (both geographical and cultural, and including the behaviour of the characters), the French translations tend to eliminate all the details that might associate the text with specific places or cultures. This approach gives the text a universal flavour, but deprives it of its British characteristics, which the author expressly wished to retain (Menzies, 1950: 3). It is interesting that strong literary systems tend to be impermeable, thereby facilitating the tendency of the translations to transform foreign repertoires (and ideologies) into those of the source nationality, especially when the source text is not considered an integral part of the original literary system's canon, which is usually the case where popular literature is concerned. In comparing the translations of Blyton's series into French and into Spanish, we can see the different responses of two literary systems that, in the case of children's literature, adopt a very different stance (dominant, like France, and weaker and historically influenced like Spain).[3] The translations of Blyton's series are representative and are, taken as a whole, quantitatively of considerable importance where studies of this type are concerned. In Blyton's case the sum of Spanish and French translations (517 and 259 respectively) represents one-third of the total number (2168) registered in the author's name in the fourth (cumulative) edition of UNESCO's *Index Translationum: International Bibliography of Translations.*

Marie-Pierre and Michel Mathieu-Colas's work (1983) on the Famous Five series in France is particularly interesting in comparison with Spanish translations. The synchronic study in both countries of the translations and of critics' reactions to them shows the tendency toward impermeability in dominant systems that avoid all exterior ideological influence.

Table 1

Original	French translation	Spanish translation
Five Run Away Together (1944)	Le Club des Cinq contreattaque (1955)	Los Cinco se escapan (1965)
Five Fall into Adventure (1950)	Le Club des Cinq et les gitanes (1960)	Los Cinco frente a la aventura (1966)
Five on Kirrin Island Again (1947)	Le Club des Cinq joue et gagne (1956)	Los Cinco otra vez en la isla de Kirrin (1965)
Five Go to Demon's Rocks (1961)	La boussole du Club des Cinq (1963)	Los Cinco en las Rocas del Diablo (1970)
Five Go to Billycock Hill (1957)	Le Club des Cinq el les papillons (1962)	Los Cinco en Billycock Hill (1969)
Five go to Mystery Moor (1954)	La locomotive du Club des Cinq (1961)	Los Cinco en el páramo misterioso (1968)

Take, for instance, the translations of some of the titles of Blyton's works. Whereas the Spanish translation respects the source text and maintains cultural elements associated with the country of origin, the French translation eliminates them systematically, as can been seen in Table 1. No less striking is the treatment given to the characters, whose names in the source text and in the French and Spanish translations appear in Table 2. Similarly, while the surnames of the source text are respected in the Spanish translation, French ones are given in the respective French version.

In addition, there is the question of geography. Although the exact location of the action is not explicitly indicated in the source text, one can deduce that it is set in the western region of Great Britain – Cornwall or Wales. The French version modifies the name Kirrin to Kernach, which the

Table 2

Source language	Target language (French)	Target language (Spanish)
Georgine ('George')	Claudine ('Claude')	Jorgina ('Jorge')
Julian	François	Julián
Dick	Mick	Dick
Anne	Annie	Ana
Timothy (the dog)	Dagobert	Tim

French reader might well associate with a French Celtic area, that of Brittany (Mathieu-Colas, 1983: 99). Although there is an equivalent Celtic locality in Spain, Galicia, the Spanish translation maintains all the cultural indicators of the original text. In the illustrated French editions of the 1970s, the nationalisation of the text is complete right down to the police who appear in the illustrations as French gendarmes.

A common phenomenon in children's literature translations, that of super-explicit textual amplification (which can be considered part of the normal use of simplified models), is found extensively in the French translations of Blyton's works. According to Genevieve Bordet, the use of textual models that are less sophisticated than the originals is due to an attempt by the editors to target readers younger than those for whom the originals were written (1985: 30). In Spain, on the other hand, the same works were published with an adolescent reader in mind, as a consequence of a different evaluation of the text. The French judgement of Blyton's work as inferior and as such liable to radical change also becomes evident when the translator of these works is sought. While in Spanish translations the translator's name is always given, only in the first two volumes of the Famous Five series, published by Hachette, does the name of the translator appear – never in any later editions (Mathieu-Colas, 1983: 157).

No less revealing is the behaviour of French and Spanish critics over the years in response to Blyton's work and that of other non-canonical British authors. In France, opinion of Blyton's work is generally negative, condemning its textual poverty and supporting the numerous anti-Blyton arguments of British critics, although we find significant exceptions, such as the work of Denise Escarpit (1985), who points out that the French texts are clearly different from the source texts. In Spain, where the translated text is generally most faithful to the original, critics are generous to Blyton, recognising her ability to interest young people in reading and to introduce other cultures (albeit from the point of view of the writer). If their criticism refers to some textual poverty, it is not to be compared to the virulent attacks by French or British critics (see, for example, Company, 1993; Colomer, 1994; Gárate, 1997; Ruzicka *et al.*, 1995).

Thus whereas there are no fundamental changes evident in the Spanish texts when compared with the first editions of the original text, the changes made in the French translations represent a reinforcement of the hierarchies and a distortion of values that are not present in the Spanish ones. Bordet (1985: 30) provides two examples: first, 'one of the farm-men' becomes '*l'ouvrier de M. Penlan*' (Mr Penlan the worker); second, while in the source text some pirates are driven by their wish for 'a bit of excitement,' in the French they are '*heureux de vivre une aventure et de gagner de l'argent*' (happy to live an adventure and gain some money). The distortion of values is obvious.

Similarly, this differential behaviour, derived as it is from the permeability of the literary system, can also be seen in Portugal, where the children's literature system is similar to the Spanish one. The translations of Blyton, for example, are analogous to the Spanish ones as far as editorial type, presentation, types of translated texts, and target market are concerned, while the translation itself falls somewhere between French and Spanish practices. The translator's name appears, as it does in Spain, but the titles of the different stories are a mixture of a faithful translation from the source text (as in the Spanish case) and a descriptive title of the adventure (as in the French case). Thus in Portugal *Five Fall into Adventure* becomes *Os cinco e a ciganita*.

In the translation of children's literature, the Spanish norm of fidelity to the original text is only displaced by other norms of greater force, such as the primacy of pedagogic and didactic considerations. If the Spanish editions still have not eliminated the racist and xenophobic elements present in the works of Blyton and Dahl, it is without a doubt because a social consciousness that rejects discrimination against ethnic minorities did not exist in Spain until the 1990s. Ethnicity and issues relating to colour had no forum in Spain, and any understanding of them was imbued with colonialist attitudes: the white man and his developed society were responsible for rescuing inferior cultures and civilisations plagued with barbarous customs arising from ignorance and underdevelopment. The only important ethnic minority in Spain during the Franco period was the Gypsies, with whom delinquency was traditionally, though wholly unjustifiably, associated.

Thus Franco Spain did not reflect the situation in Britain and the United States where, in the 1970s, the influence of the works of Wallace Hildick (1974), the Children's Rights Workshop, and, above all, Bob Dixon (1977) persuaded publishers to change some racist, sexist, and classist passages in certain works. Some of these modifications were made after the editing of the first Spanish version; still, in later Spanish editions and even in fresh translations, these passages were not modified, probably because they did not actively conflict with what Spanish society considered appropriate for young readers. For example, important modifications were made to Blyton's *Five Fall into Adventure* – in all probability as a result of Hildick's harsh criticism – in Hodder and Stoughton's English edition of 1986. The Spanish edition of 1990 did not incorporate any changes at all in the translation, and remained faithful to the original English text of 1950. The fragments that were modified in the source text refer to Blyton's treatment of

Gypsies, as characterized by an offensive lack of hygiene. Not so in the Spanish translation, in which not only characters but also the narrator of the story discriminate against a Gypsy family because of their smell: '*Al punto un olor raro, nauseabundo, alcanzó las narices de los niños ¡Que asco!*' ('Just then a strange, sickening smell reached the noses of the children. Ugh!') (p. 18). On other occasions in the 1986 English edition the ethnic reference vanishes or is changed to the English term for Gypsies common today, 'travellers': 'The girl stared at him' (p. 18) still appears as '*La niña que parecía ungitano le contempló con fijeza*' ('The girl, who looked like a Gypsy, stared at him intently') (p. 20). 'It's a big place. Don't get lost! And look out for the travellers. There's usually hordes of them there!' (p. 86) is rendered '*Es un bosque muy grande ¡Tened cuidado, no os vayais a perder. ...! y manteneos vigilantes, porque hay en él muchos gitanos*' ('It's a very big wood, so take care not to get lost! And keep a look out because there are lots of Gypsies there') (p. 99). Moreover, an offensive reference to Blacks eliminated in the English edition was also not modified in Spain: instead of 'It had nasty gleaming eyes – oh, I was frightened!' (p. 25) we find, '*sus ojos eran crueles y relucían. Todo lo demás estaba demasiado oscuro. ¡Quizás era el rostro de un negro! ¡Oh, qué miedo he pasado!*' ('Its eyes were cruel and gleaming. It was too dark to see anything else. Perhaps it was the face of a black man. Oh, how afraid I was!') (p. 28).

In both these cases the attitude is openly racist. The Gypsies, Spain's only sizeable ethnic minority when the work was translated in the 1960s, had persistently suffered harsh discrimination; although it was officially unacceptable, nevertheless in practice segregation existed. In the reference to the '*rostro de un negro*,' the treatment is different. There was no such minority group to speak of in Spain, and the popular image of the black man was closer to that of Hugh Lofting: the primitive African in need of redemption. Hence the general acceptance of black artists (mostly Latin American musicians and singers), who enjoyed warm hospitality.

A similar transformation in Britain but not in Spain occurs in the representation of strongly marked sex roles. Making clear divisions between boys' and girls' roles is characteristic of Blyton; this trait was modified in post-1970 editions in Great Britain. One example is the subtle elimination of the universal in the source text in *Five Fall into Adventure* where 'you' becomes '*niñas*' (girls): 'You can't go about fighting' (p. 19) appears as '*Las niñas no deben pelear*' (p. 21).

In England, such purification was applied not only to Blyton's works, but to others. Take the case of the story 'William and the League of Perfect Love,' which disappeared from the English edition of *William the Detective* at the same time as 'William and the Nasties,' mentioned above. Eliminated in England because it included a bloody rat hunt, rats being William's favourite animal, it has been continuously reprinted in Spain without arousing protest. And in addition to the purification of Crompton's work, in the US there is the case of *Charlie and the Chocolate Factory,* where changes occur in English editions that are not reflected in the Spanish versions. Here, the modifications are largely superficial: references to the ethnic origin of the Oompa Loompas, the workers in Willy Wonka's factory, which first appeared in the US during a period of great activity among pro-Civil Rights groups. All references linking the colour of these fictional characters with that of chocolate, contained in three paragraphs at the end of Chapter 15, have been eliminated, but no modifications were made in the corresponding Spanish translations. Similarly, at the beginning of Chapter 16, where the text talked about the geographical origin of the Oompa Loompas, 'Africa' is replaced by 'Loompaland,' and in case any doubts remained, the adjective 'black' was changed to 'rosy-white': 'His skin was rosy-white, his long hair was golden-brown, and the top of his head came just above the height of Mr Wonka's knee' (p. 85) is rendered in Spanish as: *'su piel era casi negra, y la parte superior de su lanuda cabeza llegaba a la altura de la rodilla del señor Wonka'* (p. 95) ('His skin was almost black, and the top of his woolly head came just above the height of Mr. Wonka's knee').

Parallel cases exist not only in works that critics consider on the fringes of children's literature, but also in works that some scholars consider to truly belong to the canon, as in the case of Lofting's Doctor Dolittle stories. Just as he had done with Blyton, Dixon (1977) launched a furious assault on Lofting's work in his *Catching them Young 1: Sex, Race and Class in Children's Fiction*. His complaints focused on Chapter 11 of *The Story of Doctor Dolittle* (1920), which tells the story of the Black prince Bumpo. The ascendancy that Dixon and other critics achieved in the late 1970s over the relevant editorial sectors in Britain and North America meant that Lofting became one of the children's authors whose works were most thoroughly purified. In general, 'white man' disappears or is replaced by 'man' or 'European.' The same thing happens with 'black man,' which in the purified source text appears as 'man' or 'African.' Textual purifications of the original are not limited to such minimal lexical modifications, but extend to the elimination or modification of whole paragraphs or entire chapters. The Spanish editions are not purified.

From the 1960s onward the influence of translations changed the nature of children's literature in Spain. With the end of the dictatorship in the mid-1970s came the end of censorship, which brought with it a major increase in the publication of translations of more recent works. The Spanish children's literature system continues to be highly permeable.

More than half of the published children's literature in Spain appears in translation, and nearly two-thirds of that literature is translated from English. So British and American literature is, by far, the most important area for study and the most influential in the Spanish literary polysystem. The influence of recent English-language works, incorporating themes and narrative styles from the last quarter of the century, has meant that the current literary panorama is not very different from the American, British, and German ones. The Spanish system has been strengthened thanks to the incorporation of external models into the national repertoire. This means that today racial, religious, societal, and cultural points of view are often similar to those found in other European and American narratives. By 1990, in a collection of studies carried out by reputable authors of children's literature in Spain, Pablo Barrena and his collaborators showed how the end of the dictatorship had seen an end to taboos. Similarly, realist themes, including racism, have lately been treated in an open and positive manner. The result is a powerful literature for the young that has reached a state of maturity, as Teresa Colomer (1998) and Amalia Bermejo (1999) have recently argued. Translation has meant not only the transfer of the works from those systems that have been traditionally dominant in the field of children's literature to the Spanish system, which has facilitated the revival of the field by means of new techniques and topics, but also the highlighting of ideological confrontations in studies of translator behaviour.

The influence of extra-textual factors on translation practice and, conversely, the important source that translations constitute for experts are confirmed by these few examples, which could easily be multiplied by quotations and references from many other works and authors. Contrary to the simplistic view that holds the literary study of children's literature as necessarily of less complexity than corresponding studies of adult literature, translation studies reveal yet again the richness of the field and the need for multidisciplinary research. As Tessa Rose Chester (1989: 5) has observed: 'The study of children's books touches on literary, artistic, and historical spheres, it cuts across other major disciplines such as literary criticism, education, sociology and psychology, and it is an important part of the social history'.

Notes

1. Spanish children's literature in the 19th century contains numerous accounts of the lives of child saints, who by and large were martyrs. These tales, set more often than not during the Roman Empire, were complemented by stories of others martyred for their beliefs, which were published throughout the Civil War and early postwar period by the winning faction.
2. *William the Dictator* is the title of the volume and of one of the stories. When it was

published separately in *Happy Magazine* its title was changed to 'What's in a Name?' (Cadogan, 1994: 39), probably to avoid angering certain readers belonging to the British Union of Fascists. It remains untranslated, although the reason now undoubtedly is a lack of interest on the part of publishers, with no social or political implications.

3. Until the 20th century the dominant influence on Spanish children's literature was French. Over the last hundred years, British and American works, and to a lesser extent German, have taken the place of the French. We have also witnessed a strengthening of the Spanish internal system itself, which is not as intransigent about external influence as the French system.

Tiina Puurtinen

Translating Children's Literature: Theoretical Approaches and Empirical Studies

Writing and translating for children, though often regarded as a simple and even insignificant matter, is governed by numerous constraints, which usually vary from culture to culture. The situation is also rendered problematic by the fact that a children's book must simultaneously appeal to both the genuine reader – the child – and the background authority – the adult. The translator must consider the needs of the target audience, the status of the source text and its special characteristics as well as the culture-specific norms regulating translation, and must determine a general strategy with regard to the particular book to be translated. Owing to the peripheral position of children's literature in the literary system, the translator of children's books is relatively free to manipulate the texts, i.e. the requirement of faithfulness to the original is outweighed by other constraints.

According to Zohar Shavit, translation for children is directed by the following two principles, which can be either complementary or contradictory: adjusting the source text in order to make it appropriate and useful for the child, and adjusting the plot, characterization and language to the child's ability to read and comprehend, in accordance with a society's notion of what is 'good for the child' and what the child can read and understand, respectively (Shavit, 1986: 112–113). Translational norms, which regulate, for instance, the choice of books to be translated and the formulation of the target text, are based on these two broad principles.

Translational norms are not necessarily identical with norms operating in original children's literature written in the target language, nor do the translators always conform to the norms, as a certain degree of creative freedom is normally tolerated. Therefore the type and extent of deviations from the prevalent norms, and their effect on the reception of translated children's books, form an interesting field of study.

The purpose of the present article is to relate a study on the 'acceptability' of two Finnish translations of *The Wizard of Oz* to different approaches developed by translation scholars (Toury, Shavit, Klingberg, Reiss, House,

Oittinen) with respect to the translation of literature in general or to the translation of children's literature in particular. (Studies on the latter subject are still very few in number, probably because children's literature, let alone its translation, has for a long time not been considered worthy of academic study.) Similarities and divergences will be discussed and the suitability or unsuitability of each approach to the study in preparation will be briefly evaluated. But before describing the different theoretical frameworks it is first necessary to give a short outline of the study I propose.

Outline of the Project[1]

The primary research material consists of L. Frank Baum's *The Wizard of Oz* and its two Finnish translations, *Ozin velho* by Kersti Juva (KJ) and *Oz-maan taikuri* by Marja Helanen-Ahtola (MHA). The translations were published by two different publishing houses in 1977, and both have the same function and target group (7 to 12-year-old children). There is, however, a noticeable difference in style and especially in the syntactic structures used by the translators. KJ gives an impression of fluent, natural and dynamic style, due to the translator's preference for simple finite constructions (subordinate and co-ordinate clauses), which are explicit and easy for the reader to process. MHA's style is rendered more formal and static by the frequency of complex non-finite constructions, such as contracted sentences and premodified participal attributes, which have low redundancy and therefore tend to burden the reader's short-term memory and lower the text's readability.

The purpose of the study is to compare the stylistic acceptability of the translations and to draw conclusions on the effect on acceptability of the static vs. dynamic syntax, in other words nominal vs. verbal style. The concept of acceptability, which has been adopted by Toury, is defined in terms of the norms, conventions and expectations prevailing in the language and style of Finnish children's fiction. These presumably include the requirement of high readability and natural, fluent style. This will be established on the basis of a few earlier studies on the style of Finnish children's fiction, and by examining a small corpus of secondary research material consisting of contemporary children's books originally written in or translated into Finnish.

It must be emphasized here that the study concentrates on stylistic factors and the moral, ideological and other sociocultural parameters of acceptability are ignored because of their irrelevance in this case: neither of the translators has manipulated the source text in order to adapt it to a certain ideology, nor are there any problematic culture-specific terms

requiring adjustment. The hypothesis is that the use of complex constructions in MHA decreases readability and consequently lowers acceptability,
whereas KJ is expected to be more readable and acceptable owing to its
natural, dynamic style characterized by simple finite constructions.

Two linguistic models will be applied during the analysis of those
syntactic structures. Yngve's (1960) modification of phrase-structure
grammar explains the cognitive complexity of premodified participial
attributes as a result of the direction of branching, which can be seen from
tree diagrams: a premodified participial attribute is a left-branching structure, which places a greater burden on the reader's immediate memory
than an alternative right-branching structure, such as a relative clause.
Meyer's prepositional model (1975: 25–43) illustrates the complexity of
contracted sentences as against corresponding subordinate clauses and can
be used in order to show that KJ uses more explicit means (finite constructions with conjunctions) than MHA to convey information. Finally, three
empirical tests, i.e. a standard cloze text (taken by school children), a
reading-aloud test and subjective assessment (performed by adult subjects),
will provide data about the readability and 'read-aloud' ability (my term)
of the translations as well as about adult readers' reactions to their style.
The text results are expected to reveal significant differences, whose impact
on the relative acceptability of the translations will then be evaluated.

Toury's Target Text Oriented Approach

In contradistinction to so-called 'traditional' normative and source
text-oriented theories of translation, Toury advocates a descriptive target
text-oriented approach, first and foremost to literary translation (Toury,
1980). Instead of considering translations as mere reconstructions of the
source text, he sees them as textual-linguistic products which belong
primarily to the target literary system. Every translation occupies a certain
position on a continuum between two poles, adequacy and acceptability. A
translator who aims at an adequate translation observes the norms of the
source language and the source literary polysystem, which may make the
resulting translation incompatible with the linguistic and literary norms of
the target system. The acceptability of a translation, on the other hand, is
determined by adherence to the linguistic and literary norms of the target
system (or a section of it, like a genre or subgenre).

A translation is usually a compromise between these two extremes. A
high degree of acceptability is attained when the target text is maximally
compatible with the dominant norms of the recipient literary system. The
position of a translation between adequacy and acceptability is determined

by translational norms, which according to Toury should be the main object of the study of literary translation. Toury has toppled the notion of equivalence by stating that the relationship between a source text and a text regarded as its translation *is* equivalence, and that it is the task of descriptive translation studies to establish *what kind of equivalence* exists and what are the norms determining the identification of certain relationships between a source text and a target text as 'equivalence'.

Translational norms can be divided into two larger categories: preliminary norms, which influence the choice of works to be translated and the source version of the text to be translated (possibly via intermediate translations), and operational norms, which direct the translator's decisions during the translation process. Operational norms are subdivided into matricial norms, which determine the existence and location of target language material in the target text, and the textual segmentation (omissions, additions, changes in location), and textual (proper) norms determining the actual verbal formulation of the text. Textual norms include linguistic norms (e.g. general stylistic norms) and literary norms (determining what is appropriate for literary texts in a certain genre or period, etc.). Toury calls the translator's choice between the two extremes of adequacy and acceptability the initial norm.

The advantage of the Tourian approach is that it provides a framework for the study of literary translations in their immediate environment. A translation of a children's book, for instance, generally has to operate in the target system like an original. It might be expected that in translations of children's books, which are often not even conceived of as being translations, translational norms tend to place the target text quite close to the acceptability pole. Hence the Finnish translations of *The Wizard of Oz* can also be expected to observe the linguistic and literary norms and conventions prevalent in contemporary Finnish children's fiction. As assumed above, these are likely to require a high degree of readability and a fluent, dynamic style, which are thus the main parameters for the definition of stylistic acceptability. The preference for acceptability is connected with the properties of the target group – children, with their imperfect reading abilities and experience of life, are not expected to tolerate so many strange and foreign elements as adult readers are – and with the secondary position of translated children's literature, which normally makes the translator rely on what is already conventionalised in the target system.

The static style and frequency of complex syntactic structures in MHA may imply a violation of the textual norms, namely the literary norms determining what is suitable language and style for Finnish children's books. The structures in question seem to disagree with the norms of usage, although they are probably relatively weak norms or tendencies, rather than strict, basic norms (Toury's terms, see Toury, 1980: 60). The deviations may be partly due to the fact that the translator adheres to certain target language forms or structures because of their formal correspondence to some source language forms or structures, without taking into account the possibly different distribution and/or functions of these forms in the two languages. The existence of such formal equivalents (Toury, 1980: 74) can be substantiated by comparing deviant phenomena in the target text to their counterparts in the source text, i.e. by referring translational solutions to translational problems (as suggested in Toury, 1985). In this way, it will be possible to discover whether, for instance, the complex constructions in MHA have been used more or less consistently to replace certain formally equivalent English constructions. In the following example, an English past participle has been replaced in MHA by the Finnish premodified participial attribute, which leads to a heavy left-branching structure, unfit for children's literature, whereas KJ uses a relative clause:

... but surely there is no use for a Scarecrow *stuck on a pole in the middle of the river.* (source text, no page number)

... mutta *keskelle jokea seipään päähän joutuneella Variksenpelättimellä* eitodellakaan ole mitään merkitystä. (MHA: 56)
(but in the middle of the river on a pole stuck Scarecrow is really of no significance)

... mutta *sellaisesta variksenpelätistä, joka roikkuu kepin nenässä keskellä jokea,* ei ole mitään hyötyä. (KJ: 56)
(but such a scarecrow, which hangs on a stick in the middle of a river, is of no use)

This is a clear illustration of the source text's role in the study of translations: it can obviously not be the starting point for an investigation into the acceptability of two translations, but it can supply the researcher with explanations for certain target text phenomena.

Toury's theoretical model is intended as a tool for the description of translations in general, though with special attention to literary translations. He has also applied his model to the analysis of German children's literature in Hebrew translation (Toury, 1980: 140–151). More general patterns of writing and translating for children have been suggested by Zohar Shavit.

Shavit's Behaviour Patterns of Translated Children's Literature

Shavit considers children's literature from the point of view of its peripheral position in the literary polysystem (Shavit, 1986). This position enables the translator to manipulate the text as long as two basic principles are observed: the didactic role of children's literature (the text should be educational and 'good for the child') and the adjustment of the plot, characterization and language to the child's reading ability and comprehension. Shavit (1986: 112–128) describes five comprehensive constraints or translational norms that usually dictate the translator's global approach with respect to both the content and the verbal formulation of a source text to be translated for children.

Firstly, the text must fit an existing model in the target literature. Hence a satire, for example, originally written for adults, may be changed into a simple fantasy story because the model of satire does not exist in the recipient children's literature. Secondly, it is permissible to delete parts and scenes that are not in accordance with the dominant moral values or what adults think children are able to understand. Thirdly, the thematics, characterization and main structures of the text must not be too complex (e.g. ironical elements may be left out); this norm often parallels the first and second one. The fourth constraint is based on the concept of children's literature as a didactic and ideological instrument: sometimes the source text may be changed completely in order to adapt it to the prevalent ideology. Finally, the stylistic features of the text are affected by stylistic norms. These are also in focus in the study on the translations of *The Wizard of Oz*.

The contemporary stylistic norms directing the translation of children's books into Finnish are likely to be based on the notion of children's comprehension and reading abilities as well as their likes and dislikes. Instead of a translation which is 'good for the child', the aim is an enjoyable, engaging text which encourages the reader to complete and renew the reading experience. One might even go as far as Mohl and Schlack and say that authors (and translators) of children's books should use the children's own manner of expression because this implies an attitude of solidarity (Mohl & Schack, 1981: 130). The syntactic complexities and formal style of MHA obviously disagree with these ideas.

Klingberg's Demand for Faithfulness

Contrary to Toury and Shavit, who take the target system and target text as a starting point, Göte Klingberg starts from the assumption that the author of the original work has already taken the prospective child readers, their interests, reading abilities, etc. into account, and made the text suitable for them (Klingberg, 1986). He calls the extent to which their character-istics are taken into account 'degree of adaptation of the source text', which in his opinion should be preserved in translation. Klingberg has extensively studied translations of a number of Swedish children's books into English and vice versa, investigating whether the translators have succeeded in retaining the original degree of adaptation, the main components of which are readability and content. Familiarity with the sociocultural context is often pursued in translation by adapting the cultural context of the source text to the cultural context of the target text. This procedure, which Klingberg calls context adaptation, is not relevant in the case of *The Wizard of Oz*, as I have already mentioned.

On the other hand, Klingberg's readability testing methods seem very unreliable. He has used readability formulas and word frequency lists in order to compare the readability (and thereby the degree of adaptation) of source and target texts. These methods are, however, too simple and restricted as tools for measuring readability, because they rely on a small number of separate features and, to give just one example, completely ignore the complexity of sentences. This was the main reason why I preferred the cloze method in a study on the readability of the two Finnish translations of *The Wizard of Oz* (Puurtinen, 1989a). Of course the cloze method does not directly indicate the impact of sentence structures either but, since it measures the general intelligibility of the entire text, it indi-rectly tests the effect of syntactic complexity as well.

Klingberg admits the defect of his methods. But his very starting point seems incompatible with the approach I chose. He seems to think that the degree of readability of the source text can and must simply be transferred to the target text by making some mechanical adjustments. Using Toury's terms, Klingberg can be regarded as a strong supporter of adequacy instead of acceptability. No reference is made to the possibly different norms and conventions of the source and target systems of children's literature, which may require different levels of linguistic difficulty, for instance, depending on the general principles of what is appropriate or useful for the child. Faithfulness to the original is Klingberg's main guideline. My research, on the other hand, concentrates on the comparison of certain features of two translations of the same source text, not on the discovery of differences between the source text and each translation. Both translations, produced at the same time, can be expected to conform to the norms and expectations of contemporary Finnish children's literature. The extent to which the translators' different solutions to the same translational problems influence this conformity, and hence the acceptability of the translations, is to be determined in the course of the study.

Reiss's Text Types

Katharina Reiss has discussed the specific translation problems of children's literature in terms of text types (Reiss, 1982). The informative, expressive, operative and audio-medial text types are all represented in children's literature, but fictional prose and fairy tales would normally belong to the expressive text type. Reiss states that in translations of predominantly expressive texts, the primary aim is to preserve the artistic organization, the style of the source text while conveying the content. However, most children's books are a mixture of various elements: undoubtedly expressive features play an important role, but so does narration itself, i.e. the plot and content of the story. It seems almost fruitless to divide texts into strict categories characterized by one main function, which then determines the appropriate way of translating.

Moreover, the function of the translation is not necessarily identical with that of the source text. In Reiss and Vermeer (1984), the writers actually stress the primary role of the function (skopos) of the *translation*, which can differ from that of the source text. To succeed in realizing the given function of the translation is considered more important than to perform the translation in any predetermined way. Reiss and Vermeer emphasize the interdependence of language and culture, and see translation both as linguistic and cultural transfer. Culture-bound conventions, which direct the formulation and structuring of texts belonging to different text types and text varieties, are to be taken into account to make the translation fulfil its function; the translator of an expressive text is likely to strive for analogous artistic organization in the target text, but analogy is not to be equated with identity, because language presents structural differences as well as diverging conventions and literary traditions. Thus, Reiss and Vermeer talk along the same lines as Toury, taking a prospective, target text-oriented view.

If the translator sets out to find target language equivalents for the stylistic components of a source text, there is always the danger of replacing source language forms with formally corresponding target language forms, although these may have completely different fuctions or exhibit a different level of difficulty (as in the example described earlier). Reiss also cautions us for this risk by stating that the translator of an expressive text must not slavishly imitate the source language forms but be inspired by them and use target language forms that are likely to make a similar impression on the reader (Reiss, 1971: 39–40).

House's Model

Juliane House distinguishes two basic types of translation: an overt translation is required when the source text itself is source culture linked and specifically directed at source language addressees, being tied to a specific historical event or having a unique status as a fictional text in the source culture; consequently an overt translation cannot fulfil a function similar to the one of its source text. A covert translation, on the other hand, has the status of an original in the target culture; the source text and target text have equivalent purposes and comparable target groups, which makes it possible and recommendable to keep the function of the source text unchanged. House does not deal with children's literature in connection with this model for translation quality assessment, but does mention fairy tales as an example of cases where the choice between an overt and a covert translation depends on the translator's viewpoint. If a fairy tale is seen as folklore tied to a specific cultural tradition, it is translated overtly, but if it is regarded as a non-culture-specific product intended as entertainment for the young, it is translated covertly (House: 1977: 189–204).

Hence, the Finnish translations of *The Wizard of Oz* are covert, as the original and both target texts have comparable functions and target groups. According to House, the text's function is realized by situational dimensions (including geographical origin, social class, time, medium, participation, social role relationship, social attitude and province), and their linguistic correlates, which are found on the lexical, syntactic and textual level (House 1977: 49). The choice of suitable linguistic correlates, which are naturally language-specific, is vital for the text's success. The applicability of House's model to the comparison of KJ and MHA is low, firstly because the aim of the study is not to compare textual profiles (of the source text and each target text), and secondly, because the textual profiles of the two target texts would mainly differ in syntactic structures, which is already known from the outset.

Oittinen and Dialogic Translation

In Finland, the most extensive study on translating children's literature so far was carried out by Riitta Oittinen (1988), whose theoretical and hermeneutical licentiate's thesis is written from the reader's, the child's and the translator's point of view. She questions the authority of the original work and the translator's underestimated position as an objective intermediary. The emphasis is on the translator's reading experience, which is reflected in the translation, so that every translation is seen as a new text and not as a mere reproduction of the original. The translator has to feel empathy with the source text, engage in a dialogue with it, with the child reader and the child in herself or himself, and give new life to the text in order to make it reach out for the child.

In general, Oittinen's holistic and dialogic approach provides welcome new insights into the field dominated by (source) text-orientedness, although its practical applicability is questionable. How far can a translator let the unique dialogue and his or her own idiosyncrasies take him or her before the translation becomes unacceptable? One point Oittinen has in common with the present writer is that she stresses the importance of fluency and rhythm, the 'read-aloud-ability' of children's books, without however suggesting any testing methods. In my research project, the effect of dynamic vs. static style in the translation of *The Wizard of Oz* on read-aloud-ability is to be examined by arranging a reading-aloud text during which adult test subjects will read excerpts from both KJ and MHA on tape. The recordings may indicate sentences that cause difficulties, like stumbling of hesitation, although the text is likely to reveal only minor differences between KJ and MHA.

Conclusion

Although the general theoretical framework I adopted is a Tourian one, the other viewpoints briefly discussed above also offer interesting insights into the object of study. They may even bring to the surface previously unnoticed parameters. Similarly, the test results may reveal similarly determining features. In the assessment test, for instance, where adult readers will be asked to comment on the style of the two translations, vocabulary may turn out to be more significant than expected. In the previous discussion, however, questions of vocabulary have not been dealt with, since the preliminary analysis did not reveal any major differences in lexicon between KJ and MHA. The decision to have both children and adults as subjects is justified by the two-fold status of children's books, namely the necessity to appeal simultaneously to the primary audience – children – and to the adult readers, who set the prevailing taste.

The main result expected from the comparative study on the main characteristics of KJ and MHA is information about the relative acceptability of these translations. In addition, the study is likely to give information on the possible difference between translational norms and norms operating in original Finnish children's literature. Are the translations representative of other similar texts or do they differ from the standard, and why? Finally, the results can be set into the larger context of children's culture, creativity and publishing policies, but that already goes partly beyond the limited scope of this study.

Notes

1. For a more detailed discussion of the project's objectives and methods, see Puurtinen (1989b), and for a summary of the findings of the project, see Puurtinen (1989a and 1989b).

Part 2

Narrative Communication and the Child Reader

In the set of papers reprinted in the previous chapter, scholars and critics speculate, analyse and apply theoretical perspectives to changing expectations of children's reading matter and of childhood itself. In this section, both the child reader and the translator within-the-text step into the foreground in three essays that address the interaction between the child reader of the target text and the translator. Birgit Stolt places the child reader at the heart of her discussion of ideological differences between source and target texts in the printed version of her speech at the third ISRCL symposium in 1976. By opting to confine her remarks to middle childhood, Stolt alerts us in her opening lines to the chronological range (potentially from birth to 16 when child listeners are included) covered by the general term 'child reader'– a developmental dimension often ignored in literature on translating for children.

Prefacing discussion of children's literature with a historical summary of metaphors for and quotations on the translation process, Stolt argues that the concept of faithfulness emphasised in many of them takes a back seat in translations for children. Three factors appear to take precedence in determining the nature of narrative communication with the child reader: educational intentions, the preconceived opinion of adults about what children want to read, and the sentimentalisation of matter-of-fact texts. Stolt offers telling examples in each category, closing her talk with a reference to the role of illustrations in the process of translation.

Riitta Oittinen, whose pioneering dialogic approach to translations for children is mentioned by Tiina Puurtinen in Part 1, is a children's author, illustrator and professional translator as well as a children's literature critic in her native Finland. The piece in this section, first published in 1995 and later incorporated into her book *Translating for Children* (Oittinen, 2000), examines the interplay between translator and child reader. Oittinen begins by investigating how children think and respond to the world and to what they read, asserting that in some respects children are better – sharper and fresher – readers than adults. Drawing on Bakhtin's theories of dialogism, she advocates a move away from the source text towards a new interpretation that is appropriate for the young readers of the translation. To illuminate this creative aspect of the translation process, Oittinen refers to Louise Rosenblatt's reader response model of two aspects of reading, the aesthetic and the efferent. In Oittinen's view, the translator's initial imaginative and aesthetic response continues to resonate in dynamic interaction with a closer, analytical, 'efferent' reading that is necessary in order to translate effectively. Like Stolt, Oittinen raises the visual element of translating for children that was to become central to her work. Furthermore, she emphasises performance and the read-aloud qualities of children's texts, questioning notions of 'readability' (cited in Tiina Puurtinen's article in Part 1) which depend on a linguistic analysis of the text and which do not take into account the reader's entire situation or affective response.

Emer O'Sullivan takes the notion of the addressee of translated children's texts one stage further by proposing that there is a difference between the implied child readers inscribed within source and target texts. She expands existing models of narrative communication to include both the implied child reader in the target culture, and the 'implied translator' whose voice can be detected within the translated text. In such a model the translator is the agent mediating cultural difference, often in an idiosyncratic manner, rather than the invisible and voiceless instrument of cultural exchange.

Birgit Stolt

How Emil Becomes Michel: On the Translation of Children's Books

As the problem of translation is just as old as it is boundless, this lecture will have to restrict itself to the problem of translation in general and the problem of translating children's books in particular. Both literature for young people and books for the very young must be left out of consideration.

There have been theoretical reflections on the art of translation for thousands of years. As long as there has been a cultural exchange between peoples of different languages there have been translations and translators. If one looks at what was written on this question, one gets the impression that the same problems and complaints turn up again and again, as if one had not got a step nearer a generally valid solution. Bitter puns express the fact that a translation often did not do justice to the original: *'traduttore – traditore'*, *'ein übersetzt Buch – ein verletzt Buch'*, *'traduction – trahison'*, *'libro tradotto – libro corrotto'*. Numerous also are the metaphors with which the relationship between the original and the translation is illustrated, and which all have the common conviction that the translation is not of the same value as the original. One of the oldest and most popular images of this kind is the simile of the turned carpet (Gobelin): the original is the right side on which the picture stands out clearly and distinctly, but the translation is the imperfect reverse which is full of distorting threads. The simile is to be found, among other places, in Cervantes' *Don Quixote*.

Jakob Grimm compared the task of the translator with that of a sailor: the latter mans a ship, directs it with full sails to the opposing shore, but then has to land 'where there is different earth and where different air plays.' It is this different earth and the alien air that constitute the problem on which the greater part of the debate turns and which gave rise to the above-mentioned puns: the problem of faithfulness to the original.

At the word 'faithfulness' further metaphors which have become classical immediately suggest themselves: the now proverbial expression of the 'beautiful unfaithful', the *'belles infidèles'*: the most beautiful translations, like the most beautiful of women, are not supposed to be the most faithful. *Faithfulness* towards the original text, or to use the words of the scholar Jiří Levý: the exactitude in reproduction by the translator (Levy,

1969: 84) is *the* cardinal problem in theory and practice. What a faithful translation should be like, how the faithful translator should proceed, was set out by Horace and after him Hieronymous in an expression which has become classical: a translation should not be from word to word, but from sense to sense. Nowadays 'faithful' is often replaced with other concepts. For example, one speaks of 'similar response' or of 'equivalence', whereby the demand for 'equivalence' affects both the semantic as well as the stylistic and functional area. For instance, Roman Jakobson characterizes the original message and the translation message as 'two equivalent messages in two different codes,' and Nida and Taber (1969) define translation as 'Translating consists in reproducing in the receptor language the closest natural equivalent of the source-language message, first in terms of meaning and secondly in terms of style.' The effect of the text, which should be the same in the original and the translation is also occasionally clothed in metaphor: the 'fragrance', 'taste' the 'aroma' of a work must be saved: '... no literary work is tasteless like a glass of distilled water; it has its peculiar aroma, or consistency of texture, which the translator must try to submit' (Koller, 1972: 115).

But how is this similar response to be achieved? There are two opposed ways which are called the method of alienation and that of adaptation; or the source-language oriented method as opposed to the target-language oriented; or the method faithful to words as opposed to the free method. The formulation from 1813 of the German philosopher Schleiermacher has become classical:

> Either the translator leaves the author in peace as much as possible and moves the reader towards him; or he leaves the reader in peace as much as possible and moves the author towards him. (Störig, 1963: 47)

Schleiermacher is of the opinion that one must decide for one of these two ways and then keep to it throughout the whole work. A mixture of both would only result in 'the author and the reader completely missing each other.' In a mixture of translation and 'adaptation' the reader would be thrown back and forth 'like a ball' between his own and the alien world. The philosopher himself recommended the alienation method in which alien feelings, thoughts and elements are brought close to the reader. In the adaptation method passages would often have to be left out or completely paraphrased, whereby in his opinion it was very difficult 'to set limits to the wildest arbitrariness' (Störig, 1963: 66).

Luther, however, whose Bible translation achieved fame, describes his method in the famous *'Sendbrief vom Dolmetschen'* ('Circular Letter on Translation', 1530) as a combination of the alienation and the adaptation methods, even though he does use a different terminology. Where it was necessary for dogmatic reasons he kept to the letter (i.e. translated according to the alienation method); on the other hand he 'let the letter go' i.e. used the adaptation method in other places in order to produce good German. But that not even he succeeded without exception in determining which passages permitted the adaptation method and were not falsifying, is proved by the impassioned discussion that was kindled by the individual passages.

Wilhelm von Humboldt calls the two above-mentioned methods 'cliffs' on which the translator is damned to run aground, but he considers a middle path between the two to be absolutely impossible (Koller, 1972: 74).

An impossible task, then? As far as the translation of children's books is concerned, Astrid Lindgren poses the question of its impossibility in the magazine *Babel* in 1969: 'Are children's books translatable?' (There translated into French by Malou Höjer.) She turns against the theorists who are of the opinion that children's books in particular are bound to the country in which they were written and that children with their limited experience were not able to transpose themselves into alien milieus and the people of other countries. Astrid Lindgren holds the completely opposite view and advances the argument of the phenomenal imagination of children, as well as her own experience, 'I believe,' she writes, 'that children have a marvellous ability to re-experience the most alien and distant things and circumstances, if a good translator is there to help them, and I believe that their imagination continues to build where the translator can go no further.' Thus, for example, Japanese children had been so fascinated by the thoroughly Swedish peasant children in the native Swedish milieu of Bullerby (in Astrid Lindgren's books about the children of Bullerby) that they wrote letters to the author, asking whether there really was a Bullerby, where it was situated in Sweden and whether one could move there and live there.

Thus we have come to the question of translating children's books. Does the translation of children's books differ basically from the translation of other texts? At first glance it would appear that the basic process of 'changing clothes', of 'transposing' and whatever all the other metaphors are, is exactly the same.

But then whoever has a look round at theory and practice, will discover to his astonishment that *the* cardinal problem of faithfulness to the original text which generally predominates in discussion, appears to take a back seat here. The demand for it appears to have become unimportant. We must have recourse to the tradition once again.

Translation questions and problems were in the olden times given contemporary significance above all in the translation of Holy Scriptures.

The statements of Hieronymous and Luther quoted above referred to the translation of the bible. That the problem of faithfulness to the text is central here, as falsifying the 'Holy texts' was not permissible, is obvious. Here respect for the 'author' reached its absolute limits.

Respect for the author of children's books is quite a different matter. Numerous are the complaints from children's book authors about their work being scorned as second-class, with people saying that you don't have to be so particular about children's books, a children's book can just be knocked off any old way. One can easily imagine that in such cases the respect for the original text is none too great. Bible translations can look back on a long tradition in which respect for the original text always had priority, but children's literature is a completely different tradition. In order to illustrate this, I need only refer to one single, generally known, book title: *Robinson Crusoe*. This means that the most prominent position is not occupied by the tradition of faithful translation, but that of adaptation, whereby hardly any limits are set to the arbitrariness of the adapter. I do not need to go into greater detail here as regards the adaptations of the *Robinson Crusoe* text. It is well known that not only the length of the book varied greatly, but the main character was now from Britain, now from Hamburg; the domestic animals now llamas, now goats; the narrative now in the first, now in the third person. Even Friday's father was sometimes given a name, once being called Thursday, once Sunday. Without any scruples, cuts, additions and changes were made, the style was altered and the book re-edited in accordance with the aims of the publisher in question. These were primarily didactic in nature and merely set a different accent according to whether the person responsible was most concerned with moral, religious or educational intentions. One looks in vain here for the concept of faithfulness and consideration for the author's copyright.

This taking of liberties with the original text, which was considered fully justified by the philanthropic intentions, seems to me from the standpoint of the translation of children's literature an unhealthy tradition. One can keep in mind what the great educationalist Herbart wrote over 100 years ago: 'the mere intention of educating spoils children's books' (Bamberger, 1961: 40). Astrid Lindgren, too, has observed that in her opinion a translator of children's books works under different conditions from a translator of novels for adults. She also mentions expressly the factor of faithful translation. In the already mentioned essay in *Babel* (Lindgren, 1969) she writes: 'At any rate I imagine that, for example, the translator of a novel can follow the original faithfully without him being told, "You mustn't say that, it's not good form!"' This, however, happened with children's books, and in her experience not only to the translator, but also to the author! A translator of children's books had to take into account more taboos.

In the theoretical works on translation one hardly finds anything relevant on the subject. Jiří Levý (1969) remarks in passing that a children's book translator works under special conditions, but he keeps to generalities: 'In the translation of children's books special consideration must be given to the reader,' whereby he has in mind above all the translation of book titles. Taboos of a religious or political nature cannot be dealt with here in greater detail. They are obvious and should be familiar to every publisher and translator. If a book from a strictly Catholic or from an orthodox Jewish milieu is to 'land' on an alien shore, to take up Jakob Grimm's image, adaptations will be necessary which are tailored to the 'alien coastline' in question. It is a necessary evil if the 'landing' is not to become a 'stranding'. I shall restrict myself in the following to non-necessary adaptations of a more subtle nature which are not so obvious, to which frequently little attention is paid, but which may mean a source of irritation for the author.

I shall name in particular three sources that may adversely affect the faithfulness of the translator to the original text:

- Educational intentions. These have already been named, taking the example of *Robinson Crusoe*. To this must be added the taboo-thinking stressed by Astrid Lindgren, the reaction: 'That's not good form!'
- The preconceived opinion of adults about what children want to read, value and understand. This often goes together with an underestimation of the child reader.
- A childish attitude that results in a sentimentalization or prettifying of matter-of-fact texts.

Educational Intentions

That the author is at the mercy of his translator is a fact that is often deplored. But not only the translator, the publisher too has an important word to say and some alterations from the original are not the work of the translator, but of the publisher. I shall take two 'taboo examples' from Astrid Lindgren's article; in both, a slightly drastic element in the original causes offence.

In one of her books two little girls, Lisabeth and Mattis, quarrel until one of them emerges as the winner. The whole chapter was cut by the publishers because the victorious reply seemed offensive. The exchange begins quite harmlessly with Mattis, who has recently had her appendix out, boasting in a genuinely childlike manner: 'I've got a big scar on my tummy, how about that. You haven't!' Lisabeth pays her back in her own coin: 'I've got a pea in my nose, how about that. You haven't!' (She had in fact been sent to the doctor together with her elder sister Madicken for this reason.) This, however, does not make the slightest impression on Mattis: 'I've got so many peas at home that I could stuff my whole nose full. That's nothing at all!' Lisabeth is at a loss for a moment, then she sees Mattis wiping her nose on her sleeve. Then the crushing reply occurs to her: 'Your nose is already so full up that you couldn't even get a single pea in it, you snot-nose!' The whole chapter, writes Astrid Lindgren, had been cut because of Mattis' snot-nose and yet it was true that the noses of children all over the world ran now and again – she at any rate had met quite a few. Apparently there were taboos of which people had no idea. In this case it was a translation into American English. One would think that some less draconian solution could have been found, even though, admittedly, Lisabeth's behaviour cannot be called exactly exemplary for dear little girls (as the publishing firm no doubt imagined they should be) and thus a suitable object of identification for other little girls. That children often themselves experience positively drastic scenes and therefore like to read about such things, is apparently not important. In another book Astrid Lindgren tells the story of little Lotta who yearns to grow up very quickly. She has heard that dung and rain hasten growth and on a rainy day she stands on the middle of a dung-heap and thinks that she will now grow big very quickly. In the American translation Astrid Lindgren discovered to her great surprise that the dung-heap had turned into a pile of withered leaves! This time she wrote to the publishers and asked whether American children really did not know that there were other means, much better than withered leaves, of hastening growth. If it were not so, she didn't think much of American agriculture. This time she was successful: 'I was allowed to keep my dung-heap – what a triumph!' she writes.

    It cannot be distinguished exactly whether it was the aesthetically refined taste of the publisher (or of the translator) that took offence, or the educational principle according to which the taste of children should be refined, or that children in the book are only allowed to appear as exemplary children – possibly all these three together. In addition to which, no attention is paid to the fact that the 'aroma' of the original is weakened, the taste is insipid, the whole impression made tame and thus the danger of boredom is precipitated.

Preconceived Opinions of Adults about Child Readers

    We are now coming to the second question: the preconceived opinion of adults about child readers, their imagination, their humour, and in quite general terms also what one can credit them with and expect from them. Here too one can observe how the prejudices of the publishers help to make the translation paler and tamer, less effective, quite simply more insipid than the original. The French Pippi Longstocking, for example, is not allowed to pick up a horse, only a pony! In this case the correspondence of the author with the publishers was without success. She had to swallow the reply that perhaps little – and, as was clear from reading between the lines, stupid – Swedish children could be persuaded that Pippi was strong enough to lift a whole horse. But French children, who had just been through a World War, were much too realistic to be taken in by something like that. 'Sometimes I think,' writes Astrid Lindgren, 'that publishers don't understand all that much about children!' [1]

People often underrate what can be expected of children, of their imagination, of their intuitive grasp of matters, of their willingness to concern themselves with what is new, strange, difficult, if only it is described excitingly. Names and book titles belong in this category, too. We are now coming to Astrid Lindgren's *Emil I Lönneberga* (*Emil in the Soup Tureen*) which in German has a name and a title that have been changed so that they are no longer recognizable: in Germany it is *Michel in der Suppenschüssel*. Why Emil was renamed, although the name is German too and not at all difficult to pronounce, can only be guessed. That it is not modern nowadays ought not to be so important in view of the fact that the story is set in the countrified past. But the name had already been taken by another famous Emil, the considerably older boy with the detectives in Kästner's well-known books. Michel is not a Swedish name, even the ich-sound is alien to the Swedish language. Consequently, in making this selection the translator is interfering with the local colouring. Perhaps he had a dim recollection of the 'German Michel', the awkward farmer's lad who, depicted in his cap and breeches, was exposed to ridicule, not a very felicitous association, which the child readers would completely overlook. The other first names in this book, which also have exact German equivalents, have been taken over without any changes: Ida, Lina, Anton, Alfred. One can argue about whether the substitution of Michel for Emil was absolutely necessary; at any rate it would have been better to find a name which was also common in Swedish. In my opinion children can very well be credited with being familiar with the fact that there are a whole lot of quite different children with the same name. The consequences of interference of this sort with the text can often not be foreseen. In Holland, for example, where the German model has been used and the hero renamed 'Mikkel', there were difficulties later on when the (Swedish) film was running and it turned out that the film hero had the unchanged name of Emil! I was told that after that the books were provided with a little sticker which informed the children that Mikkel and the Emil in the film were one and the same boy.

To take another example from a French translation of a Swedish children's book: in Edith Unnerstad's book *Farmorsresan* (i.e. the *Journey to Grandmother*) the main character is called 'Pelle Göran', popular forms of 'Peter George'. In this case there was understanding for the fact that French children could not be expected to grasp such a difficult, almost unpronounceable name, and so a Swedish form of a name was substituted: 'Erik'. That was perfectly all right, but did not suffice; Uncle Folke was given the Norwegian name of Olaf, and the friend Katarina, who in the book is called by the abbreviation 'Kaja' which is unusual in Swedish too, is named 'Cathie' in the translation, which sounds more English than Swedish. It is naturally very difficult for any local colouring associated with names to emerge when there is such a hodge-podge. The apparently generally accepted and widespread custom of substituting names should, in my opinion, be applied more restrictedly and should more frequently be questioned. One wonders how, in view of the unrestrained renaming, it came about that Johanna Spyri's 'Heidi' was able to make such a triumphant advance without the name needing to be substituted or at least the spelling being subjected to local rules. Or who would ever have thought of changing the name of, say, Nils Holgersson (from the book by Selma Lagerlöf) to Hans Schneider, for example? Were children credited with more in those days, or is it the other way round: is the endeavour to make it too palatable for them nowadays? English and American editions of *Heidi* offer aids to pronunciation, and it is not clear why this path is not followed more frequently. If the contents of the book are exciting enough, the child will also put up with difficulties and the strange name, to which one quickly gets accustomed, is a part of the strange milieu. As a child, for instance, the surname of Robinson seemed to me strange and difficult to pronounce (Cruso-e or Crusö?), but I cannot recall that this had any adverse effect on my interest in the book.

Helen W. Painter from the Kent State University (1968) deals with the problem of adaptations in the translation of children's books. She is of the opinion that in general too much is altered, and unnecessarily, and adapted to local conditions, where the strange and the exotic in particular would have been of charm, interest and not least of all educational value. She therefore recommends as aids to comprehension notes, aids to pronunciation, explanations of important foreign words and terms, and maps in the case of travelogues; also information about the author, and an explanation of the often difficult foreign names, their pronunciation and mention of the fact that, for instance, Tove Jansson and Gunnel Linde are women. All this introductory information should be inside the book and not on the dust-cover blurb, as jackets very quickly get torn and lost. Short explanations in the text itself are recommended, too. With these aids to reading as much as possible of the foreign milieu could be saved and kept in the translated text. The charm of what is new and strange, the broadening of the reader's horizons would be lost if everything were made too effortless and palatable and adapted to one's own milieu. E.W. Rosenheim (1969) is also an energetic adherent of the same view. He stresses in particular the loss of suspense and charm caused by adaptation: 'The commonplace is the commonplace and therefore the most unexciting object to the imagination,' is his opinion and in his emphasis on the child's imagination he touches on the already quoted view of Astrid Lindgren. One should seriously tackle the problem of the degree of adaptations. It is, as always, a matter of the cardinal problem in translation: faithfulness to the original.

Sentimentalization and Prettifying

Astrid Lindgren speaks of the ambition of many a translator to make everything a bit more beautiful and more full of genuine feeling than the author has succeeded in making it. Theoreticians of translation have several times pointed out the danger of an ambition in the translator to be an author (Koller, 1972: 126). The translator's own style may prove stronger than the will to reproduce the style of the author to be translated. But a translator can also unconsciously colour a style in a personal manner by allowing adult perceptions arising while reading the text to be carried over into the translation. Children are matter-of-fact and realistic. They seldom find each other moving, 'nice' or even sweet – these feelings are mainly reserved for adults. Astrid Lindgren writes that her German translator was gripped by tender feelings for little Lisabeth, the little girl with the pea in her nose mentioned above, the little sister of Madicken. In a play-scene seven-year-old Madicken tries in vain to free herself from Lisabeth's embrace. Lisabeth has put her arms round her neck and does not want to let go. The translator makes of these arms: 'Lisabeth throws her podgy, round little arms round Madicken's neck.' As the whole story is written from the viewpoint of Madicken, and Madicken sees nothing podgy, round or little in the embracing arms that she wants to get rid of, i.e. she experiences no nice or tender feelings, but interference which irritates her, this tender emotional value is completely out of place here. According to the author's intention the reader should experience everything through the eyes and feelings of the seven-year-old. What appears at first to be an insignificant matter, turns out to be a shift in the point of view of the narrative and is in fact a grave case of interference with the text. One must understand the position of the author who speaks of the irritation beyond words that an author experiences as a result of this sort of 'improvement'. In this case she was able to take action at the manuscript stage, but she says: 'sometimes one wonders with concern how many podgy, round, little arms and similar things slip into translations, the language of which one does not understand and which one can therefore not keep under surveillance.'

Such interference is particularly grave when it affects the final words of a book. Astrid Lindgren gives an example of this from an American translation, too, where right at the end a single word is added that brings an element of mood into the text that Astrid Lindgren does not want there at all. I shall do no more than refer to her article here and would myself like to give a different example of changing the final accent, this time from a translation into French as so far mainly German and English translations have been mentioned.

The example is Edith Unnerstad's *Journey to Grandmother*, the French translation of which has already been mentioned because of the renaming of characters. Even the change in title [to *Patte de tigre sur le sentier de la guerre*] overrides the original very freely, inasmuch as a minor episode, the kitten with which the boy plays at his grandmother's, among other places, is moved into the foreground. It is suggested to the child that it is a book about the escapades of a kitten named Tiger's Paw. It is, however, about the already mentioned Pelle Göran, renamed Erik, whose mother is hospitalized for a long time after a serious road accident. The boy is therefore sent to southern Sweden to his grandmother. The book begins sadly, with the accident, a visit to the hospital, pain, fear and the parting from his mother which is unbearable for the boy. Behind the happy days that the boy spends with his grandmother, there is also the reminder of homesickness and worries about his mother. She has to have an operation, and the grandmother promises to bake a big pyramid cake for the surgeon, if and when the operation is successful and the mother is home again and in good health. The sympathies of the child reader are led by way of a successive development from the accident to a gradual reassurance and finally to pure bliss; the book ends with a scene depicting the doctor and the boy sitting together on the carpet and eating pyramid cake, both relaxed and happy. It should be added that in spite of all the warm sympathy the book is completely free of any sentimentality or even tearfulness.

> *'Men oj, vad vi har smulat på fina mattan! Sa han sen. Blir hon inte ond på oss, hon som slöppte in mej?'*
> *Professorn skrattade.*

'Kanske, sa han. Men hör du, det byr vi oss inte om. Vi tar en bit till, eller hur?'
'Mm, sa Pelle Göran.'
Och så tog de varsin bit till.
Och har de inte slutat så sitter de väl där än och äter spettekaka. (Edith
Unnerstad: *Farmorsresan*)

'But oh dear, we've made crumbs on the nice carpet!' he said presently.
'Will she be cross with us, the lady who showed me in?'
The doctor laughed.
'Perhaps,' he said, 'but never mind, we won't take any notice. Shall we
have another bit?'
So they each had another slice.
And if they haven't finished it they are still sitting there eating
spettecake. (*The Spettecake Holiday*, English translation by Lilian Seaton)

*– Oh! Mon dieu! Noius avons fait des miettes sur le beau tapis. Est-ce que la
dame qui m'a amené ici va être très fâchée?*
Le docteur rit de bon Coeur:
– Je ne le pense pas. Encore un morceau, Erik?
*Et c'est ainsi que finit, dans la joie, un été qui avait si mal commence pour le petit
Erik.* (*Patte de tigre sur le sentier de la guerre*, French translation by G.
Hoppe)

Through the short discussion in the original about a scolding nurse
much becomes obvious: between the doctor and the boy there emerges a
slightly impish, conspiratory palliness. With the marvellous pyramid cake
they celebrate the fact that a great misfortune has been averted: life as an
invalid for the mother or even her death. On such a joyful day a slight
annoyance such as a nurse scolding about crumbs is of no significance.
Thus the child learns to keep things in proportion, and the cause of being
happy is set in relief.

In the French translation text, apparently the reaction 'Not good form'
was at work, for here the nurse never grumbles, not even 'perhaps'. The
reproofs of adults should apparently not be treated lightly on such a day.
But the suggestion of the fairy tale 'and if they are still alive' of the original
has vanished too. Instead, the anxious opening of the story is recalled once
again, whereas the original text closes light-heartedly, almost in high
spirits. Through the word *'petit'* the boy is sentimentalised and prettified,
which is quite alien to the original. Because of this sentence the book does
not end with a tone of light-hearted, almost fairy-tale joyousness, but a
tearful-sentimental trait is introduced and determines the concluding
emphasis.

Illustrations

In conclusion I should like to mention a problem that is quite specific to children's books: the question of illustrations. One may argue that illustrations are not part of the problem of translation. However, I would like to claim that they pose a very special translation problem, as they convert texts into pictures. In theoretical scholarly discussions of the question of translations in general adult literature is at the centre of interest, which is why in professional literature hardly anything relevant is to be found on the problems of illustrations.

The importance of illustrations in children's books cannot be rated high enough, especially in the case of books for small children. Ideas of fairy tale characters, castles, princes and princesses are frequently formed for life from childhood picture books. Thus great emphasis must be put on the quality of illustrations.

There are a number of books, the original success of which has been considerably assisted by the congenial illustrations of an artist, books in which there is no seam between the text and the pictures, in which the style of the author and the style of the illustrating artist are in perfect harmony. I mention as such an artist Ernest Shepard who died at the age of 97. His illustrations for Winnie-the-Pooh have achieved such fame that they have been exhibited in the Victoria and Albert museum in London. Other books have been illustrated by the author: 'Who but Tove Jansson could draw a Moomintroll?' writes Helen W. Painter. In other cases the illustrations vary with the different editions.

As an example of how the character of a book can change with the illustrations, let us take Emil alias Michel again. The original illustrations are by Björn Berg and have been kept in the English and American translation. To connoisseurs of the Swedish milieu the pictures appear congenial, genuine and 'right': the countrified milieu of yore, people, landscape and interiors with clear, firm lines and a sure grip, humorous and slightly burlesque, without however becoming caricatures. They fulfil the demand that Levý makes of a good translation: they are the same in effect, which means here that in the reader there is aroused the illusion of a certain historical national milieu. Both children and adults enjoy this, and one thinks involuntarily: these illustrations build a bridge for the children of other countries so that with their imaginations they can break through to the shore of the original and breathe in foreign air. That is, apparently, how the British and Americans thought, too. Helen W. Painter (1968: 42) quotes as an American principle: 'Book editors insist that neither text nor art are Americanized by their companies. Instead, the national characteristic of the book is retained in illustrations as much as possible.'

Figure 1 From the original edition of Astrid Lindgren's *Emil i Lönneberga*

This is not how the Germans thought. They had new illustrations done. Let us have a look at what happened. It should be mentioned marginally that there are in some cases pure plagiarism with elements of the artist's own taste (there is a long children's book tradition in this respect, too!). In general one can say of these drawings that the original powerful peasant milieu has been transformed into a prettified bourgeois small-town milieu.

Figures 1, 3 and 5 are by Björn Berg for the original edition of Astrid Lindgren's *Emil i Lönneberga*, 1963 (reprinted by permission of Rabén &

Figure 2 From the German translation *Michel in der Suppenschüssel*

Figure 3 From the original edition

Sjögrens bokförlag, Stockholm). Figures 2, 4 and 6 are by Rolf Rettich for Astrid Lindgren's *Michel in der Suppenschüssel,* 1971 (reprinted by permission of Verlag Friedrich Oetinger, Hamburg).

The black moustache makes the Swede into a southern European (Figures 1 and 2), the peasant women are made into bourgeois wives with their curly hair, ruffled aprons, lace peeping from under their skirts and heeled boots (Figures 3 and 4); the military parade ground in Hultsfred is turned into a central European fairground (Figures 5 and 6), the positively gripping realism is turned into an artificially playful world of appearances. In brief, the reader is 'thrown back and forth like a ball' between the world as it is depicted in the text and the world of the illustrator. Instead of a humorous replica of historically possible reality, the eye is offered a friz-

Figure 4 From the German translation

Figure 5 From the original edition

Figure 6 From the German translation

zled, prettified world of appearances overloaded with unnecessary details and artificially made childish and playful, whereby the powerful 'taste', the 'aroma' of the original is diluted and over-sweetened. Rendering the book puerile is at work here, too. The frilly and ornamental style is in crass opposition to the narrative style of Astrid Lindgren, with its matter-of-fact, realistic, positively gripping manner and the clear and firm tracing of lines. The question of artistic quality, of personal taste, is here of secondary importance. Decisive is the fact that the illustrations do not have the same effect, that there is a lack of congeniality between the author and the illustrator, that leading children by the nose is a disservice to their imagination. The same personal modesty is demanded of the illustrating artist as of the translator: to submit to the style of the original. It appears that faithfulness to the original in the field of illustrations is threatened from the same sources as we have shown above: by preconceived opinions, personal taste, the puerility of adults whose job it is to select illustrations. The culturally pre-formed personal taste determines what is suitable and what is not, without child readers themselves being asked.

We are returning to the complaints of children's book authors about the lack of respect for their work. Each publisher or editor apparently has his own opinion on what a children's book should be like, and above all, on what it should not look like.

Astrid Lindgren takes the field passionately against this attitude. She heatedly defends the right of the children's book author to write as he wishes to. She dismisses the question of what a good children's book should be like as being just as meaningless as that as to what a good book for adults is. With the same right with which an author writes a book for adults completely according to his own lights at the risk of failing, a children's author should also 'have freedom, freedom, *freedom* to write as he wants to, without recipe.' Only one sort of children's literature should never ever be written: books which were botched together in an early morning break, by a writer who thinks it isn't of any importance, as it is 'only a children's book' ('Orm barnböcker:' Lindgren 1972: 367).

That means:

• respect for children:
• respect for children's books: and thus,
• respect for the authors of children's books.

The conclusion is that the original text must be accorded just as much respect as in the case of adult literature, therefore the endeavour should be a translation as faithful, as equivalent as possible. Where adaptation is absolutely necessary, it should be done with a gentle hand, as little as possible and in collaboration with the author. The translator of children's books does not have an easier job than the translator of books for adults.

Note

1. A subsequent translation of *Pippi Longstocking* into French by Alain Gnaedig (1995, Paris: Hachette) takes a different approach.

Riitta Oittinen

The Verbal and the Visual: On the Carnivalism and Dialogics of Translating for Children

We create texts for different purposes, different situations, and different audiences, so any 'text' to be translated is much more than a mere text. It is the unity of the original text in words and pictures, the creators, and cultural, social and historical milieu, and text contexts such as the child images, which mirror our cultures and societies. It involves a whole situation with several different perspectives, and includes what the translator brings to the situation as a human being with her/his[1] own background, language, culture, and gender.

Thus translation is not 'producing sameness'; it is not what Jacques Attali (1985) calls normalized reproduction or repetition, but composing that lies 'beyond repetition' and frees us. The pleasure of repetition and similarity is based on a hypnotic effect. Through abstraction, power has been made incomprehensible and conformity to rules and norms 'becomes the pleasure of belonging, and the acceptance of powerlessness takes root in the comfort of repetition.' Attali's views could well be applied to translation, too. By tradition, translators are supposed to strive for repetition. If they start composing, re-creating, they are blamed for not being 'faithful' to the original. Yet I consider translating an act of composition; I consider it a dialogic, carnivalistic, collaborative process carried out in individual situations.

In this paper, it is my intention to address some fundamental assumptions in the situation of translating for children, taking into account that translators never translate words on paper alone, but whole situations including texts in words and pictures as well as their different readers, writers, and users.

Carnival and Children

The Russian philosopher Mikhail Bakhtin's ideas about carnivalism and dialogics apply quite well to translation, especially translating for children: on the one hand, translation is a carnivalistic act as such; on the other, even children's culture can be considered carnivalistic.

In one of his essays, 'Discourse in the Novel' (1990a) Bakhtin deals with the key points of his literary theory: the problematics of the alien word, authoritative discourse, and dialogism. In *Rabelais and his World* (1984) Bakhtin discusses the issue of carnivalism, which is closely connected with dialogism and a very interesting phenomenon, especially with regard to children and their culture.

In his *Alkukuvien jäljillä (Tracing the Origin of Images)*, the Finnish semiotician Henri Broms (1985) characterizes modern children's culture as an underground culture. Here 'underground' is understood as some kind of a carnivalistic culture of laughter outside the establishment described by Bakhtin in *Rabelais and His World*. I, too, see several similarities between children's culture and carnivalism: like carnivalism, children's culture is nonofficial with no dogma or authoritarianism. It does not exist to oppose adult culture as such, but rather lives on in spite of it.

Carnivalism originated in Antiquity and had its golden age in the folk cultures of the Middle Ages and the Renaissance. Carnival is 'festive laughter,' it is 'the laughter for all the people,' it is ambivalent, triumphant and deeply philosophic, and everybody can join in it. There are no outsiders, there is no audience, as the carnival is universal in scope; it is directed at all and everyone: 'footlights would destroy a carnival, as the absence of footlights would destroy a theatrical performance' (Bakhtin, 1984: 7).

In literature, carnivalism and laughter belong 'to the low genres, showing the life of private individuals and the inferior social level,' as Bakhtin points out (1984: 67). During the 1980s, there was growing interest and awareness of non-appreciated literature, popular literature, and books written by women authors. The same applies to children's literature. These kinds of literature can be considered 'low genres' from the publisher's point of view, for instance, although I do not consider children's literature a genre as such.

The relationship between carnivalism and language is very interesting. For instance, like writing for children, feminist writing has certainly belonged to 'low genres' (in the sense of non-appreciation). In feminist writing, we can find attempts to create new (in the sense of non-suppressed) ways of writing and experiencing literature.[2] As Bakhtin points out, 'the verbal norms of official and literary language, determined by the canon, prohibit all that is linked with fecundation, pregnancy, child-birth. There is a sharp line of division between familiar speech and 'correct' language' (Bakhtin, 1984: 320). A new form of culture always evokes a new way of writing. In my own writing I have noticed how the subject and content have influenced my way of expression. Carnivalism frees the language of science, too. A new type of communication always creates new forms of speech or a new meaning given to the old forms:

> The principle of laughter and the carnival spirit on which grotesque is based destroys this limited seriousness and all pretense of an extra-temporal meaning and unconditional value of necessity. It frees human consciousness, thought, and imagination for new potentialities. For this reason great changes, even in the field of science, are always preceded by a certain carnival consciousness that prepares the way. (Bakhtin, 1984: 49)

Children, too, use ritualized speech and comic, even vulgar language, which is not considered acceptable in (official) adult language.

In addition to breaking the immovable, absolute, and unchanging norms, carnivalism (folk culture) and children's culture have many other things in common: love for the grotesque (the devil), ridicule of anything that is scary, curses as well as praise and abuse, games, and the mouth and eating. As Bakhtin (1984: 316) points out, 'of all the features of the human face, the nose and mouth play the most important part in the grotesque image of the body.' The belly is also a central 'figure' in carnivalism – and we know how important eating is in all children's literature.

Eating and the names of food are very central issues in children's books in general – Göte Klingberg (1986) and Bakhtin note the companionship of children and food: the eating child is an idyllic character. Food is magic, it means happiness and safety. It is used as a device, for instance, to rhythmize narration: Carroll's *Alice's Adventures in Wonderland* gets its rhythm from Alice eating and drinking and growing and shrinking and growing again. The whole story is based on eating. As Alice herself points out: 'I know *something* interesting is sure to happen [...] whenever I eat or drink anything' (Carroll, 1981: 23).

The supper served in Grandgousier's castle, 'highly detailed and hyperbolized in Rabelais,' like 'water-hens, teal, bitterns, curlews, plovers, heath-cock, briganders,' (Bakhtin, 1990a: 180) has much in common with the picnic meals that the Famous Five eat during their adventures, like 'tea, rolls, anchovy paste, a big round jam tart in a cardboard box, oranges, lime juice, a fat lettuce and some ham sandwiches,' and, of course, 'ginger-beer' (Blyton, 1981: 26) .

The Finnish scholar Kaj von Fieandt, who has carried out extensive studies on the child's perception, describes the peculiarity of her/his sense of taste. During her/his first ten years, the child has far more taste receptors in her/his mouth than the adult. The ability to taste sweet things greatly depends on the amount and function of taste receptors. This means that children tend to prefer all sorts of sweets, while adults favor spices, where smell components are more significant (von Fieandt, 1972). This may be why food and drink are such popular themes in children's literature (cf. Blyton's *The Famous Five*).

Tastes are part of the child's world of experiences, part of her/his emotional life. Tastes are never 'as such,' as von Fieandt points out: they always refer to something experienced before, in our childhoods, in some special situation, which is one reason why people taste things differently. On the basis of these early likes and dislikes people remember and feel things in different ways, even if they are 'in the same situation' smelling and tasting 'the same things.'

But where does the comparison of carnivalism and children's culture take us? In my view it gives us a new point of view on children's culture. It encourages us to acknowledge the value of something other than adult phenomena: this unofficial culture might have something to offer us, as adults, and not just the other way around, as we are used to thinking. The temporal quality of carnivalism makes it easier for the participants to communicate. There is no etiquette, at least not in the adult sense of good and bad manners. Carnivalistic communication is not authoritarian but dialogic, where 'you' and 'I' meet. Children have their own carnivalistic way of speech, 'abusive language,' as Bakhtin calls it, but there is no reason to feel strange in this setting: we were part of the culture once, too.

What is also important in carnivalistic laughter is its victory over fear. Rabelais' devils are funny fellows and even hell is a comical place. In the Middle Ages, anything frightening was made grotesque and ridiculous:

The people play with terror and laugh at it; the awesome becomes a 'comic monster.' Neither can this grotesque image be understood if oversimplified and interpreted in the spirit of abstract rationalism. It is impossible to determine where the defeat of fear will end and where joyous recreation will begin. Carnival's hell represents the earth which swallows up and gives birth, it is often transformed into a cornucopia; the monster, death, becomes pregnant. Various deformities, such as protruding bellies, enormous noses, or humps, are symptoms of pregnancy or of procreative power. Victory over fear is not its abstract elimination; it is simultaneous uncrowning and renewal, a gay transformation. Hell has burst and has poured forth abundance. (Bakhtin, 1984: 91)

Similar things happen in old fairy and folk tales: when devils, ogres, and witches are ridiculed, they become less dangerous. These evil creatures usually come to an unhappy end, too. In a similar way, Francisco Goya combined the frightening and the comic in his art, especially his graphic arts series about the nobles, priests, doctors, and other well-to-do people, who had money and power and were thus awesome: he depicted them as donkeys and parrots.

In carnivalism, the grotesque is bodily, in a positive sense, since it is not egoistic but universal and dialogic: 'The material bodily principle is contained [...] in the people, a people who are continually growing and renewed. This is why all that is bodily becomes grandiose, exaggerated, immeasurable' (Bakhtin, 1984: 19). Grotesque realism is 'the lowering of all that is high, spiritual, ideal, abstract; it is a transfer to the material level, to the sphere of earth and body in their dissoluble unity.' The grotesque is a continuous process of re-creation and metamorphosis (Bakhtin, 1984: 19–20, 24–25).

The grotesque is paradoxical, which is well depicted in the birth of Pantagruel, one of Rabelais' characters: 'Gargantua (Pantagruel's father) does not know whether to weep over his wife's death or to laugh with joy at the birth of his son. He now laughs 'like a calf' (a newborn animal), or moos 'like a cow' (birth-giving and dying) (Bakhtin, 1984: 331). This paradox, the combination of the grotesque and laughter, makes carnivalism very radical: through victory over fear it reveals the mysteries of power. Laughter is directed against all boundaries, hypocrisy, and adulation, and it liberates a human being from any internal censor:

> It liberates from the fear that developed in man for thousands of years: fear of the sacred, of prohibitions, of the past, of power. It unveils the material bodily principle in its true meaning. Laughter opened men's eyes on that which is new, on the future [...] Laughter showed the world anew in its gayest and most sober aspects. Its external privileges are intimately linked with interior forces; they are a recognition of the rights of those forces. This is why laughter could never become an instrument to oppress and blind the people. It always remained a free weapon in their hands. (Bakhtin, 1984: 94)

Laughter or pantagruelism means the ability to be happy, gay, and benevolent. It also extends to foolishness, even madness. Like Plato, Bakhtin underlines the importance of madness, abnormality, drunkenness, and deviation from ordinary language. This is what happens in children's culture and children's language. Bakhtin points out that children's language often deviates from the beaten path: children's speech, free as it is from abstract structures and rules, is life itself.

Our starting point in the discussion of the child and childhood could be positive. We could ask: *what abilities does the child have?* What is typical of a child's thinking? Few people adapting stories for children seem to start from this premise. Jill Paton Walsh, however, appreciates what children bring to the reading experience. She grants that adults have more experience, which makes them to a certain extent 'better' readers than children, but as she says, 'the other side of the coin' is 'the ways in which adults are likely to be *inferior* to children as readers': While the adult response is 'dull' and 'weary,' children's response is fresh and 'sharp'– carnivalistic. Adults have norms and expectations, but children 'just drown,' as they 'don't know what books are supposed to be like.'[3]

What is most interesting here is that many of our adult abilities turn out to be liabilities, and children's 'inabilities' make them better readers and listeners. It is also interesting to note that this conforms to the ideas of the German professor Hans-Ludwig Freese: he asserts that children's abilities are not weaker but different from adult abilities. Children's thinking is not naive, illogical, or 'wrong,' but mythical and logical in a different way than adult thinking (Freese, 1992: 54–5).

As a whole, children's culture could well be seen as one form of carnivalism – imagine the situation where we as translators for children join the children and dive into their carnival, not teaching them but learning from them. Through and within dialogue, we may find fresh new interpretations, which does not mean distortion but respect for the original, along with respect for ourselves and for the carnivalistic world of children.

Dialogue and Coming-together

Bakhtin points out that every word is born in a dialogue. Everything in life can be 'understood as a part of a greater whole.' He says, 'there is a constant interaction between meanings,' and all these meanings 'have the potential of conditioning each other.' In every translation the reader, as an individual 'I,' meets the 'you' of the text (Bakhtin, 1990a: 246–7). Dialogue may be described as a kind of context, a situation that occurs between texts and human beings and the world around.

Dialogue is closely connected to 'heteroglossia.' All utterances are 'heteroglot', which means that 'at any given time, in any given place, there will be a set of conditions – social, historical, meteorological, physiological – that will ensure that a word uttered in that place and at that time will have a meaning different than it would have under any other conditions (Bakhtin, 1990a: 428). To divorce word and dialogue, word and context, would be artificial, because words are always born between the own and the alien. Detached from its context, a word is empty or rather, it simply does not exist; but when a word is in a dialogic interaction with an alien word, it continually takes on different meanings. Thus Bakhtin does not consider languages and texts to be linguistic systems, but he speaks of metalinguistics instead: 'Stylistics must be based not only, and even *not as much*, on linguistics as on *metalinguistics*, which studies the word not in a system of language and not in a "text" excised from dialogic interaction' (Bakhtin, 1987: 202). This means that we cannot own meanings, which always escape final definitions. Understanding is always carnivalistic and dialogic interaction.

Dialogue can be both external and internal: it takes place between persons or between persons and things. In reading, for example, it takes place between the reader and a book. The dialogue may also take place within one person. For instance, when a translator translates for the child, she/he also reads, writes, and carries on a discussion with her/his present and former self. She/he also discusses with her/his audience, the listening and reading child (Bakhtin, 1990a: 426). Every text, every translation, is directed toward its readers and listeners. Every listener, every reader, is also directed toward the text. In a dialogue, the reader is active and responsible for what and how she/he reads and understands.

The same thing happens when a text is being translated. If our focus is the purpose of the translation, the original is left in a shadow, and the aim of the new interpretation is to convince readers of its legitimacy. The goal to assure the reader, the internal dialogue of a word, may even become more important than the text material. Thus the translation is a credible whole, a logical entity.

With any translation, and the translation of fiction even more so, we necessarily deal with the issue of reading. The translator always starts out as a reader. Reading is an especially interesting issue within the situation of translating for children, because we need to take both child and adult readers into account. The child as a reader has a key role to play. Where does the child fit into the story, into society? What are the cultural definitions of childhood? Besides the differences between children and adults, other questions also arise, such as the translator as a reader and involvement while reading.

Reading is involvement, as Saskia Tellegen (Tellegen & Coppejans, 1991) points out. It is an emotional state: the more we read, the more we become attached to the text. Accomplishing something and deriving pleasure are an important part of reading: the more the child gets out of the reading situation, the more the child wants to read. Reading is an active, carnivalistic process, an event, which is guided, to a great extent, by the reader. The reader uses texts; she/he reads for many different purposes. Sometimes she/he needs information, sometimes she/he reads for pleasure; sometimes a parent or translator, for instance, reads for other people, too.

The translator is a very special kind of reader, as she/he is sharing her/his reading experience in one language with readers of another language. The translator is a specialized reader, who travels back and forth in and between texts, the original text and her/his own text. Christiane Nord describes the movements in translation as 'looping.' Thus translation 'is not a linear, progressive process leading from a starting point [...] to a target point [...] but a circular, [...] recursive process' with feedback loops (Nord, 1991: 30). While translating, the translator is influenced by previous words and passages – the whole reading and viewing situation – which in their turn influence the words and passages to come, and the other way around. As Mary Ann Caws (1989: 17) would describe the situation, 'seeing anything twice means reorienting the vision as well as the object seen and ourselves in relation to it.'

Nord's model is not far from Nicole Brossard's, where the movement does not take place within any unbreakable or unbreachable circle (the circle of the 'original' and its culture) – it extends in all directions, three-dimensionally. The movement is not center-oriented. It is 'sense renewed, through excursions into and explorations of non-sense,' as Brossard (1988: 117) describes it in her *spiral model.*

Reading and translation can well be seen as this kind of spiral movement reaching toward what is new in an attempt to understand what is old, dialogically. Thus translation could be described as Brossard (1988: 116–7) describes female culture: 'New perspectives: new configurations of woman-[translator]-as-being-in-the-world of what's real, of reality, and of fiction.'

Louise M. Rosenblatt describes reading as *coming-together.* For her, reading is a two-way street: it is transaction between a reader and a text. When a reader reads a text, she/he actively evokes 'the poem' out of the text. For Rosenblatt (1978: 12, 75), the poem, the reading experience, is an event in time and place and situation, not an object, but something happening 'during a *coming-together* of a reader and a text.'

From a translator's point of view, Rosenblatt's ideas are of great interest. She describes two different reading strategies, aesthetic and efferent reading, which differ in at least two key aspects – time and experience. In aesthetic reading, the reader's whole attention is attached to the experiences she/he has while reading; in efferent reading, on the other hand, what will happen next is important, 'what will be the residue *after* the reading,' what kind of information, what kind of instructions the reader has internalized (Rosenblatt, 1978: 23).

When a child studies history, the goal is to be able to answer her/his teacher's questions, so the child tries to memorize as many dates, places, and names as possible. The child is thus reading the book in an efferent, non-aesthetic way. Since the same material could be read in an aesthetic way, Rosenblatt always speaks of different kinds of readings, not different text types or text functions.

As a whole, translators are mainly supposed to be thoughtful, analytical readers – but uninvolved. For me, each way of reading makes its own contribution to the translation process. During the first, aesthetic and involved reading, the translator may be fascinated by a story that appeals to her/him emotionally (or she/he may hate it from the very beginning). I believe this happens to some extent every time a translator reads texts, even if she/he usually knows that she/he will be translating the text later on.

During an efferent, more critical reading, the translator starts the translation, reading the text backward and forward, analyzing and synthesizing it; she/he studies the text closely, wanting to be sure of the legitimacy and coherence of her/his own interpretation. She/he is now using the text for a certain purpose. Yet, it is worth pointing out that I do not see these readings as two or more separate events, but, rather, as several successive and overlapping readings, where one reading influences the other.

When translating a story, the translator has the memory of the first reading experience constantly in her/his mind, even if it fades, and her/his subsequent readings begin to dominate. So even at the more analytical, critical stages, the first reading experience is always present in the background. The earlier readings can also be seen as parts of the translator's experience, as parts of the whole translation situation. As a whole, translators are mainly assumed to be thoughtful, analytical readers – some writers even consider involvement harmful to the translation process. Yet I find that both of these ways of reading are equally important.

The Verbal and the Visual

Performance is an essential, quite inseparable, part of art, whether a novel, painting, composition, or film. Performance can also be understood in relation to time, as something happening here and now. Every dialogic situation of translating and writing for children, for instance, is unique and thus ephemeral – the time, place, mood, and the readers involved are different. The reading and listening child and the adult reading the story aloud to the child all bring themselves to the situation. Even the channels used may vary: translations are performed for different media in speech and writing.

In her *Translation Studies* (1991) Susan Bassnett considers the performance of translations and uses the terms *performance-oriented* and *reader-*

oriented. Translations may also be *auditive* and *visual.* Bassnett's ideas may well be applied to translation for children: when an adult is reading aloud, she/he is performing, acting, the story to the child. Her/his own interpretation is interwoven in the performance and the listening child is her/his audience. In this situation, as in theater translation, many of the same principles apply. As Bassnett (1991: 131–2) says, 'the role of the audience assumes a public dimension not shared by the individual reader whose contact with the text is essentially a private affair.'

As art forms, theater and film are closely related to picture books. In an illustrated book, the reader participates in the dialogue of the rhythm of words and pictures, which gives her/him an idea of the scene, characters, and the whole setting of the story – just like in theater or film. In the same way, we must pay attention to the readability, even 'singability' of the text when translating an illustrated text for a small child.

Sharing, performance, and reading aloud are also characteristic of children's books and their translations. The human voice is a powerful tool, and reading aloud is the only way for an illiterate child to enter the world of literature. Jim Trelease, the American reading advocate, points out in his *The New Read-Aloud Handbook* (1989) that listening comprehension comes before reading comprehension. He even says that we all become readers because we have seen and heard someone we admire enjoying the experience of reading. Thus the translator is responsible for contributing to the aloud-reader's enjoyment of the story in every way possible. For instance, the translator should use punctuation to give rhythm to the text. I even go as far as to insist that a translator, especially when translating for small children, should not necessarily punctuate according to the rules of grammar, but according to rhythm. The translator of a fairy tale – whether a novel, a poem, or a play – must take into consideration which senses she/he is translating for. When we are translating for children below the school-age (seven in Finland) we should translate, not just for the eye and the ear, but also for the adult's mouth.

Here we also encounter the question of the readability of texts, which is not easy to define. I believe that the 'readability of a text' is determined not only by the 'text' in the abstract or by the meanings *in* the text, as words on paper, but by the reader's entire situation. The concept 'readability of a text' is even misleading, as it often refers to texts being easy or difficult, regardless of how the individual reader responds to them. It would make more sense to speak of the 'readability' of the reading situation, which is not far from the idea of 'acceptability' advocated by the Israeli scholar Gideon Toury (1980).

In addition, as translators, we must pay attention to the illustrations, which are a kind of set design for the text; as in the theater, they have an effect on the audience, the listening child. In the concrete sense, we, as translators, try to make the text and illustration fit each other, and in another sense, we – either consciously or unconsciously – have internalized the images from our reading of the text and illustrations.

The visual appearance of a book is important for the child and always includes not only the illustrations and selection of scenes, but even the cover, the end pages and title pages, the actual typeface, the shape and style of letters and headings, and the book's entire layout. All these elements have an emotional impact on the reader. The illustrator sets the scene and shows what the characters and their situations look like. Illustrations also add to the excitement of the reading experience and give the reader a clue about what may happen on the following pages. Or the illustrations may simply decorate the story. All this enriches and complicates the reader's interpretation of the characters and events in a book. Unconsciously, illustrations both free and capture the dialogics.

Yet an illustrated text, like a picture book, is not just a combination of text and illustration. It has both sound and rhythm, which can also be heard, when books are read aloud. But even if they are read silently, texts also have an inner rhythm that the reader can feel. The American Cecily Raysor Hancock has given 'Musical Notes to *The Annotated Alice*' (1988). Referring to the well-known song, Jane Taylor's 'Twinkle, Twinkle, Little Star' she points out:

> most English-speaking readers will echo internally Alice's 'I've heard something like it,' and for most of them the tune that comes to mind will be the familiar *do do sol sol la la sol* tune [...] an international nursery tune with a printing history going back to eighteenth-century France. (Hancock, 1988: 4–5).

Having read quite a few books aloud to children, the situation is familiar to me: every time there are songs in the stories, I sing the texts – for the songs uncomposed or unfamiliar to me I create tunes of my own. When I read aloud a translation of *Alice's Adventures in Wonderland*, I expect the songs to be singable, too. 'The tunes are part of the intended effect,' as Hancock (1988: 22) concludes her article. Even if I am reading silently, just for pleasure, I may sing the songs in my mind, that is, I audiate them. The music, even inaudible, is part of the emotivity of the reading situation; it is part of the non-verbal text elements, the phonological gestalt, as Christiane Nord (1991) describes it.

The translator of a picture book must be able to interpret these auditive and visual messages to understand the dynamics of text and illustration.

Just as the translator translating from English into Finnish must be a specialist and know both languages, the translator of illustrated literature must know the language of illustrations. The more prominent the illustrations are, the more important it is for a translator to have the ability to read this language. It is difficult for me to understand why publishers are in the dark about the demands placed on translators of picture books. This also shows up in the publishers' attitudes to children's literature in general: they find it 'easier' than literature created for grown-ups. I would describe translating illustrated texts as a special field with its own language. It is a field that requires specialization and training.

Moreover, as interpretive tasks, reading a poem and reading a picture, for instance, are not as different as they may seem at first – much depends on the reader/viewer and her/his point of view. Illustration can be understood as a form of translation, in the sense that it is another channel for interpreting the original, though visually. As Joseph Schwarcz (1982: 104) describes the illustrator's work, 'the illustrator, consciously or unconsciously, tastefully or crudely, interprets. The illustrator of children's books, like any artist, suggests meanings which he recognizes in the text and wishes to communicate through the content and style of his work.'

As a whole, the issue of the relationship between text and illustration becomes far more complicated when translating is taken into consideration. In an original work, the author, illustrator, source-language readers, and publisher are involved in a dialogic relationship. In a translation, the dialogic constellation expands and involves a translator interpreting the text and illustrations, target-language readers with a different cultural background, a new publisher and, possibly, even a new illustrator participating in a collaborative dialogue with the translator.

As a reader, the translator has many responsibilities, too: she/he is responsible for her/his reading, not only with respect to her/himself, but also with respect to all the participants in each dialogic situation. The good of the future reader of the text is the reason behind the whole translation process: we are translating stories for target-language children to read or listen to. The rights of the original author and those of the future readers of a translation do not conflict. The original author benefits if her/his books are translated in a live, dialogic, and fearless (i.e. carnivalistic) way so that they live on in the target-language culture. This is loyalty, not only to the target-language readers, but to the author of the original, too.

Of course, no speaker or author can be absolutely sure of perfect understanding of her/his messages: the reader and listener always bring along their own personality and background to the reading/viewing/listening situation. On the other hand, authors, including translators, are addressing their words and images to someone, to whom they speak 'directly,' someone who does not exist in the flesh. This someone might be called a 'superaddressee,' whom Bakhtin (1990a: 135) describes as one 'whose absolutely just responsive understanding is presumed, either in some metaphysical distance or in distant historical time.'

The child image of the translator for children could be described as this kind of a 'superaddressee.' The translator is directing her/his words, her/his translation, to some kind of a child: naive or understanding, inno-cent or experienced; this concept of child influences her/his way of addressing the audience – the choice of words, for instance. Later, in a real dialogue, a real child takes up the book and reads, and new, perhaps unin-tended, meanings arise. Yet, without any 'superaddressee' the book would not be a coherent whole (Iser, 1990: 285).

Translation as Carnivalistic Action

To translate well, for her/his target-language audience, the translator needs to encounter the original fearlessly. The lack of fear entails a new kind of attitude, 'a free and familiar attitude' that 'spreads over everything: over all values, thoughts, phenomena, and things,' as Bakhtin (1987: 123) describes what happens in carnival. Through carnivalistic laughter, the translator defeats her/his fear of the original. Laughter is therapeutic by nature (Bakhtin, 1990b: 452).

Carnivalism signifies being universal, freedom, and defeat over fear. Carnival is also ephemeral, it is a ritual of crowning and uncrowning. As Bakhtin points out, carnival includes a ritual act, which he calls 'the mock crowning and subsequent uncrowning of the carnival king' – or queen. It is a dualistic act, where a carnival queen/king is crowned and given the 'sym-bols of authority.' It symbolizes 'the joyful relativity of all structure and order.' Bakhtin (1987: 124–5) goes on, 'from the very beginning,' an uncrowning 'glimmers through the crowning.'

Translation is in many ways this kind of carnivalistic action: it is crowning and uncrowning. As Bakhtin points out, it is an issue of 'shifts and changes, of death and renewal.' The idea of uncrowning is immanent in the idea of crowning: today the author is the queen/king, tomorrow she/he is uncrowned and the translator becomes the queen/king; the day after tomorrow the translator loses her/his crown and the target-language reader receives 'the symbols of authority.' For Bakhtin (1987: 124–5), the process is never-ending; interpretation is unfinalizable and fearless.

A thought, a sentence, a text, a picture – they are all involved in a never-ending, carnivalistic dialogue. They are continuously changing, moving, and they never meet in a vacuum. In different reading situations, readers interpret these signs in various ways – they turn away from what they read – depending on the situation itself, which involves the text, interpreter, time, place, and so on. Translating, too, always includes the act of turning away from the original, which is the starting point for a new, fearless interpretation based on the translator-reader's reading experience.

All this makes translating rewriting, alteration and positive manipulation. As Hans-Georg Gadamer (1976: 360) says, it is adapting a work of art into a new art form: 'it is the awakening and conversion of a text into new immediacy.' In a dialogic, carnivalistic situation, the translator reads and writes her/his reading in another language for her/his future audience in another culture: the child.

Notes

1. As a female myself, I decided to 'put the feminine first.'
2. Compare the Canadian literary feminists like Nocile Brossard (1988) and Susanne de Lotbinière-Harwood (1991) and 'writing in the feminine.'
3. Jill Paton Walsh, letter from author, 8 March 1992.

Emer O'Sullivan

Narratology Meets Translation Studies, or The Voice of the Translator in Children's Literature

When scholars or critics identify 'changes', 'adaptations' or 'manipulations' in translations of children's literature, they often rightly describe and analyse them in terms of the differing social, educational or literary norms prevailing in the source and the target languages, cultures and literatures at that given time (See Ben-Ari, 1992; Du-Nour, 1995 and Wunderlich, 1992 for examples). A rich source of such observations are the many translations of Astrid Lindgren's *Pippi Långstrump* (1945), which give a good indication of what was perceived by the target cultures, at the time of translation, to be unacceptable for child readers. In a scene in the novel Pippi, Tommy and Annika are playing in the attic when Pippi finds some pistols in a chest. She fires them in the air and then offers them to her friends who delightedly accept. In the German translation (Lindgren, 1965: 205), Pippi doesn't give the pistols to her friends, instead she instructs them – and the readers – by changing her mind, putting them back in the chest and declaring '*Das ist nichts für Kinder!*' (That's not right for children!) a sentiment totally out of character. She herself had made fun of such moralising just a few moments previously when firing the pistols. A possible explanation for this change in the German translation could be that post-war Germany didn't want its children to be encouraged to use weapons.[1]

The point of focus of this article will not be changes and manipulations in translated children's literature and the reasons motivating them, whether social, educational or aesthetic. Instead I want to concentrate on the agency of such changes, the translator, in order to identify her/his presence in the translated text.

The translator's visibility has been a much-discussed issue in translation studies since Lawrence Venuti used the term 'invisibility' to describe both the illusionistic effect of the translator's discourse and the practice by publishers, reviewers, readers, etc. in contemporary Anglo-American culture of judging translations acceptable when they read fluently.[2] Venuti's 'call to action' to translators has been for visibility by use of non-fluent, non-standard and heterogeneous language, by producing foreignised rather than domesticated texts. He rightly insists on talking about translators as real people in geopolitical situations and about the politics of translation and ethical criteria (cf. Venuti, 1995). But the translator's discursive presence can, I submit, also be identified in texts which aren't non-fluent, non-standard and 'foreignised.' It can be located on a theoretical level in a model of narrative communication as shown by Giuliana Schiavi in 1996, and on the level of analysis of the text based on such a model, where the translator's presence is evident in the strategies chosen, in the way s/he positions her/himself in relation to the translated narrative.

My guiding questions are: What kind of translator is making her/himself felt in the text? Where can s/he be located in the act of communication which is the narrative text? How does the implied reader of her/his translation (the target text) differ from that of the 'original' (the source text)? To address this, I will present a theoretical and analytical tool, a communicative model of translation which links the theoretical fields of narratology and translation studies. Before doing so, however, I have to emphasise two points. Firstly, the model applies to all fictional literature in translation. Owing to the asymmetrical nature of the communication in and around children's literature where adults act on behalf of children at every turn, the translator as s/he becomes visible or audible as a narrator is often more tangible in translated children's literature than in literature for adults (where Venuti likes to talk about visibility, my preferred metaphor is audibility, the voice that is heard in the text). I will, secondly, be talking about narrative texts only. A model for drama or poetry would call for appropriate modifications.

Narrative Communication: A Model

The point of departure for the model to be presented in three steps is the basic narrative structure proposed by Seymour Chatman in *Story and Discourse* (1978) (Figure 1).

In this well-known and commonly applied model six different parties form three pairs. The narrative text – indicated by the box in the middle – is the message transmitted from the *real author* to the *real reader*, from the one who physically wrote the text of the book to the one who holds it in her/his hands and reads it (or has it read to her/him). These parties are not to be found within the book itself, nor does the real author communicate directly with the real reader, the communication takes place between the constructed pairs within the narrative text. The first of these pairs is the *implied author* and the *implied reader*.

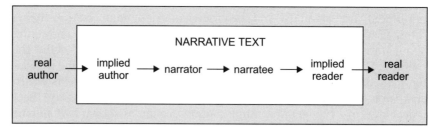

Figure 1 Six part model of narrative communication
Based on Chatman (1978)

The real author, according to Chatman (1990: 75), 'retires from the text as soon as the book is printed and sold', what remains in the text are 'the principles of invention and intent.' The source of the work's invention, the locus of its intent is the implied author, whom Chatman (1990: 75) calls a silent instructor, the 'agency within the narrative fiction itself which guides any reading of it.' The implied author, an agency contained in every fiction, is the all-informing authorial presence, the idea of the author carried away by the real reader after reading the book. The implied reader is the implied author's counterpart, 'the audience presupposed by the narrative itself' (Chatman, 1978: 149f), the reader generated by the implied author and inscribed in the text.

The asymmetrical nature of the communication in children's literature is reflected in this model as follows: an adult implied author creates an implied reader based on her/his (culturally determined) presuppositions as to the interests, propensities and capabilities of readers at a certain stage of their development. The implied author is thus *the* agency in children's literature that has to bridge the distance between 'adult' and 'child.'

The next, innermost, pair in the model is the *narrator* and the *narratee*. The narrator is the one who tells the story, hers/his is the voice audible when a story is being told. The narratee, in the words of Barbara Wall (1991: 4), is 'the more or less shadowy being within the story whom ... the narrator addresses.' The narrator is not always sensed as a persona in the text; Chatman distinguishes between the 'overt' and 'covert' type. Overt are the narrators who feature as figures in the narrative, an example being Oswald Bastable in Edith Nesbit's *The Treasure Seekers,*

> There are some things I must tell before I begin to tell about the treasure-seeking, because I have read books myself, and I know how beastly it is when a story begins, ' "Alas!" said Hildegarde with a deep sigh, "we must look our last on this ancestral home"' ... (Nesbit, 1899: 3f)

or Christopher Robin's father who tells the stories and features in the frame in Milne's *Winnie-the-Pooh* (1926). Equally overt are narrators who feature not as characters but as an authorial presence in the text, such as the one who declares in Nesbit's *The Enchanted Castle*: 'the sensible habit of having boys and girls in the same school is not yet as common as I hope it will be some day' (Nesbit, 1907: 7). The overt narrator has become less common in children's literature over the past few decades, but even without saying 'I', s/he can be no less revealing of character and attitude.

The narratee, too, can be a character in the novel – Christopher Robin in the frame of Milne's *Winnie-the-Pooh* is an obvious example, or the social worker for whom Hal writes the account of his story in Aidan Chambers' *Dance on my Grave* (1982); more often s/he isn't actually portrayed but evoked. The overt first-person, authorial narrator occasionally addresses her/his narratees with questions or appeals like 'You know the kind of house, don't you?' or 'You may imagine their feelings' – both examples from Nesbit's (1907) *The Enchanted Castle*.

The narrator is created by the implied author and is not to be confused with that agency. Similarly the narratee should not be identified with the implied reader. In some cases there will be some overlap. If we again take *Winnie-the-Pooh* as our example: Christopher Robin of the frame is the narratee, but the implied reader (or rather implied readers) includes older children and adults reading the story to children. There are elements in the text that appeal to and can be understood only by them, indeed which are written specifically with an older audience in mind. In this case we can speak of a text with dual or even multiple address[3].

Translation and Narrative Communication

The second of the three steps, moving from general narrative theory to the specifics of translation, looks at translation in terms of narrative communication. The model in Figure 1 applies to an original (non-translated) text and its readers. Taking Erich Kästner's *Emil und die Detektive* (1929) as an example: the real author is Kästner, the real reader is someone who reads the original novel in German. Only those who read German can be real readers of that specific text. Where does this leave those who read Kästner's *Emil* in Spanish, Swahili or Swedish? They aren't accounted for in Chatman's model, which can represent only an original text.[4] In the case of a translated text, however, the message transmitted by the real author in the source language is read by the real reader in the target language. Kästner wrote *Emil* in German, but a Spaniard reads it in Spanish. To account for what has happened in translation the model has to be expanded.

Translation is depicted in Figure 2 as two sequential processes of communication. On the left side of Figure 2 is the source text (the 'original') with the already familiar parties. Where the real reader was situated at the end of the process illustrated in Figure 1, we now have the translator. The translator acts in the first instance as the real reader of the source text. As someone familiar with the source language as well as the conventions and norms of that culture, s/he is in a position to slip into the role of the implied reader of the source text. Above and beyond that s/he tries to identify 'the principles of invention and intent' of the text – the implied author and the implied reader. (This is particularly significant for the process of translating children's literature. As an adult, the translator does not belong to the primary addressees of most children's books. S/he has to negotiate the unequal communication in the source text between adult (implied) author and child (implied) reader in order to be able to slip into the latter's role.)

Parallel to the source text is the target text (the translation). As the creator of the translation, the translator acts, in the second half of the process shown on the right side of Figure 2 as a counterpart to the real author of the source text; s/he is the one who creates the target text in such a way that it can be understood by readers in the target culture with language, conventions, codes and references differing from those in the source culture. However, the translator does not produce a completely new message, as Giuliana Schiavi (1996: 15) who identified the translator's presence in narratological terms writes, s/he 'intercepts the communication and transmits it – re-processed – to the new reader who will receive the message.' By interpreting the original text, by following certain norms, and by adopting specific strategies and methods, the translator, according to Schiavi (1996: 7), 'builds up a new [...] relationship between what we must call a "translated text" and a new group of readers.' In doing so s/he also creates a different implied reader from the one in the source text; *the implied reader of the translation.*[5] This implied reader can be equated with the implied reader of the source text to different degrees, but they are not identical. The implied reader of the translation will always be a different entity from the implied reader of the source text. This statement applies to all translated fictional texts.

If the implied reader of the translation differs from her/his counterpart in the source text then the question has to be asked: what is the agency that creates the difference? The implied reader of the source text, the reader inscribed in the text, is generated by the implied author. By the same token the implied reader of the target text is generated by a similar agency: *the implied translator.*

Based on these deliberations, the final, complex model of the translated narrative text[6] and all its agencies can be described as shown in Figure 3:

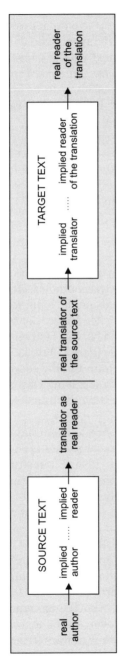

Figure 2 Translation in narrative communication, incorporating the implied translator and the implied reader of the translation

Note: '……denotes narrator and narratee]

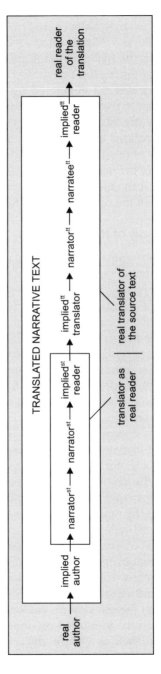

Figure 3 Communicative model of the translated narrative text

Note: st = source text, tt = target text)

The communication between the *real author of the source text* and the *real reader of the translation* is enabled by the *real translator* who is positioned outside the text. Her/his first act is that of a receptive agent, who then, still in an extra-textual position, transmits the source text via the intra-textual agency of the *implied translator*. The *narrator, narratee* and *implied reader* of the target text, all generated by the implied translator, can be roughly equivalent to their counterparts in the source text; however they can also differ greatly, as the following examples will reveal.

In translated texts, therefore, a discursive presence is to be found, the presence of the (implied) translator. It can manifest itself in a voice that is not that of the narrator of the source text. We could say that two voices are present in the narrative discourse of the translated text: the voice of the narrator of the source text and the voice of the translator.

The Voice of the Translator

The translator's voice can be identified on at least two levels. One of them is that of the implied translator as author of paratextual information such as prefaces or metalinguistic explanations such as footnotes. Here 'the translator' can be heard most clearly. When, for example, s/he tells the readers of the German translation of Barbara Park's *My Mother Got Married (and other disasters)* (1989) that *Thanksgiving Day* is a harvest festival which takes place on the fourth Thursday in November (Park, 1991: 115), it is clearly not in translation of an explanation to be found in the source text (American readers hardly need to be told what Thanksgiving Day is). It is information composed for readers of the target text by the translator and proffered in her/his own voice.

In his 'companion piece' to Schiavi's with concrete examples of the implied translator, Theo Hermans locates the translator's voice as an 'index of the Translator's discursive presence' (Hermans, 1996: 27) in situations where s/he has 'to come out of the shadows and directly intervene in a text which the reader had been led to believe spoke only with one voice'. These are primarily moments of paratextual intervention where explanations are crucial, self-reflexive references to the medium of communication itself, moments where (the source) language itself is the theme and 'when "contextual over-determination" leaves no other option' (Hermans, 1996: 23). Hermans' Voice of the Translator is therefore primarily a metalinguistic one, in principle 'wholly assimilated into the Narrator's voice'. I would argue that the translator's voice is not only heard in such interventions, it can be also be identified on another discursive level, on the level of the narration itself as a voice 'dislocated from the one it mimics' (Hermans,

1996: 43), one which is not assimilated into the voice of the narrator of the source text. This specific voice, hitherto largely unrecognised by translation studies or narratology, is what I call the *voice of the narrator of the translation*. Two examples will illustrate how this voice can manifest itself and the consequences it has for communication within the text.

The first is a passage from the classic Swiss children's novel first published in 1881/2, Johanna Spyri's *Heidi*. It occurs in the novel just after Heidi has completed the difficult task of teaching the young goatherd Peter to read, so that he can be a source of comfort to his blind grandmother by reading her beloved hymns aloud when they are snowed in during the winter and Heidi is unable to visit. The grandmother nonetheless prefers Heidi's rendering of the hymns, and the following reason is given:

> *Das kam aber daher, weil der Peter sich beim Lesen ein wenig einrichtete, daß er's nicht zu unbequem hatte. Wenn ein Wort kam, das gar zu lang war oder sonst schlimm aussah, so ließ er es lieber ganz aus, denn er dachte, um drei oder vier Worte in einem Vers werde es der Großmutter wohl gleich sein, es kämen ja dann noch viele. So kam es, daß es fast keine Hauptwörter mehr hatte in den Liedern, die der Peter vorlas.* (Spyri, 1978: 276)

The manner in which Peter shortcuts his reading and how he justifies it to himself is related by a 3rd-person narrator briefly focalising Peter's point of view. This is reflected in the use of colloquial language ('er's'), the particles *'gar'* and *'wohl gleich'*, the subjunctive relating his thoughts as indirect speech (*'werde'*, *'kämen'*) and in the uncommented report of his naive logic. The authorial description of the result is understated and mildly ironic but the narrator neither remarks upon nor judges Peter's actions or thoughts.

In an anonymous translation published in 1949, the voice of the narrator of the translation tries, largely, to emulate that of the narrator of the original, even though the colloquial tone is muted.

> The reason (...) was that Peter used to tamper with the words a little, so as to make the reading slightly less trouble. When he came to a word that was too long, or in some other way seemed difficult, he simply left it out; for he thought that Grannie wouldn't notice the absence of two or three words in a verse – after all, there were so many of them. The result was that the hymns, as read aloud by Peter, had scarcely any nouns. (Spyri, 1949: 224)

The version of the same passage in M. Rosenbaum's popular and much issued translation is compressed, with the final authorial dictum omitted:

> The reason was, of course, that Peter was rather lazy about reading for

the grandmother, and if a word were too difficult or too long he just skipped over it thinking it would not matter very much to the grandmother seeing there were so many words! (Spyri, 1955: 210)

The narrator of this passage, unlike the one of the source text, passes judgement on Peter ('rather lazy'). With the phrase 'of course' a bond of agreement is insinuated between the narrator of the translation and the implied reader and the final exclamation mark is a comment on Peter's thoughts, signalling to the reader that they should be regarded as hilarious. The narrator of this translation therefore appeals directly to the implied reader and makes what s/he has to say more explicit. The implied translator obviously has a reader in mind who may not grasp the subtle irony of Spyri's narrative, whose reading of the text has to be guided with authorial asides and exclamation marks, thus transforming the laconic explanation of the source text into an overstatement.

Less subtle is the amplification to be found in a German translation of Lewis Carroll's *Alice in Wonderland*, published in 1949 (for an account of this translation, see O'Sullivan, 2001)' in the passage in which the 'Mock Turtle' is first introduced. In the original it reads as follows:

Then the Queen left off, quite out of breath, and said to Alice, 'Have you seen the Mock Turtle yet?'
'No', said Alice. 'I don't even know what a Mock Turtle is.'
'It's the thing Mock Turtle Soup is made from,' said the Queen.
'I never saw one, or heard of one.'
'Come on, then', said the Queen, 'and he shall tell you his history.'
(Carroll, 1865/1949)

Franz Sester, one of 32 translators to have produced unabridged German versions of *Alice in Wonderland*, apparently found this too short on explanation. What were his young readers supposed to think a Mock Turtle was? He therefore added a lengthy passage with no equivalent in the English original in which Alice is, culturally adapted, a well-behaved German girl who learns English at school. In the course of the explanation of what a Mock Turtle is, the reader is introduced to Alice's teacher and Alice's aunt and is given a recipe for Mock Turtle soup:

'Wie kann man mich zu einem Tier führen', so dachte Alice, 'das es doch gar nicht gibt?' Alice hatte schon im zweiten Jahre Englisch. Die Lehrerin hatte den Kindern bereits beigebracht, daß 'turtle' auf deutsch 'Schildkröte' bedeutet, während 'mock' auf deutsch 'nachgemacht' heißt. Mock-Turtle-Suppe war also nichts anderes als eine 'nachgemachte' Schildkrötensuppe, die gar nicht mit Schildkrötenfleisch zubereitet war. Die Folge des guten englischen Unterrichts,

den die Lehrerin gab, war also, daß alle Mädchen der Quinta genau wußten, was eine Mock-Turtle war und aus Dankbarkeit der Lehrerin gleich den schönen Spitznamen 'Die Mockturtle' gaben.

Bei der Hochzeit ihrer Tante hatte Alice auch einmal in der Küche zugesehen, wie die Mock-Turtle-Suppe zubereitet wurde. Sie erinnerte sich noch genau, daß in die Suppe ein halber Kalbskopf, ein Ochsengaumen, Suppengrün und andere Zutaten kamen. Später bei Tisch hatten der kleinen Alice die Kalbskopf- und Ochsengaumen-würfelchen in der Suppe besonders gut geschmeckt, denn, wißt ihr, wenn es sich um Essen handelte, hatte Alice immer ein besonders großes Interesse und ein ausge-zeichnetes Gedächtnis. So etwas behielt sie immer viel besser als englische oder französische Vokabeln. (Carroll, 1949: 69)

('How can I be brought to an animal which doesn't even exist?', thought Alice. This was Alice's second year learning English in school. The teacher had already told the children that 'turtle' was 'Schildkröte' in German and that 'mock' meant 'nachgemacht'. So Mock Turtle Soup was nothing other than an imitation turtle soup which wasn't made with turtle meat at all. Thanks to the excellent English instruction by their teacher, each girl in the sixth class knew exactly what a Mock Turtle was, and out of gratitude to their teacher they gave her the lovely nickname 'the Mockturtle'.

At her aunt's wedding Alice had also seen how Mock Turtle soup was made in the kitchen. She could remember exactly that half a calf's head, an ox's gum, some carrots, onion, celery, leeks and parsley and other ingredients were used to make the soup. Later, during the meal, little Alice especially savoured the small pieces of calf's head and ox's gum in the soup because, you know, when it came to eating, Alice was always very interested and remembered anything to do with that much better than English or French vocabulary.) [My translation, Emer O'Sullivan]

The voice of the narrator of this translation overrides that of the narrator of the source text, the tone is heavy-handed and pedantic. The work of the implied translator was informed here, as always, by the time and place in which the translation was carried out (the detailed descriptions of food and eating must have been particularly attractive to readers during the hungry post-war years in Germany) and especially by his notion of the implied reader based on assumptions as to the interests, propensities and capabilities of readers at that stage of their development. He obviously envisaged the implied reader of his translation as a child devoid of the fantasy necessary to imagine what a mock turtle might be, a child to whom everything had to be explained. His implied reader can't cope with a 'foreign' setting, any action has to be transported to familiar, German, territory. It could be claimed that this implied translator missed the point of the book and produced a nanny translation devoid of nonsense. Unlike the source text, it holds absolutely no attraction for adults, any incidental humorous effect is involuntarily. The implied translator of this *Alicens Abenteuer im Wunderland* and the implied author of Carroll's *Alice in Wonderland* come from entirely different planets in the universe of children's literature, and the implied translator is sure that his is a safer place for child readers than Carroll's one.

The discursive presence of the translator can be located in every translated narrative text on an abstract level as the implied translator of the translation. The translator's voice can make itself heard on a paratextual level as that of 'the translator' and is inscribed in the narrative as what I have called 'the voice of the narrator of the translation'. This particular voice would seem to be more evident in children's literature than in other bodies of literature due to the specific, asymmetrical communication structure which characterises texts which are written and published by adults for children. In these texts, contemporary and culture-specific notions of childhood play some part in determining the construction of the implied reader: what do 'children' want to read, what are their cognitive and linguistic capabilities, how far can/should they be stretched, what is suitable for them. These are only some of the questions implicitly answered by the assumptions evident behind the 'child' in children's literature and behind the child in any specific children's book. The same questions are asked again by the translator and by the publisher of the translation. The strategies chosen by translators for children are, as Riitta Oittinen (2000) reminds us, primarily dictated by their child image. Assumptions about 'the child' and the ensuing construction of readers of specific children's books and of their translations can lead to vast divergences between implied readers of source and target texts for children, as the few examples here have illustrated. Using a model of narrative communication it is possible to locate and name the place and agent of this divergence, to identify exactly where 'changes' and 'manipulations' happen and how these can be described in terms of narrative strategy, in terms of the construction of implied readers of the translation.

André Lefevere and Susan Bassnett describe translation as one of the most obvious, comprehensive, and easy to study 'laboratory situations' for the study of cultural interaction, because a comparison of original and translation:

> will not only reveal the constraints under which translators have to work at a certain time and in a certain place, but also the strategies they

develop to overcome, or at least work around those constraints. This kind of comparison can, therefore, give the researcher something like a synchronic snapshot of many features of a given culture at a given time. (Lefevere & Bassnett, 1998: 6)

One of these features is doubtlessly child image as one of the most influential factors determining the strategies developed by translators of children's literature. The model of narrative communication presented here offers a tool with which varieties of implied readers of source and target texts at certain times and in certain places can be identified by analysing the narrative strategies chosen by the translator as indicative of her/his idea of the reading child and the kind of literature appropriate for that child. These strategies manifest themselves in audible form in the voice of the translator in children's literature.

Notes

1. The first edition of the German translation of 1949 actually translates the scene as it is in the source text; it was altered in a subsequent edition (cf Surmatz, 1998).
2. Theo Hermans (1996: 27) calls this illusion of transparency and coincidence 'the ideology of translation,' it is the illusion of a single voice which blinds critics to the presence of the other voice, the translator's.
3. How some of these addressees can go missing in translation is shown in O'Sullivan (1993).
4. The main narratological models available fail to distinguish between original texts and translations. As Theo Hermans (1996: 26) rightly says, they 'routinely ignore the translator's discursive presence.'
5. This term, and that of *the implied translator*, was introduced by Guiliana Schiavi (1996) who theoretically located these agencies in the translated text. She did not, however, provide examples of the discursive presence of the implied translator in actual translations.
6. This model is loosely based on the diagram in Schiavi (1996: 14) but has been further developed, for example by placing the real translator in an extratextual position (cf. O'Sullivan, 2000: 247).

Part 3
Translating the Visual

One of the most notable differences between translating for adults and translating for children is the challenge of what Anthea Bell has called a third dimension to the translation process. In addition to source and target languages, a translator for children often works with images, either illustrations that punctuate a prose text or, in the case of the modern picture book, an intricate and vital counterpoint between image and text. An understanding of the role of the visual in children's texts is essential for any translator working for a child audience. Indeed, Riitta Oittinen, who has written extensively on the translation of visual texts (see Oittinen's article in Part 2), has argued in her book *Translating for Children* that: 'Translating illustrated texts is a special field, or a special language, and requires specialization in translation studies, combined with art for example' (Oittinen, 2000: 114). In the first essay in this section, Emer O'Sullivan demonstrates in two telling examples what can happen to the integrity of a picture book when translators are not sensitive to this 'special field'. A translator who ignores the orchestration of word and image limits the active and intelligent participation of the child reader that is required by the source text.

An active reader is central, too, to Mieke Desmet's analysis of the translation of both intertextuality and intervisuality in the Dutch translation of the Ahlbergs' *The Jolly Postman* series. Texts that are intertextually and intervisually rich and highly culture-specific are often deemed untranslatable. To deal with the intertextual and culture-specific elements in the source text, the translator of *The Jolly Postman* books into Dutch uses a variety of translation strategies: literal translation for shared intertexts, substitution for intertexts likely to be unknown to the intended target audience, and addition or compensation. In this way he has created Dutch target texts with plenty of opportunities for readers to forge their own interpretations and play their own intertextual games.

Gillian Lathey pursues one of the 'delicate matters' raised by Anthea Bell (for the full text of Bell's article turn to Part 5 of this Reader) as well as Riitta Oittinen's emphasis on the 'performance' of the picture book (in Part 2) in analysing the effects of a shift from present to past tense in the British translation of Jean de Brunhoff's *Histoire de Babar.* With reference to theories of narrative time, this essay invites speculation on the impact of such tense

111

shifting on the dynamic interaction of text and pictures in the original, on the dramatic and playful event that constitutes a shared reading by child and adult and, finally, on the relevance of the young child's developing understanding of the role of tense in narrative.

Emer O'Sullivan

Translating Pictures

The 'language' of pictures is generally regarded as international, capable of transcending linguistic and cultural boundaries. How, then, can we speak of translating pictures in picture books when, in most cases, these remain materially unaltered? It seems to me that in the translation of picture books, neither element – words or pictures – can be isolated, nor are they isolated when the translator translates. I think that, in a genre combining words and pictures, an ideal translation reflects awareness not only of the significance of the original text but also of the interaction between the visual and the verbal, what the pictures do in relation to the words; it does not verbalize the interaction, but leaves gaps that make the interplay possible and exciting. The reader of the ideal translation is left to do the same work as the reader of the original. This paper looks at how translation changed this interaction in two picture books: Michel Gay's *Papa Vroum* (French into English) and John Burningham's *Granpa* (English into German).

First, a general point. The communication in children's books and around children's literature is asymmetrical; indeed asymmetry is one of the defining characteristics of this branch of literature. As is frequently observed, adults write, publish and sell books for children, adult critics write about them, librarians recommend them, and teachers bring children's books into school. Adults act on behalf of children at every stage in this literary communication. In itself this is not a bad thing but it is not always easy to distinguish between adults enabling children and controlling them.

The asymmetrical communication is mirrored when children's literature is translated: the various steps from the selection of texts to the details of how individual lexical items are to be translated are subject to the assumptions of publishers and translators as to what children can understand, what they enjoy, what is suitable and acceptable. These norms and suppositions function on educational, sociocultural, ideological and aesthetic levels. An example of a text being altered in translation to conform to views on suitability can be found in the German translation of Astrid Lindgren's *Pippi Långstrump*. In the original Swedish Pippi and her friends play in the attic with pistols; in the German edition Pippi declares that children shouldn't play with guns and that she will put them back into the chest.[1]

Picture books present a special challenge to the translator, as the presence and interaction of two media make the process more complex. The more intricate the interplay between words and pictures, the more complex the task of translating. Difficulties arise when pictures and words tell different stories or when the text consistently does not refer to what can be seen in the pictures.

A translator's reading of the original text is bound to be influenced by the pictures, though it is not always easy for her to disentangle the elements that contribute to the complexity.[2] The result can be problematic: the pictures stimulate the creative linguistic powers of the translator, who may in turn make elements explicit in the narrative where originally these were seen only in the pictures. In other words: gaps in the source text may be filled by translators in the target text.

Papa Vroum

The American edition of Michel Gay's *Papa Vroum* (*Night Ride*) reveals how the character of a picture book can be substantially altered in translation. In this night-time adventure Gabriel and his father, stuck in traffic, decide to spend the night in their van. While the father is asleep in the back, the van is towed away and Gabriel, who is joined by various animals as the night proceeds, is left 'driving' the car. The present-tense narrative consists of direct speech for the most part and, though in the third person, is focused on Gabriel's point of view and thus relates directly what Gabriel is seeing, thinking and feeling. He thinks he is driving the van, and the reader is not told anything to the contrary. The pictures reveal that Gabriel is not the agent of the action, however, and the point of the story is that this is not made explicit so the reader shares Gabriel's trepidation and surprise.

A lorry, which Gabriel hasn't noticed, reverses close to the van and hits the front bumper. Gabriel thinks the noise is someone knocking at the door. In Figure 1 Gabriel tells the kittens not to wake his sleeping father, which implies that he believes they have made the noise. The kittens smell sausage in the van and ask to come inside. In the picture we see a monkey, again unnoticed by Gabriel, jumping onto the van. The text is narrated in the present tense with liberal use of direct speech, making action and words immediate for the reader/viewer.

The American text accompanying the same pictures describes what can be seen and interprets it, thus causing a shift in the relationship between picture and text. Whereas in the original the narrative is frequently constructed as dialogue, in the translation Gabriel is made into the main actor, the narrative is now about him. What he perceives and how he reacts are now described rather than indicated in his own words. Immediacy is reduced by the elimination of direct speech and the substitution of past tense for present tense. Explaining that the kittens couldn't have made the noise because they are too small and that Gabriel didn't notice the monkey violates a central device of Gay's picture book: the variance between what is shown and what is said.

When the van begins to move – the monkey has just been shown playing with the steering wheel – the French text exclaims '*Oh là là! Ça démarre!*' ('Oh no! It's moving!') but the American text spells it out: 'Suddenly the van jerked forward. They were moving! It wasn't the monkey's fault. The trailer was pulling out of the parking lot – and dragging the van behind', thus ruining the surprise of the later picture showing the van being towed by the lorry.

The narrative of the American translation also differs from the original in the stated reassurance that Gabriel is in control and that he is not afraid. Constant verbal reminders of the father's presence in the van – in the

Il ouvre la portière et regarde.
«Moins de bruit, les petits chats.
Papa dort!»

«C'est ta voiture? On peut monter?»
demandent les petits chats. «Miam!
la bonne odeur de saucisson!»

Figure 1 From *Papa Vroum* by Michel Gay © l'école des loisirs, 1986
American translation (left-hand page): He opened the door and looked out. There were three kittens all by themselves in the parking lot. They were too little to have made that sound. *(right-hand page):* Gabriel decided to let the kittens into the van. He did not see the monkey that quickly, silently, climbed down to see what was going on.

pictures he is visible only as a sleeping shape, until the final pages – further reassure the reader that there is no cause for alarm.

In the original the pictures tell a different story from the words, the text doesn't divulge more than Gabriel knows, but readers can experience the thrill of noticing more in the pictures than the words have told and draw their own conclusions. They can savour Gabriel's fear, excitement and surprise from a perspective of knowledge. The American translation eliminates the tension and, instead of playful irony, we have a nanny text that removes challenge and unexpectedness. Even the cover blurb tells all: 'And when the van jerks forward – hooked by accident to the huge trailer parked in front of them – Gabriel bravely stays at the wheel as they roll faster and faster through the night.' Much is lost in translation by everything being explained.

Granpa

John Burningham's *Granpa* is a collection of episodes about a girl and her grandfather, presented as scenes in a greenhouse, on a beach, sitting at home. In most of the double spreads a full-colour picture in a distinctly naïve and childlike style, showing a situation experienced by the pair, faces a faint sepia picture depicting the old man's memories, the child's imaginings, or some form of association that illuminates or elaborates what is shown in its partner.

The links between the pictures are generally as open as those between pictures and fragmentary text,[3] which consists of snippets of dialogue between the old man and the girl. Different typefaces indicate the two speakers; they are shown in word and picture to have two distinct but equal subject positions. The same attention is given to their differing modes of perception, levels of experience, types of fantasies, their means of thinking and communicating. There is no narrator, no explicit commentary and, other than roughly following the pattern of the seasons, no apparent sequence of events until the final pictures portraying the grandfather's illness and death. The text is distinctly undercoded, and there are substantial gaps between the text and the pictures. What does a translator make of it all?

Two things are striking about the title page of the German translation (Figure 2). The first is that equal billing is given to John Burningham and Irina Korschunow. The translator – a figure traditionally ignored in children's literature – is elevated to the status of author. Irina Korschunow is a children's book author in her own right (it is quite common for German authors to translate children's literature) and has written extensively for all age groups from beginner readers to young adults. The double billing can, therefore, be seen as effective marketing of a name familiar to German readers and especially to those who buy the books. It also indicates that the German product is no longer a visual and verbal composition by Burningham but an amalgam of pictures by Burningham and text by Korschunow.

The second striking element is the title, 'My grandfather and me.' The girl is now clearly the focus of the story, which has become one about her relationship to her grandfather. The dialogue of the original is replaced by a text narrated in the past: the soundtrack is no longer immediate; what is being told happened a while ago. Where the first picture in the original shows the girl running into the arms of her grandfather, accompanied by the direct speech of the man, 'And how's my little girl?', the German text, translated, runs: 'Me and my grandpa, that was nice. "Do you still love your old grandpa, my little girl?" "You aren't old at all, grandpa."' The past tense ('that was nice') tells us that their relationship is a thing of the past. The old man's death in the final pages is pre-empted by the tense used in the translation. The mode is sentimental: the grandfather wants to be assured of his granddaughter's love while she is at pains to tell him that he isn't old. As being old is not regarded by children as negative but simply as a fact, we find here placed in the mouth of the young girl an adult sentiment

Mein Opa und ich

John Burningham
Irina Korschunow

PARABEL

Figure 2 Title page of the 1984 German translation of *Granpa*

which seeks to evade the inevitable end associated with old age. The pattern of communication – the simultaneity of the two discourses – has changed. Granpa has become the object of the girl's concern and no longer features as an autonomous subject of the text. Korschunow also verbalizes obvious details in the pictures. The first sentence accompanying the fishing scene reads 'We also went fishing.' By supplying this superfluous information, Korschunow degrades the picture to an illustration of her text.

The translator's reading of the text has begun with its ending, the grandfather's death. A popular topic in German children's literature in the 1980s, death is elevated to being the central theme around which the translator builds a continuous narrative. This has consequences for the characterizatin of the girl. Gone is the unburdened child perspective. Korschunow's girl is defined solely by what she thinks about and feels for her grandfather; she is fixated on him in an overprotective, anxious way.

The illustration in Figure 3 shows the grandfather, who has been taken ill in the previous scene, and the girl indoors watching television together. Her plans and hopes for their continuing adventures are expressed in her question, which remains unanswered by the grandfather. A ship sailing

Figure 3 From *Mein Opa und ich* (Parabel, 1984)

In the original *Granpa* (Jonathan Cape, 1984), John Burningham's text for this doublespread was '*Tomorrow shall we go to Africa, and you can be the captain?*' The above translates as (*left-hand page*): 'I painted a ship and we sailed to America. "Do you want to be captain, Granpa?" "Yes please, if I may." "I love you, Granpa." "I love you too, my little girl."' *Righthand page*: '"Mama said that soon you'll be going away forever, Granpa." "Maybe. I am already so old. But when I'm no longer here, all you have to do is close your eyes and think of me. Then you'll be able to see me. "Is that true, Granpa?" "Have I ever lied to you, my little girl?"'

away under gloriously billowing clouds can be seen in the sepia picture. We can't see whether the two of them are on board, as the girl probably imagines, or whether the old man, in what is more likely to be his association, is embarking alone on his last trip. The openness of picture and text allows a multitude of possible interpretations. The text of the German translation crowds this simple scene and closes most of the gaps.

The indeterminate ship has become one which the girl in the translation claims to have painted herself. In addition to reducing Burningham's pictures to mere illustrations, Korschunow makes one of them be explicitly drawn by the girl and then used as an illustration. The scene is taken by the translator as a cue for a discussion about the impending death of the grandfather and about how the granddaughter will cope. Exclamations of mutual affection verbalize in an almost unbearably sentimental manner the closeness so eloquently expressed by the body language of the two people in the pictures.

In the final double spread of the original the symbolic force of the empty chair is strengthened by the visual expression of silence on the textless page. The grandfather's chair is empty, the girl is left alone staring at it. There can be no words because words, in this book, have only ever been part of a dialogue, part of the pattern that characterized the communication. Once the grandfather is gone, dialogue is no longer possible. The almost deafening, and certainly moving, silence on this page is a fitting expression of loss. It also leaves room for the reader to grasp and respond to the death of the grandfather. There is no room for sorrow. Not so in the German translation (Figure 4).

The translator obviously believes that the antidote to the final silence of death is garrulousness. On this page she tries to undo the grandfather's death or, at the very least, not to leave the reader alone to digest what has happened. The translator fills the vacuum with words and succeeds in bringing him back to life by having him talk in the familiar manner with the girl. The tone is one of hope for the future, the girl has coped quickly with bereavement. The picture is no longer an autonomous expression of loss but an incidental illustration to go with what the narrator of the German translation wants to tell us about death and how to deal with it.

Rather than translating the words of *Granpa*, Korschunow uses Burningham's pictures to tell a different story – a story about old age, death and mourning – in a different way. She clearly thought the original text far too open and thus not suitable for young readers who couldn't or shouldn't be expected to understand the complex narrative interaction between pictures and fragmentary text. Her translation fills all possible gaps with elements of continuity, with a narrative focus and with numerous explana-

Und dann war mein Opa wirklich nicht mehr da.

Zuerst war ich traurig. Aber später nicht mehr.
Mein Opa hat mir nichts vorgelogen.
Immer, wenn ich die Augen zumache und an
ihn denke, ist er weider bei mor.

„Mein kleines Mädchen!"
„Ich bin gar nicht mehr so klein, Opa.
Ich bin bald so groß wie du."

Figure 4 From *Mein Opa und ich*

In the original *Granpa* no words appear on this double spread. The above translates as: 'And then my granpa really wasn't there any more. First of all I was sad, but after a while I wasn't. My granpa hadn't lied to me. Whenever I close my eyes and think of him, he is with me again. "My little girl!" "I'm not that little any more, Granpa. Soon I'll be as big as you!"'

tions, thus delivering an infinitely less interesting and less skilfully told story than Burningham's.

Korschunow's translation has had unusual repercussions. It is one of the rare instances where a license has been withdrawn by the originating publisher. A second, 'authorized', translation under the simple title *Grosspapa*, true to the spirit of Burningham's text, was undertaken by Rolf Inhauser, who has served not only Burningham but many other celebrated picture-book artists well with his translations into German. It was published by Sauerländer Verlag in 1988, four years after the first translation.

The American edition of *Papa Vroum* and the first German edition of *Granpa* reveal how, even while remaining materially unchanged, pictures are indeed translated when their contribution to the dialogic whole of the original is usurped by translators and fed into the text. The implied readers of these translations are not identical to the readers of the originals, that much is made clear by the analysis. The translators obviously felt that they could not or did not want to reproduce a text in their language that trusts children to be able to read between the lines and the pictures, to be able to resolve the sophisticated connections between the verbal and visual elements of the books. Their solution was to resolve these connections themselves in the re-narration of the stories.

Criticism of literature in translation – both for children and for adults – tends to speak of 'changes', of 'omissions' or 'additions' in translations without identifying an agent in the text responsible for the changes. A translator is never invisible – despite the ideology of translation that insists that she is. Each translation has its own implied reader, and its own narrator, one who was not present in the original: the narrator of the translation. Two examples of clearly identifiable narrators of translations have been discussed here. The variations are infinite, but that is a different story, one that has been told in more detail elsewhere by the narrator of this paper.

Acknowledgement

I am grateful to Reinbert Tabbert for drawing my attention to the American translation of *Papa Vroum* by some remarks made in his article 'Bilderbücher zwischen zwei Kulturen', in Reinbert Tabbert (ed.) (1991) *Kinderbuchanalysen II. Wirkung – Kultureller Kontext – Unterricht*, Frankfurt: dipa 1991, 130–48.

Notes

1. Astrid Lindgren (1945) *Pippi Långstrump* (172ff). Stockholm: Rabén & Sjögren. Astrid Lindgren (1965) *Pippi Langstrumpf* (p. 205), translated into German by Cäcilie Heinig, Hamburg: Oetinger.
2. The Finnish translation scholar Riitta Oittinen was one of the first to point out the function of illustrations in the translation of children's literature. See Riitta Oittinen (1990) The dialogic relation between text and illustration: A translatological view. *TEXTconTEXT* 5, 40–53.
3. Peter Hunt writes of *Granpa* that 'the relationships between the fragmentary text and between the full-colour pictures and the sepia pictures ... are as important as whether the book is read in a conventional sequence or not' (Hunt, 1991: 183ff).

Mieke K.T. Desmet

Intertextuality/Intervisuality in Translation: The Jolly Postman's Intercultural Journey from Britain to the Netherlands

Intertextuality and intervisuality, hallmarks of many children's books being published at the moment, can survive in translated texts even though the intertextual and intervisual references, which are sometimes unknown in the target culture, may provide difficulties for the translator. Moreover, a translator may translate intertextual aspects of source texts so that they not only survive in some way, but also contain the seeds for gain through creating target culture oriented intertextual games. It follows that cultural specificity as exemplified by intertextuality need not defeat the translator, but may, on the contrary, be the catalyst for a new, differently intertextual text. How this can be achieved will be explored through the Dutch translations of Janet and Allan Ahlberg's intertextually and intervisually rich and culture-specific books on the jolly postman: *The Jolly Postman or Other People's Letters* (1986, 1997) and its translation *De Puike Postbode of: Briefgeheimpjes* (1987, 1997), *The Jolly Christmas Postman* (1991, 1996) and *De Puike Pakket Post* (1992), and finally *The Jolly Pocket Postman* (1995) and *De Piepkleine Puike Postbode* (1996).

In the first part of this paper I discuss translation from a theoretical viewpoint, while part two will take a closer look at specific translation problems and their solutions in the translations of *The Jolly Postman* books into Dutch.

Viewpoints on Translation

When discussing translations, attention is usually focused on the original (the source text) rather than on the functioning of the translation (the target text) in its new environment, the target culture. This is borne out in the vocabulary used to describe and evaluate translations; terms such as 'faithfulness' and 'equivalence' betray the inherent bias towards the 'sacred' original, which the translator can never equal. This view is still widespread today and as Emer O'Sullivan argues:

we are more inclined to speak of losses than gains in translation; it has something to do with the perspective of comparison. If we read a text first in its original language and then in the language of translation, we risk setting out to hunt for 'errors of translation,' concentrating on the passages in the translation that represent problems in the form of cultural references, wordplay, and so on. (O'Sullivan, 1998: 186)

This view on translation, although still widespread, is being superseded by a variety of new approaches. Among these, reader–response theory has for some time stressed the input of the reader as actively processing texts, and hence as generating rather than merely reconstructing the meanings embedded in texts; as a result, the original text has lost some of its traditional authority. Emphasizing the role of the reader in creating meaning from a text leads to the recognition of multiple legitimate interpretations of any one text. Translators of source texts are in the first place readers of that text, and it is their particular interpretation of the original that will guide their translation. The translator will note some aspects of the source text but may overlook others, and this is obviously also the case for the researcher of children's literature. This manipulation of the text by the translator or researcher as reader is unavoidable. What is interesting is the particular form that manipulation takes.

Another approach to the study of literature that undermines the originality of the text is a text-based approach such as intertextuality, which John Stephens defines as 'the production of meaning from the interrelationships between audience, text, other texts, and the socio-cultural determinations of significance' (Stephens, 1992: 84). Maria Nikolajeva further notes that 'no artistic texts can be produced without an intertextual confrontation' (Nikolajeva, 1996: 154), and in this sense all forms of discourse, whether intended for adults or children, whether traditional or alternative, derive their significance from relationships to texts that precede them and texts that follow them. The concept of intertextuality also questions the authority of any one text over another because essential to an intertextual analysis is the equality of the confrontation of texts. In an intertextual approach readers do not think in terms of 'one author "borrowing" from another, but instead are intent on discovering hidden echoes and latent links' (Nikolajeva, 1996: 154). What is important is not just the link but the use the author makes of that link – consciously or unconsciously. Although intertextuality emphasizes the creative input of the author, at the same time it stresses that:

a text is available only through some process of reading; what is produced at the moment of reading is due to cross-fertilisation of the packaged textual material (say, a book) by all the texts which the reader brings to it (Worton & Still, 1993: 1–2).

That reading process may be quite different for adult readers/writers as opposed to child readers. The adult reader/writer and the child reader will be exposed to different texts: adults have access to a repertoire of adult books not necessarily accessible to children, but children too may have read works unfamiliar to the adult writer/reader. The intertextual web available to the adult writer/reader and that available to the child reader will thus include a common area as well as areas available only to one or the other; that common ground may be large or small depending on individual reading experience. These differences in reading experience mean that allusions may remain dormant or that different connections will be made.

Helen Bromley describes how she introduced the concept of intertextuality to her class of 6-year-olds, turning it into a spy game, and explains how the pupils then tried to find examples in picture books. One pupil, Matthew, used the illustrations and a rhyme known to him to create meaning, although the actual reference in the words of the text was to another rhyme which he was not familiar with (Bromley, 1996: 105). It is clear that the nature of intertextuality is one of silences and of echoes or dialogue; with highly intertextual narratives this may lead to a perpetual deferral of meaning and an essentially open text not bound in any one direction. In the same way, translators as readers of an intertextual source text may remain oblivious to particular intertextual references while at the same time creating their own. That which remains dormant in the translator's own reading and that which is created personally obviously colours the translation of the intertextual text. Although adult translators may, consciously or unconsciously, pick up many of the intertextual references, a complete and full understanding of all references is even here an impossibility. A translation will necessarily reflect the translator's interpretation in his/her actual rendering of the text. Moreover, the extent to which a translator consciously processes intertextual references and his/her consideration and assessment of the intended audience's differing degrees of familiarity with these intertextual references will also affect the actual form of the translation.

Two main strategies for translating a text which is highly intertextual suggest themselves, based on what is characteristic of intertextuality. On the one hand it is possible to argue that the likelihood of intertextual references remaining dormant in a particular reading of a text, either in the translator's personal reading or in the predicted reading of the intended audience, leads translators to a standpoint where they do not worry about those references. A possible translation strategy here would be one where all the references are just translated literally, that is, going for the closest equivalent phrase in the target language. For example, a reference to 'Jack and the Giant' in the *Jolly Postman* books could be rendered as '*Jack en de reus*,' even if that might hamper interpretation of the target text and make it difficult to understand and create meaning in the text because '*Jack en de reus*' is an unknown intertextual reference to the target audience. It is also possible to copy these cultural references verbatim, and to treat, for example, 'Mad March Hare' as a proper name leaving it as 'Mad March Hare' in the translation, again making interpretation more difficult for a target text reader who does not have the required language knowledge to understand the phrase and its reference. Another translation strategy with regard to references that translators predict will remain dormant in the target audience would be to delete them as they would not be understood anyway – robbing the target text reader of the references altogether. This would imply deleting River Dee, London Bridge, and so on.

On the other hand, a different approach based on another aspect of texts seems equally possible. The multiplicity and variety of interpretation implied in highly intertextual texts that leads to a more open text can be recreated by translators who may try to focus on creating an equally, but differently, open text. Translators may be aware of gaps in their own reading, may observe that certain intertextual or cultural references do not work in the target culture, and therefore recognize that particular references would remain dormant for most of the intended audience in the target culture. Yet, since translators are committed to creating their own version of an open intertextual text, they may decide to use substitution, whereby intertextual or cultural items that would remain dormant and close off a text are substituted by different references of a similar kind that work in the target culture and create a similar effect in the target reader. An example of this would be changing 'Mr McDonald's Farm' into 'Groen Knollenland'. Substitution as a strategy may be linked with compensation, that is, where it is impossible to create the same effect translators can compensate by creating that effect in a place where the source text does not have a reference, thus creating its own links, for example adding 'Dr Leukoplast' (a local brand name of plasters) to the Humpty Dumpty episode. In this view of translation what matters is 'to retain the play of ideas' (O'Sullivan, 1998: 201), and substitution and compensation are useful strategies to achieve this goal.

Intertextuality may be understood as a process of text creation where a text is infused with echoes from a variety of sources. References ring through and permeate the text, while at the same time opening up a dialogue with other texts; being in the form of an echo they imply both amplification and distortion of the sources. This view also applies to the translation of a text, which is an echo of the source text – in this particular case, into a different language. The translated text gives a new lease of life to the source text (amplification) but also transforms its meaning potential (distortion). To see how this operates in practice, I look at the translation of Janet and Allan Ahlberg's *Jolly Postman* books, a marvel of intertextuality, into Dutch.

The *Jolly Postman* Books and their Translations into Dutch

The *Jolly Postman* books offer particular examples of intertextuality at work. All three books are conceived as narratives about a postman delivering letters; the actual letters are interleaved between the pages of the books in open envelopes for exploration by the reader. *The Jolly Postman or Other People's Letters* (1989, 1997), the first book in the series, maintains tight control over its form. A 6-line partly rhyming stanza is found on the left page of the first spread, then an envelope containing a letter makes up the right side of the first spread, followed by a 4-line partly rhyming stanza on the right page of the second double spread. This pattern is repeated throughout. Letters include Goldilocks' apology to the Three Bears, junk mail to the Witch from Hansel and Gretel, a postcard from Jack to the Giant, and a lawyer's letter to the Wolf from Little Red Riding Hood and the Three Little Pigs among others. The second book in the series, *The Jolly Christmas Postman* (1991, 1996), is built around the idea of gift giving for Christmas. The format of this book is similar to the first one but is not as rigidly controlled: more pages go between envelopes, the number of lines on each page changes, as do the rhyme patterns. Letters, again six, include a goose board game to Little Red Riding Hood, a Christmas annual to the Gingerbread Man, and a letter of Little Red Riding Hood to the Wolf. The last book in the series, *The Jolly Pocket Postman* (1995), starts off with a letter to the reader; the envelope also contains a lens to be used in reading the book. All the other letters are addressed to the postman himself and contain, among other things, advice on how to proceed, a route to escape from the wolf, a map of Oz, and an alternative story telling what would have happened if the tyre of the postman's bike had not been flat. These examples, which are far from exhaustive, show that the books abound in intertextual references to fairy tales, nursery rhymes and children's novels; moreover, internal intertextual links between the three books are also maintained.

It is important to assess the role intertextuality plays in a text when considering how to translate it. The examples cited above make it obvious that intertextuality is an essential feature of the books and that, if their meaning potential is to be recreated in some form, an attempt to render their intertextuality in the target text should be undertaken. However, a balance must be found as the target text also needs to function in the target culture environment. The particular character of the intertexts used in the *Jolly Postman* books is clearly British. Although fairy tales have an international background, the fairy tales in the books are very much located in the British cultural sphere; this is even more true of the nursery rhymes alluded to.

The Dutch translator needs to strike a balance between rendering the Britishness and local colour of the source texts and positioning the target texts in the target literary culture. In order to do so, he combines straightforward translation with substitution and compensation strategies. However, the intertextual and metafictional aspects of these texts are not the only elements to consider in translating them. The relationship between the illustrations and the verbal text is crucial, and the verbal text is reinforced by visual interpretation, but at the same time the illustrations on their own sustain further intertextual links not mentioned in the text. Other elements taxing the translator's creativity and putting constraints on the translation are the use of typeface, the register (that is, the choice of vocabulary, style and grammar patterns used), the rhyme pattern, the rhythm or read-aloud quality of the texts, the verbal information in the illustrations, and the graphic design of the pages and letters.

Dutch is the official language of the Netherlands and Flanders, the northern part of Belgium. Both regions share certain cultural practices, icons, texts and folklore, yet they are also very different, using their own currency, foods, customs, newspapers. As Dutch is a relatively small language, of some twenty million speakers, large numbers of books are translated and imported into the culture. However, when translating into Dutch a translator may have to opt for one cultural background rather than the other (Dutch versus Flemish), but could also mix and provide references from both cultural spheres. The translations of the *Jolly Postman* books are brought out by a publisher based in the Netherlands, whose books are also distributed in Flanders, and the translator, Ernst van Altena, is Dutch as well. The factor is relevant: The substitution and compensation strategies used clearly locate the text as a Dutch intertextual text, and not Flemish.

All three *Jolly Postman* books are translated by Ernst van Altena, a much respected writer and translator of adult poetry, and all three books acknowledge the translator on the title page or on the back cover and in the bibliographic information. Van Altena has clear views on translation and considers the translator to be the key person who opens foreign cultures and literary texts, which would otherwise remain closed to the target public. He stresses that it is the translator's responsibility to remain respectful to the style and rhythm of the source text author, but also to expand the target culture and language (Van Altena, 1985: 51). He sees himself as a 'subjective' translator and considers it impossible to efface his personality when translating (Van Altena, 1985: 55).

The translation strategies Ernst Van Altena uses for the *Jolly Postman* books include literal translation, substitution, compensation (or addition), and very occasionally deletion. The title of the first book stresses the friendly postman and draws attention to the game of reading other people's letters. The Dutch title, *De Puike Postbode of: Briefgeheimpjes* (1987, 1997), uses *'puik'* ('excellent', 'first-rate') for 'jolly', which has a slightly different meaning from the English, but adds alliteration to the title improving on its read-aloud quality. *'Briefgeheimpjes'* refers, with an endearing diminutive (*'-pjes'*), to the privacy of letters and the secrecy that this book will break. This pattern of alliteration is also exploited in the titles of the two following books: In *De Puike Pakket Post* (1992), the translator deletes the reference to Christmas, which is obvious from the illustrations anyway, substitutes it with 'pakket' ('gift' or 'package') to create additional alliteration and also deletes *'bode'* from *'postbode'* for reasons of rhythm, whereas in *De Piepkleine Puike Postbode* (1996) alliteration and rhythm again create a fluent title. This translation strategy links the three books together just as is the case with the three source texts. The addition of alliteration and assonance is not limited to the book titles, but occurs throughout the texts. For example 'The Complete Book of Foul Curses' is translated as '*Het Volkomen Vuile Vervloekingen Boek*' (JP1/PP1[1]: letter 2).

A prominent feature of all three books is the device of envelopes with handwritten addresses, postmarks, and stamps. The graphic design of the envelopes remains almost identical – addresses are handwritten, different typefaces are used to characterize the different kind of letters, the hand drawn stamps are the same. The time on the postmarks is changed to continental use of time, for example 4.15 p.m. becomes 16.15 U (JP1/PP1: letter 1). Postmarks also carry verbal information and this information is translated literally, substituted by a target culture reference, and even compensation in the form of additional punning can be found. The reference 'East of Sun West of Moon' (JP1: letter 3) is rendered literally as '*Ten oosten v/d zon Ten westen v/d maan*' to denote the same fairy tale and is thus a culturally equivalent phrase. Substitution can also be found: The reference to the nursery rhyme 'Banbury Cross' (JP1: letter 1; JP2: letter 1), which would most definitely remain dormant in the target culture, is rendered as

'Krentebolsward', a combination of *'krentebol'* and *'Bolsward'*. *'Krentebol'*, which is a kind of bun, retains in this sense a tenuous link with the source text, and 'Bolsward' is an existing Dutch city located in Friesland (northern part of the Netherlands). With this substitution the translator has created a different reference, definitely Dutch, not Flemish, which sets off its own intertextual games to Dutch children's books and culture. Another example of substitution is the change of 'The Barracks' (JP 2: letter 3), a reference to all the King's Horses and all the King's Men from the Humpty Dumpty rhyme, into 'De Hoftimmerman' which refers to a similar, but slightly different Dutch rhyme. This nursery rhyme also has a Flemish version, which is not alluded to. Additional punning may be added: 'Far Away' (JP1: letter 6) is translated literally as 'Heel Ver', but the postmark follows it with the words *'Engel-land'* ('Angel Land'), yet at the same time puns with *'Engeland'* ('England'), which is an intertextual/metatextual reference to the country of origin of the source text for this Dutch translation. The translation has here created additional links obviously not present in the source text.

The translator has also used substitution where this was not strictly necessary. A postmark with 'Wonderful Copenhagen' surrounding the drawing of the statue of the famous little mermaid (JP3: letter 4), an obvious reference both to contemporary Copenhagen and to Hans Christian Andersen, author of *The Little Mermaid* and *The Constant Tin Soldier*, the story that is rewritten in the letter, is replaced by *'Geef mij maar Amsterdam,'* a local reference to a song. However, this source text intertextual reference would have worked in the target culture and need not have been substituted. The purpose of this local reference may be to create more Dutch feeling in the text.

The addresses are also translated in different ways. Straightforward translation is found in 'The Woods' (JP2: letter 1) becoming *'Het bos,'* or 'Postman' turning into *'Postbode'* (PP3: letter 3). Target culture references are used as substitution: 'Horner's Corner' from the nursery rhyme is changed into *'Tussen Keulen en Parijs'*, a reference to a target culture children's song (JP1/PP1: letter 5). As noted above, the books are also internally intertextual and letters from different books are often written to the same address; it is obviously desirable that this internal logic, an extra intertextual feature, should be reproduced. In most cases the translator has retained the internal logic, but in two cases he has not. In the first example, 'McVitie House' located on 'Little Toe Lane' (JP2: letter 4; JP3: letter 4) has once been rendered as *'Sinterklaashuis'* ('Saint Nicholas House') on *'Pinkieteenlaan'* (PP2: letter 4) and once as *'Het Koekblikhuis'* ('Cookie Tin House') on *'Klein Duimpjelaan'*, a reference to the story of *Seven League Boots*

(PP3: letter 4). The substitutions chosen by the Dutch translator do make sense in the target culture: '*Sinterklaashuis*' is chosen because it is linked to '*Koekemannetje*' (translation of gingerbread boy), who is the recipient of the letter and shown in the illustrations, and which is usually eaten on the feast of Saint Nicholas (celebrated on 6 December). The translation '*Het Koekblikhuis*' is clearly influenced by the illustrations and the reference to the story of *Seven League Boots* is relevant as it foreshadows the Postman's escape from the wolf. The translator has prioritised the creation of different intertextual references over internal consistency between the different books of the series. The second example concerns PP2 letter 3 and PP3 letter 6, both addressed to the same hospital, where the translator adds a street name and city to the address of the hospital in PP3: letter 6. This added address is actually that of the Dutch publisher. The reference cannot be identified from the colophon, which only lists a PO Box address for the publisher; the 'real' address is thus both a metatextual link to the real world and very much an insider joke.

The main body of text also uses the strategies of straightforward translation, substitution and addition. References to *Alice in Wonderland* and *The Wizard of Oz* are rendered in Dutch (PP3), as these texts have been translated into Dutch and are quite well-known. The story of *Jack and the Beanstalk*, on the other hand, is not widely known in the Netherlands and Belgium, so the translator introduces the story of *Seven League Boots* which is familiar and has a giant and a small boy as main characters (PP1: letter 3), matching the source text characters. This substitution of one fairy tale by another is sustained by the references in the illustrations, although parts of the illustration, such as the beanstalk, will remain dormant references which may provide the target reader with fuel for taking the interpretation of the text in another direction. Other references to tales and nursery rhymes such as *Tom Thumb*, *Tiny Tim*, and *Wee Willie Winkie* are substituted by references to fairy tales which are better known in the target culture, such as *Klein Duimpje* (*Seven League Boots*), *Duimelijntje* (*Thumbelina*), and *De gelaarsde kat* (*Puss in Boots*, PP2). References to nursery rhymes and songs are substituted with references to Dutch rhymes, songs, or children's classics: In this way *Little Miss Muffet* becomes *Biebelebonse Berg*, a reference to a poem by Annie M.G. Schmidt, one of The Netherlands' best known writers for children (PP1: letter 6).

Another feature of the text is the different styles and vocabulary used in the letters. Goldilocks writes a letter of apology full of grammar and spelling mistakes, and this is recreated in the Dutch with grammatical errors and spelling mistakes geared to Dutch; for example, the difference between words spelled with 'ei' and 'ij' which are pronounced identically

(PP1: letter 1). The legal letter of Red Riding Hood's lawyers imitates official jargon and the translator adds official terms, not used in the source text, such as '*onroerend goed*' ('real estate') to refer to the houses of the three little pigs. The lawyers also change names from Meeny, Miny, Mo & Co (JP1: letter 5) to *Olleke, Bolleke, Rubisolleke & Co* (PP1: letter 5), a Dutch nursery rhyme.

The rhyme pattern constitutes an additional constraint upon the translator. In the first book it is quite strict and follows the pattern *abbcbd* on the left side of the first spread and *efgf* on the right side of the second spread (with the same pattern but different rhyme words used for each following set of two spreads), which the Dutch translator recreates almost exactly. In two cases the Dutch rhyme pattern becomes *abcbbd efgf*, and two lines of rhyme could not be recreated. In the second book the number of lines on each page is different, and the rhyme schemes show much more variation in the source text. The English text has 64 rhyming lines on a total of 105 lines, whereas the Dutch translation shows 86 rhyming lines on a total of 109. The translator has clearly compensated by adding more rhymes to the target text. In the third book in the series, the English text features 156 rhyming lines on 183 lines, where the Dutch has 156 rhyming lines on 181 lines. Although the number of rhyming lines is the same, the lines do not always occur in the same places in the English and Dutch texts. In some cases rhyme constraints have led to substitution of semantic elements to make the rhyme pattern work. These books are picture book texts and although older children may read them on their own, it is also very likely that adults will share them with younger children, so that the read-aloud quality is an important element to consider when translating. The additional alliteration and assonance and the rhythmic rhyming give the Dutch texts extra zest and are appraised in a review of *De Piepkleine Puike Postbode* as enticing to young readers (Vanhalewijn, 1997: 10).

The illustrations themselves have not been changed at all, and they contain many elements which may remain dormant in a target text reading or be interpreted differently – such as the Christmas crackers, a typical British Christmas pudding, the mince pies, and the cow over the moon. However, the text items in the illustrations have been changed, again using the translation strategies of literal translation, substitution and compensation. For example, the newspaper '*Mirror, Mirror*,' with a pun on the British newspaper as well as a reference to Snow White (JP1), is substituted by '*NHC Heksenblad*,' a similar pun on a newspaper from the Netherlands '*NRC Handelsblad*' where the 'R' is replaced by 'H' for '*heks*' ('witch') and '*Handelsblad*' ('commercial paper') is replaced by '*Heksenblad*' ('witches' paper') (PP1) but with loss of the Snow White reference. The newspaper reference may occasionally remain dormant in the reading of some Dutch children, but will more certainly remain dormant in the reading of most Flemish children, who are exposed to different newspapers from their counterparts in Holland, although adult Flemish readers may recognize it. The same holds true for the money Goldilocks receives for her birthday: a one pound note becomes a five guilder note, not Belgian Francs (JP1/PP1: letter 6). Other changes include 'Tweedledum' and 'Tweedledee' (JP2, children's letters to Santa Claus) which are rendered as 'Jip' and 'Janneke' (PP2), two characters from an Annie M.G. Schmidt book. Changes in the map of Oz (JP3/PP3) include the 'Hispaniola' turning into the *'Zilvervloot'* ('Dutch Silver Fleet') and 'Far Away' becoming *'Verwegistan'* where the suffix *'-stan'* is added to create the impression of an exotic country as is typical of fairy tales.

Conclusion

The quality of mixing and matching different intertextual elements in the source texts has been recreated in the Dutch target texts through a variety of translation strategies. Substitution of intertextual features that are specific to the source culture and would remain dormant for the target culture audience with intertextual references based on the target culture is a sensible strategy. It creates differently intertextual texts and solidly positions the translation as a Dutch text with Dutch intertextual links and echoes. More features may remain dormant in the reading of Flemish children depending on their knowledge of and familiarity with the Dutch cultural references that are used to substitute for the original source culture references. Although in some cases the substitutions used were not entirely necessary, as the source culture reference might not have remained dormant in the target audience, overall the effect of the three Dutch books looks very similar to that of the source texts. Other strategies, such as addition of target culture intertextual features, straightforward translation of shared intertexts, and compensation make these Dutch translations very effective and productive. The balance between adherence to the source text and the embedding of the target text in the target culture is successful. The success of the translations can also be measured through the Dutch literary prizes awarded: *De Boekensleutel* (Book Key), an award for a book which brings surprising perspectives to techniques and contents (Piek-van Slooten, 1990: 218), was awarded to *De Puike Postbode of: Briefgeheimpjes*, and De Kinderjury (Children's Judges) recommended *De Piepkleine Puike Postbode*. These three Dutch translations demonstrate that the intertextual and playful elements which seem to characterize so much of children's literature at the end of the 20th century can be rendered successfully in translation – even if they perform a somewhat different intertextual game.

Dialogue with the intertextual sources of a text is open only to readers who are familiar with them; other readers may make their own intertextual links based on their reading experience. Readers of translated texts who do not have access to the source text or source language will forge their own interpretations and intertextual links based solely on the target text. Only readers fluent in both languages and cultures can understand the particular form of dialogue between the source text and the target text. In this sense the translation is a gain, as without the translation the source text would not be able to achieve its new lease on life in this other language and would be unable to reach a whole new audience.

Acknowledgements

I appreciate the valuable responses of Prof. Theo Hermans and Dr Gillian Lathey on an earlier draft of this paper, as well as the comments of the British editorial committee of *Children's Literature in Education*.

Note

1. JP1 refers to the first book *The Jolly Postman or Other People's Letters* and PP1 to its Dutch translation; JP2 will refer to *The Jolly Christmas Postman* and PP2 to that translation, and JP3 to *The Jolly Pocket Postman* and PP3 to the translation.

Gillian Lathey

Time, Narrative Intimacy and the Child: Implications of Tense Switching in the Translation of Picture Books into English

Anthea Bell is one of Britain's most highly respected translators and a past recipient of the Marsh Award for Children's Literature in Translation in the UK. When reflecting on her extensive experience of translating children's books in 'Translator's Notebook' (Bell, 1986: Chap. 5), she drew attention to the 'delicate matter' of translating the historic present – that is the present tense as basic narrative mode – of French and German children's stories into English. In Bell's opinion the historic present in English is an exciting, but unusual, narrative strategy:

> I am most reluctant to use the historic present in English in a middle-of-the-road kind of children's novel, even if it is the main tense of a French or German original. In English, the historic present seems more a tense for a stylist than is necessarily the case in other languages. I like it myself; I like its immediacy. But I feel it needs to be approached with caution in translating children's fiction. (Bell, 1986: 17)

Bell's cautious response to the translation of the present tense is challenging. It suggests that tense in narratives is linked to dominant literary conventions within languages, and that tense shifting in translation is one means by which a text is assimilated into the target culture. It also provokes speculation on the imaginative and aesthetic effects of the narrative present in children's texts, and the consequences of a change of tense in the process of translation. One striking example of a transposition of tense is to be found in the British edition of Jean de Brunhoff's picture book *Histoire de Babar*, where the unacknowledged translator[1] has changed the present tense of the original French to the past in English. By analysing the causes and effects of this shift on the British *Babar*, and exploring the relationship between language, narrative and the perception of time in the original French edition, I hope to establish some of the qualities of present tense usage in the picture book that are potentially lost in translation and, finally, to relate this discussion to the young child's developing understanding of the role of tense in narrative.

Since, as Paul Ricoeur has asserted, our experience of time is 'constitutive of human reality' (Onega & Landa, 1996: 129), its apprehension is reflected in language at both lexical and grammatical levels. European languages superimpose a system of verb tenses and aspectual contrast ('I live in London' as opposed to 'I am living in London') on the fluidity of real time. In narrative, that 'primary act of mind', tense naturally plays a pivotal role, as human beings tell each other about their past, present or potential future experiences, and exchange information in narrative form. As Ricoeur (1984: 52) has argued: 'time becomes human to the extent that it is articulated through a narrative mode, and narrative attains its full meaning when it becomes a condition of temporal existence'. When time is articulated in narrative, tense has less to do with an attempt to express the physical laws of time than with the registration of subjectivity. What matters in narratives is not the accurate recording of real time, but the significance of events within the story for its protagonists. Hence the distinction first made by Müller (1968) between narrative time – the time it takes for the narrator to tell his or her story – and narrated time, that is the time narrated events would take to unfold in real time. Real time may be condensed, 'folded', slowed down or accelerated in narratives encompassing a few minutes, hours, years, decades or even centuries.

All narrators, from the gossip to the bard, manipulate real time in this way; they must deftly orchestrate tense and the apprehension of time by an audience in order to ensure maximum impact of the story to be told. When a writer or storyteller decides to adopt the present tense to relate events that happened in the past, there is a merging of narrative and narrated time either for the whole of the narrative or for substantial passages, as events are related by an 'on the scene' narrator. A synchronicity of narration and events is, of course, impossible; there is a time lag even for the sports reporter with microphone in hand or the surrealist scribbling down fragmentary thoughts in 'automatic' writing. Nevertheless, in present tense narratives such as *Histoire de Babar*, narrator and reader collude in ignoring this paradox: they are united in an illusion of presentness.

To regard the historic present as a mere substitute or stylistic flourish, however, is to ignore the qualities that make it special. Suzanne Fleischman (1990: 285), in her comprehensive study of tense and narrativity, examines these qualities in narratives from medieval performance to modern fiction. One aspect she addresses is the visual qualities of the present tense which 'in ordinary language is primarily a descriptive tense' as well as the immediacy of the narrator as spectator. Surprisingly, she makes no reference to the frequent use of the present tense in children's literature; yet it is precisely these visual attributes, together with the nature of the interaction between adult reader and child listener, that are particularly relevant to the picture book.

Jean de Brunhoff's classic picture book, *Histoire de Babar* (1931), is a present tense narrative in French that was first published in English in two separate editions. Merle Haas, translator of the American version of 1933, retained the present tense of the original. The translator of the British *Babar*, on the other hand, opted for the past tense in an edition that appeared a year later. Two translators, translating into the English language at about the same time, made quite different choices. Merle Haas decided to align her translation with the French cultural practice of using the present tense in children's stories, whereas the British translator of *Histoire de Babar* appears to have shared the unease Anthea Bell expresses at using the present tense as a basic narrative mode, and chose instead to follow the dominant convention in contemporary British children's stories.

Why should this be so? A closer look at the original French text of *Babar* reveals a possible narratological reason for the British translator's tense shift. There is a retrospective narrative viewpoint underlying Babar's story; an organising narrative entity is at work that is in command of the story material and knows the outcome. This becomes apparent when the narrator jumps forward two years from one page to the next during Babar's Parisian *séjour*; despite the present tense, narrated time and narrative time are not synchronous throughout the story. An occasional use of the past perfect – by the second page of the book Babar '*a grandi*' (has grown) – also interrupts the present tense reportage and indicates omniscience. Such intimations of the inherent pastness of events recounted in a present tense narrative may well have determined the British translator's choice of the past tense.

De Brunhoff's French text for *Histoire de Babar* therefore exemplifies a function of the historic present addressed by Dorrit Cohn in her discussion of the representation of consciousness in fiction. Cohn describes the eyewitness account of events by Darl in William Faulkner's *As I lay Dying* as: 'a retrospective narration in the evocative present tense' (Cohn, 1978: 206). In *Babar*, too, the present tense is instrumental in the 'calling forth' of past events into the present. So the French narrator of *Histoire de Babar* operates on two levels, both as orchestrator and controller of time and action within the story in the role of all-knowing storyteller, and as eyewitness reporter on events within the illustrations to which the child has immediate visual access. The narrator in role as eyewitness, a voice assumed by whoever is reading the book aloud to the child, and the child listener share the same time frame as they activate de Brunhoff's illustrations in the present. This dual use of the present tense both to recount events as they unfold visually, and as an 'evocative' strategy for breathing life into past events, accounts for the common usage of the present in illustrated books for young children, particularly on the European continent.

But the picture book is also a dramatic medium. Babar's story, first told to her children by de Brunhoff's wife Cécile, is clearly intended to be read aloud to a young child. The book becomes a catalyst for a kind of play-acting that includes gesture, physical contact and dialogue, all inspired by the joint interpretation of pictures as well as by the reading aloud of the written text. Philip Pullman (1989: 167), in an essay on the reading of images, has asserted that: 'Pictures have a present-tense quality which anyone who has shared a picture book with a child will recognise'. Pullman alludes to the shared animation of pictures as the story progresses. The present tense of the French *Babar* is therefore entirely in keeping with this act of narrative elicitation. Anthea Bell, too, cites visual narratives as an exception to her general wariness of the historic present in English. As co-translator with Derek Hockridge of the *Astérix* series into English, she regards the strip cartoon as a present tense genre because it resembles: 'a dramatic performance unfolding before the reader's eyes' (Bell, 1986: 17). The present tense as a narrative mode does, after all, have its historical roots in orally performed epics or the enactment of human experience in drama.

As *Babar* is read aloud, the adult reader becomes the narrator and acts as guide, taking the young listener by the hand as together they activate the static images of the text. Although the British translator uses the past as the basic narrative tense, it is clear that s/he too is aware of this animating function of the present tense. On the second page of *Histoire de Babar*, the French narrator indicates which elephant is Babar by pointing to the action in which he is engaged: '*C'est lui qui creuse le sable avec un coquillage*' (de Brunhoff, 1979: 9). In a scene immanent with movement, the British translator (Figure 1) is compelled to abandon the narrative past by using the deictic 'look' and the present participle: 'look at him digging in the sand with a shell' (de Brunhoff, 1989: 5).

The present tense in French, and the elision of the continuous present form in English, set in motion a repeated action in the imagination. Later in the story, when all the elephants run to greet Babar on his return to the jungle, the British translator again resorts to the present participle. The French narrator addresses his audience directly, asking the child reader what he or she sees: '*Qu'est qu'ils voient! Babar qui arrive dans son auto et tous les éléphants qui courent en criant*'. In English the present participles avoid the loss of immediacy that would result from maintaining the past tense: 'What

*Babar grew fast. Soon he was playing   with the other baby elephants.
He was one of the nicest of them.   Look at him digging in the sand with a shell.*

Figure 1

a wonderful sight they saw! It was Babar arriving in his car, with all the elephants running and shouting' (de Brunhoff, 1989: 34).

In these instances the requirements of the image force the translator's hand, but he or she resolutely maintains the past tense throughout the rest of the narrative. In addition to the inevitable distancing of events, the inter-action of pictures and text is affected in less obvious ways. Picture book authors and artists make careful choices to ensure a counterpoint between written text, narrative perspective, layout and image; the orchestration of tenses can make a subtle but significant difference. The death of Babar's mother on the fourth and fifth pages of *Histoire de Babar*, for example, is one of the most memorable and shocking moments in children's literature (see Figure 2), and de Brunhoff momentarily switches tense between the two pages of the double spread to create a dramtic effect. On the first of these two pages a child listening to the French original effectively watches *as the huntsman shoots* thanks to the present tense, *'tire'* (shoots):

But then de Brunhoff introduces a cinematic cut between this scene where the hunter is shooting at Babar and his mother, and the second page of the double spread where Babar weeps on his mother's corpse: there is no image of the bullet striking home. On this right-hand page there is a rare instance in the French text of the use of the past perfect to jump forward in

Babar se promène très heureux
sur le dos de sa maman,
quand un vilain chasseur,
caché derrière un buisson,
tire sur eux.

Le chasseur a tué la maman.
Le singe se cache, les oiseaux s'envolent,
Babar pleure.
Le chasseur court pour attraper
le pauvre Babar.

Figure 2

the narrative: *'Le chasseur a tué la maman'* (de Brunhoff, 1979: 11). De Brunhoff deliberately bridges the messy process of injury and death both visually and linguistically by creating a hiatus in the narrative flow[2]. In the British version this entire event is consigned to the past, from: 'a cruel hunter, hiding behind a bush, shot at them', to 'He killed Babar's mother' (de Brunhoff, 1989: 6–7). The jarring effect of the tense switch in the original is therefore lost.

Changing the basic narrative tense of *Histoire de Babar* and the corresponding interplay of tenses is, then, likely to have an effect on the narrative triangle in a read- aloud event. The intimacy of the relationship between the narrative voice of the adult reading aloud, the child who listens and imagines, and the images quickened by both adult and child, are enhanced in the case of the French original by the present tense.

In turning my attention finally to the child listener's own usage of tense in narratives, I wish to suggest two points for consideration in relation to the broader issues raised by Anthea Bell's discussion of the historic present. Firstly, it has become a commonplace to assert that adults and young children experience time differently. Whilst it is certainly true that children younger than five or six do not share adult concepts such as day, year, 'sooner' or 'later' (to tell a sobbing child on its first day at school that its mother will be back that afternoon or in a few hours is no comfort at all) adult and child nevertheless share the subjective apprehension of time. The sensation of time 'dragging' or 'flying' – what Martin Heidegger has called 'within-timeness'– is common to all human beings whatever their age; it is the linguistic reckoning with time in the form of vocabulary and grammatical structures such as tenses that children only gradually assimilate. A child may therefore not locate narrative events temporally in quite the same way as an adult. My second point, which concerns children's use of tense in dramatic play, throws some light on this developmental question.

Young children begin to use the past tense as a narrative mode quite early, adopting the language of anecdotes or stories read and told to them by adults[3]; yet at the same time they engage in dramatic play where stories are created or re-enacted in the present. Child players move seamlessly in and out of participant and spectator roles, with tense sometimes acting as an indicator of the degree of engagement. A child takes on a role, whether as Cinderella, a character from a favourite soap opera or a superhero; he or she becomes that figure and speaks in the present tense. Yet at any moment the child may move outside the story to act as spectator, and the shift into narrative mode is often reflected in a change of tense to the past. In transcripts of children's play, such as those collected by American kindergarten teacher Vivian Gussin Paley (1981: 192–193), it is possible to see this movement into and out of the text created in play. One particularly revealing example occurs in Gordon Wells' longitudinal study of pre-school language development, where three five-year-old boys are taking an imaginative journey on a boat. One of them, David, introduces a note of distress:

> **David:** All our luggage is—is—One of, er—one of our boyfriends is crying in a corner [*pretends to cry.*] Pretend one of the—the—their children was crying in a corner (Wells, 1987: 199)

Not only does David switch tense from 'is crying' to 'was crying', but he also articulates the reason for doing so. His instruction to the other players to 'pretend' that one of the children 'was crying' indicates a move from inside to outside the story, and from participant to spectator and initiator of the dramatic scenario. Such an approach to time and narrative, while echoing adult conventions, also demonstrates the child's ability to immerse himself instantaneously in an imaginary world as though it existed in the present. This suggests that the more frequent use of the historic present in French and German narratives noted by Anthea Bell is in fact in tune with the younger child's usage of tense in play. Misgivings about maintaining the historic present in translation into English may therefore be unfounded, at least as far as a young child audience is concerned.

The next step in investigating the translation of tense in children's fiction is a large-scale comparative study; translation of the historic present into English in longer prose fiction, for example, raises a different set of questions from those posed by the translation of a picture book. The focus in this paper has been on the younger child, and it is pertinent to my conclusions that Riitta Oittinen (2000: 32), in her discussion of translation issues specific to children's literature, privileges read aloud qualities. Surely the narrative intimacy of the present tense, which potentially affords the closest possible relationship between narrator and addressee, is one of these qualities that a translator should preserve, particularly when pictures contribute a third dimension to the read aloud performance. In the great forest a little elephant *is* born; or: 'In the Great Forest a little elephant *was* born' (de Brunhoff, 1989: 3) – the present tense lends a tone and an aura to a narrative that *do* matter.

Notes

1. Despite extensive research I have been unable to trace the translator of the British edition.
2. In an early draft de Brunhoff included both scenes on one page and used the present tense '*tue*'; it can only be assumed therefore that the separation of images and change in tense was designed to enhance impact. See Fox Weber (1989: 25)
3. Arthur Applebee in *The Child's Concept of Story* (Chicago: Chicago University Press, 1978) cites an earlier, extensive study by Evelyn Goodenough Pitcher and Ernst Prelinger (*Children Tell Stories: An Analysis of Fantasy*, New York: International Universities Press, 1963) where analysis demonstrated an increase in the consistent use of the past tense in storytelling by children between the ages of two and five.

Part 4

The Travels of Children's Books and Cross-cultural Influences

The focus in this section is on the nature, extent and effects of the international dissemination of children's literature. At the 1976 ISRCL symposium, Richard Bamberger (1978) sketched a number of instances where translated children's books had inspired individual writers or the emergence of entire genres. Oscar Wilde's stories for children, for example, owe a direct debt in tone and sentiment to Hans Christian Andersen (to compare the ending of Andersen's 'The Steadfast Tin Soldier' to that of 'The Happy Prince' is to recognise Wilde's debt) just as James Fenimore Cooper's *Leatherstocking Tales*, albeit in abridged form, are responsible for the tradition of '*Indianergeschichten*' (stories about native Americans) in Germany that continues to this day. Bamberger concluded his address with a strong plea for further international and comparative investigation of children's literature.

Emer O'Sullivan took up the same theme at the 23rd International IBBY (International Board of Books for Young People) Congress in 1992. O'Sullivan begins the keynote speech reprinted here with a survey of changing views of international exchange in children's literature from Paul Hazard's 'world republic of childhood' to Shavit's polysystem theory of cultural transmission. Taking Carlo Collodi's *Pinocchio* as a case study, she asks whether the international exchange of 'classics' is not pared down to basic elements – in this instance a wooden puppet with a long nose in many retellings and film versions. In conclusion she suggests two routes of transmission: firstly 'literary' translation, and, secondly, what Alieda Assmann (1983) has called 'written folklore', namely the numerous retellings, revisions and multimedia adaptations of children's classics that depend to a large degree on a visual element. O'Sullivan also provides examples of the cultural hegemony of Western 'classics' that constrains the development of indigenous children's literatures in parts of South America, Asia and Africa. We would do well to remember that some of the best-known Western tales to enter the international children's canon originate outside Europe: Neil Philip (1989) and Alan Dundes (1982), for example, have traced the Chinese origins of the Cinderella story.

The most widely known of all stories to enter the children's canon at an international level, at least until the advent of Harry Potter, were probably those of Cinderella, Sleeping Beauty, Hansel and Gretel and other fairy tale characters. But how, historically, did this international progress begin, and what resemblance do early collections of Grimms' tales in English, for example, bear to the multiple editions published by the Grimm Brothers themselves? How many tales are lost (or censored) in translation? An edited version of David Blamires' article on the Grimms' *Household Tales* reveals a complex textual history both in the German language, and subsequently in selected 'literary' translations. Omissions, alterations, and additions to the Grimms' texts in Edgar Taylor's highly successful and influential 1823 translation have resulted in a skewed picture of the collection and of individual tales in the minds of English-language readers. Once again the image plays an important role, as Blamires points our that it was George Cruickshank's illustrations that secured the longevity of Taylor's translation.

In her case study of *Sleeping Beauty*, Karen Seago locates translations of fairy tales within the political and socio-historical context of the target culture, 19th-century England. *Sleeping Beauty* is of particular interest because of the merging of elements of Perrault's *'La belle au bois dormant'* and the Grimms' *'Dornröschen'* in the English tradition. Perrault's tale first crossed the Channel in Robert Samber's 1729 translation, but the late 17th and early 18th-century emphasis in England on socialisation, manners and rational education delayed its acceptance as a story for children. Seago offers an overview of 13 translations of the Grimms' *'Dornröschen'*, demonstrating how changes were made for didactic and moral reasons, and how elements of Perrault's tale were incorporated in the course of the 19th century into a tale that became generally known as *Sleeping Beauty*. In addition, Seago alleges that changes in legislation, the class system, gender roles and the development of industrialisation had a profound effect on the social behaviour depicted in successive translations.

To bring discussion of international exchange up to date, Nancy K. Jentsch reports on the rapid and accelerating global success of the Harry Potter series. In contrast to the sometimes delayed or halting progress of earlier international classics, J.K. Rowling's books have achieved international fame in a short space of time thanks to global marketing, merchandising and film adaptations. At the height of 'Pottermania' there was enormous pressure on translators to complete contracts, so that foreign language editions could follow the UK publication of the latest volume of the series as soon as possible (Lathey, 2005). Jentsch provides sales figures for the first three volumes of the Potter series in French, German and Spanish to illustrate the extent of Harry Potter's European success. She then offers a cultural and linguistic analysis of translations into these three languages to establish how translators have addressed what is, after all, a culture-specific text in its references to English boarding school traditions or the suburban milieu of the Dursleys. Rapid and widespread dissemination of the series has inspired a varied corpus of work on translations of the Potter books. A reading of Philip Nel's (2002) analysis of differences between American (*Harry Potter and the Sorcerer's Stone*) and UK (*Harry Potter and the Philosopher's Stone*) versions, Lathey's (2005) account of an international seminar on the same text, and Eirlys E. Davies' (2003) analysis of compensation strategies would all complement Jentsch's detailed account of translation losses and gains.

Emer O'Sullivan

Does Pinocchio have an Italian Passport? What is Specifically National and what is International about Classics of Children's Literature

> *Children's books keep alive a sense of nationality; but they also keep alive a sense of humanity. They describe their native land lovingly, but they also describe faraway lands where unknown brothers live. They understand the essential quality of their own race; but each of them is a messenger that goes beyond mountains and rivers, beyond the seas, to the very ends of the world in search of new friendships. Every country gives and every country receives – innumerable are the exchanges – and so it comes about that in our first impressionable years the universal republic of childhood is born.*
> Hazard (1944: 146)

This quotation is from the pen of the French comparative literary scholar, Paul Hazard, written in his influential book *Les livres, les enfants et les hommes* first published in 1932.

Children's literature, and especially classics of children's literature to which I would like to confine my comments here, are frequently regarded and spoken of as products of an international culture of childhood, mono-lingual, monocultural, in which international understanding is the order of the day. This 'world republic of childhood' as Paul Hazard (1944: 145) called it knows no borders, no foreign languages. On the other hand he, and others, like to take recourse to the very nationalities of the authors, to prove, by mentioning the origin of the works, that in the real world with borders and foreign languages, a large variety of nations is represented.

> If you note down the name of the child classics, you will see that Germans, English, Americans, Russians, Danes, Swedes, Italians and French are all the most friendly of neighbors. ... You will not find a single country that does not admire ... books that come from the four quarters of the globe. ... Smilingly the pleasant books of childhood cross all the frontiers; there is no duty to be paid on inspiration. (Hazard, 1944: 147)

To speak in this nice, rather cosy and certainly very idealistic way about children's literature, is to ignore both the conditions influencing its production and those underlining its cultural transfer. That the works change considerably in the course of time and on their ways across linguistic and cultural frontiers is an inevitable consequence of these conditions. Each book is produced in a specific culture at a specific time, and it naturally bears the marks of the region, time and literature of its origin. By examining questions of cultural transfer and cultural exchange, I would like, at least partially, to explode some of the myths surrounding the simultaneous internationality and specific nationality of children's classics.

By children's classics are generally meant books that have been commercially successful over several generations in several countries. Their status is not permanent: the assessment of what a classic is changes with altering tastes and assessments. Their value is based less on aesthetic qualities than on inscribed moral and social values, inherent images or even myths of childhood and – and this is my addition – they reveal a basic narrative moment, situation or constellation of characters which lend themselves to being retold and reinterpreted in different forms.

Classics are books that could be called the household names of what is regarded as 'good' children's literature. They are the books that are constantly reprinted in editions and series of varying size and quality. No two lists of classics will be absolutely identical, but there are titles that are guaranteed to find a place on each of them. One of the oldest is almost 400 years old – *Don Quixote*, one of the youngest – depending on the list – is not yet 50: *Pippi Longstocking*. The consensus is that their number is between 30 and 50. The books, figures, authors meant are, amongst others, *Don Quixote*, *Robinson Crusoe*, *Gulliver's Travels*, *Baron Munchausen*, Grimms' fairy tales, the fairy tales of Hans Christian Andersen, *Struwwelpeter*, *Alice in Wonderland*, *Tom Sawyer*, *Huckleberry Finn*, *Heidi*, *Pinocchio*, *Treasure Island*, *The Jungle Book*, *Peter Pan*, *Emil and the Detectives*, *Mary Poppins*, *Pippi Longstocking* ... and many more can be added to this incomplete list.

They are a motley lot, reflecting the three different origins of children's literature itself. Firstly the oral tradition of folklore – fairy tales, legends, myths and sagas. Secondly literature which was originally written for adults and adapted for children – that covers Don Quixote, Robinson Crusoe, Gulliver and others. The third group represented – which is now probably the most dominant source of children's literature altogether – is that written intentionally for children, a source that postdates the other two.

It is, I hasten to say, not my intention to take each one of the titles mentioned to examine, in accordance with the title of my paper, what elements in them can be seen to be specific of their culture of origin, to proclaim Pinocchio identifiably Italian, Pippi Longstocking strikingly Swedish or Emil of the detectives a genuine German. What I would like to do, in three steps, is first of all to consider, using a few selected examples, the processes involved in the transfer of these works into a culture other than their own, to look at the patterns that determine this transfer. That the titles we usually accept as classics, contrary to Hazard's claims, cannot be called representative of all the continents of the world shall lead me to reflect, in the second step, on what is commonly taken to be the international character of the origin of the classics. In the third and final step I shall, as a consequence of the discussion of the traditions of handing down these texts through time and across borders, consider how their status, how their relationship to the works which originally bore their name, is to be defined.

The central moment, the pivot between cultures when a work passes from one into the other, is translation. It is here that a product of one linguistic and cultural territory is transformed into one understandable in another. Since its inception, translation theory has concerned itself with questions about the literary status of translations: are they to be seen as creative works in their own right, or are they secondary products? How is the relationship of a translation to an original to be described? To what extent is the expression of a culture so closely bound to its own linguistic means of expression that it is impossible to achieve a correspondence in another? What is meant by equivalence, when an equivalent rendering of a text is sought? Equivalence on the level of single lexical items, equivalence on the level of the reconstruction of the communicative situation reproduced, equivalence of the entire rendition? The much-quoted pronouncement made by Friedrich Schleiermacher in 1813 when writing on the different methods of translation: '*Entweder der Uebersetzer läßt den Schrifts-teller möglichst in Ruhe, und bewegt den Leser ihm entgegen; oder er läßt den Leser möglichst in Ruhe und bewegt den Schriftsteller ihm entgegen*' ('A translator either leaves the author as much alone as is possible and moves the reader towards him; or he leaves the reader as much alone as is possible and moves the author towards him' trans. S.S. Prawer, 1973), sets out two poles whereby either as much of the 'foreignness' of the text as possible is retained in the translation, without many concessions being made to the culture into which it is translated, and linguistic and aesthetic idiosyncrasies are imitated so that the reader is constantly aware that it is the product of another culture which he or she is reading in translation, or the text is translated in such a way that the illusion is created that it has been written in the culture of the reader.

These and other questions posed in studies of translations, using the original or source text as the central point of reference against which possible deviations in the translated or target text could be registered and measured, frequently concentrated on shortcomings of translations and the means by which these could be avoided or at least lessened, while accepting the premise that a translation can never replace an original text. Frequently prescriptive in nature, the ideal of a good, equivalent or at best adequate translation informed the analysis and discussion.

In the last few years a different approach has developed in the area of translation studies, one which is primarily product rather than process oriented, descriptive rather than prescriptive, in which a discussion about what an ideal translation should be has no place. Pioneered, amongst others, by the Israeli scholar Gideon Toury, this semiotic, polysystem theory approach reveals translation to be as much of a cultural process as a linguistic or literary one (Toury, 1980; Hermans, 1985). It is target text based, concentrating on the translations themselves, to examine how norms governing the target literary system – that is the literature into which the text has been translated – influenced or even determined the process of translation.

Using a theoretically related model Zohar Shavit, in her study *Poetics of Children's Literature* (1986), has shown how the position and status of children's literature within the literary polysystem determines its production and especially the conditions pertaining to its translation. She reminds us of the special character of children's literature which is not only governed by literary norms at a given time, but because it belongs simultaneously to the educational as well as to the literary systems, the changing educational norms, too, have to be taken into consideration in an analysis of children's literature and its translations.

I would now like to move on to take a look at what the translation of a children's book can involve, how different literary and educational norms, traditions, expectations and ideologies can influence the cultural transfer of children's literature.

Over a hundred years ago, the Tuscan puppet Pinocchio saw the light of day in print and since then Collodi's book has been translated, adapted, abridged, turned out in film and comic form and marketed in a variety of ways for a host of purposes in all the corners of the world. More than 220 translations have been made into at least 87 different languages – there are 40 versions in German alone, as the extensive study of Sonia Marx (1990) on the German adventures of Pinocchio reveals. The history of Pinocchio in German starts almost 25 years after his Italian birth with Otto Julius Bierbaum's version, *Zäpfel Kerns Abenteuer*, published in 1905 and ends – at least for the moment – with Christine Nöstlinger's *Der neue Pinocchio* (1988), a contemporary Pinocchio in terms of behaviour, consciousness and language. Here the main character has been given an explicit psychological dimension, key incidents in the story have been altered and the basic pedagogical concept is turned on its head. Children, small and weak, have to see to it that they can get what they need, have to look out for themselves; all they can expect from the adult world is lack of understanding and exploitation. Pinocchio's decision to do only what he wants is applauded by the author. He has clear notions of what his rights are and what demands he can make of his father and the world. It is an interpretation firmly rooted – obviously – in the ideas of the author on the relationship between children and adults, but they are ideas that mirror an aspect of late 20th century West-European and American thought, following a few decades of intensive research on the history and conditions of childhood itself. Nöstlinger's name and not that of Collodi is given as the author, and it has been translated, as such, into Italian.

Bierbaum as the first and Nöstlinger as the latest are the two cornerstones of translations/adaptations of Pinocchio into German and both clearly declare their purpose in a preface, stating that theirs is a retelling with appropriate adjustments. Bierbaum wrote that he could not provide his readers with a straight translation of the Italian original: the strict national character of the book made a translation impossible,[1] but it also made the prospect of a very free, independently German treatment of the wonderful, invented theme a most attractive one. His adaptation was not undertaken in the spirit of pedagogical change, it was rather the prospect of being able to 'Germanize' the aspects which attracted him to the work: Collodi's ironic stabs and satirical treatment of figures of authority – the law, medicine, etc. – and indeed expand them by satirizing aspects of the German monarchy, of academic life and the military. This can be seen most clearly in Bierbaum's augmentation of the narrative incident of the '*paese dei balocchi*', the country in which the children are for ever playing games, to expand it, in the guise of a fantastic incident, into a satirical attack on – amongst other things – the hooray nationalism of the Germany of his day, going even so far as to invent a national anthem for that country which parodied that of Germany under Emperor William II.

This adaptation was, then, as the scholar Erwin Koppen (1980) has pointed out, a 'Williamization' of Pinocchio. But other elements were culturally adapted, too. On the most primitive level, the food becomes German, as do the unfamiliar animals – the cricket becomes a may beetle, a Professor Dr may beetle, no less. But most obvious is the adaptation of that achievement with which Luigi Santucci (1964) credits Collodi, that of having acclimatized the fairy tale to the bright Mediterranean climate with all its playful jokes and its cosy probabilities, of having shown that fairies could also exist in bright sunshine and not just in dark woods and turreted castles. This achievement is reversed in Bierbaum's version in which the magic quality of the piece of wood that is to become Pinocchio, or Zäpfel Kern, is implied by the manner in which it is brought to the carpenter, Meister Gottlieb: it is presented to him by a little hunchback with a long white beard and bright, bright blue eyes: a figure who had just emerged from a German fairy tale forest. In this, as in later German versions, the tradition of the *commedia dell'arte*, of Pinocchio's connection to Arlecchino and Pulcinella, is replaced by that of the German Kasperletheater.

These adaptations to suit the tastes and traditions of the target culture were not only undertaken in the book which proclaimed itself to be a 'Germanization' and thus an adaptation of Collodi's story. In the successful German translation published in 1913, eight years after Bierbaum's version, by the educationalist Anton Grumann (1913), amongst the reasons for its success, as pointed out by Sonia Marx, were additions that referred to popular children's books in Germany at the time – Wilhelm Busch's *Max und Moritz* and *Robinson Crusoe*, for example – and the Grimms' fairy tale tone can be heard in this version, both stylistically and in terms of descriptions of places. The fairy from Italian folklore with the turquoise hair is now blonde as is the boy into whom the puppet turns in the end.

Here we have had just a few examples of how an original or source text can be changed to adapt to literary norms and traditions in the target culture, to make it more acceptable to readers there. How the text can be adjusted to conform to ideological and pedagogical norms, is illustrated in a study of various American versions by the sociologist Richard Wunderlich (1992: 198) in which he shows that 'The popular image in the United States of what Pinocchio is all about bears little or no relation to Collodi's original.'

The first American translation[2] of 1904 by Walter S. Cramp (Collodi, 1904) was written to accommodate the new social order that resulted from the reorganization brought about by the industrialization of America in the late 19th century and the new public sense of morality which had to develop to enforce that reorganization. It involved an emphasis on self-discipline, self-denial, industriousness and respect for authority. Scenes from Pinocchio involving violence, social criticism and any disparagement of adults in the text – especially when it involved showing children ridiculing adults – were systematically removed. The tone of this first American translation is 'harsh, punitive and unsympathetic. Pinocchio, the child, is an annoyance' (Wunderlich, 1992: 202).

What Wunderlich calls the 'industrial moralism versions' died out in the 1920s, gradually making way for a more endearing puppet who arouses less anger. The image of Pinocchio which was created in the late 1930s in America, which gradually took hold and still defines Pinocchio in popular culture today is one which, again, can only be explained in terms of the norms and projections of American society. It is the Disney Pinocchio – although two other versions of the 1930s, similar in tendency, appeared before and, indeed, probably influenced Disney[3] – 'docile, loving and innocent, incapable of provoking anger and more lovable precisely because of his "pranks", which have now become innocuous and cute' (Wunderlich, 1992: 207). His becoming a real live boy in the end is not motivated, as in the original, by Pinocchio's desire to grow up. Here the goal of the child is no longer to reach adulthood, but to be a good child and to celebrate family unity and harmony. The image of Pinocchio has changed from Collodi's egoistic, headstrong puppet child to a personification of childhood innocence and loving acceptance.

This development was undoubtedly influenced by experiences of the Depression and the pending World War in which the only safe world was seen as the world of the family: children were better off, perhaps, not growing up. Wunderlich also sees a political message of the time in the versions of the 1930s. Unlike the empowering original in which Pinocchio is not expected to simply obey – as we know, the instances of state authority are explicitly satirized in the novel – but to assume responsibility for himself and his deeds as a precondition of adulthood, an illustration, in other words of the notion that people should have some control over their own lives and destinies, the American versions of the 1930s, in a time of heightened political consciousness and social activism, proclaimed the message that family harmony was crucial and to be strengthened, not threatened by the child, and, 'just as the child should be in harmony with the family, so should the citizen be in harmony with the state – for that is the natural order' (Wunderlich, 1992: 215).

When asking what is specifically national and what is international about Pinocchio, we assume that by the specifically national is meant: what is Italian about the book and its main character. But looking at translation/adaptations we must state that the question as to how specifically the culture into which he has been imported has been imprinted upon him, is equally valid and interesting. How German – or Austrian – is Pinocchio in any translation into that language? How American is he in a US translation? Or, to take these considerations one step further, using the passport metaphor given in the title of my talk, we might not just ask whether the docile Pinocchio has lost his Italian passport while crossing cultural borders, but whether he hasn't lost his passport altogether, being left to toss and turn on a sea of constant reinterpretation and instrumentalization taking him further and further away from his culture of origin and indeed from his original state of being. Some might claim that, despite all the chopping-up, sanitization and changes, the authentic story of Pinocchio has not been lost. Something about it endures and can never be ultimately changed, and that is the essential nature of the story. John Cech (1986: 176) is one of these. He writes about its mythoic core: it is a 'tale about one of the most basic and universal of transformations: the process of growing up, of moving towards conscience and consciousness.'

I do not believe that this is true. This was not the tale told by Disney and it is not the tale told in the countless sequels, series and television programmes that are based on the figure. If we reduce what Pinocchio has become in popular culture today to a common denominator, we will find that the only similarity he bears with the original is the fact that he is a wooden puppet with a long nose. And that this puppet has little or nothing to do with genuine international exchange in terms of elements of one culture being accepted in another in the area of children's literature should be evident.

Children's literature is necessarily characterized by the asymmetry of its communication structure: it is written, published, reviewed, bought, etc. by adults. The translation process represents another filter through which a text has to pass before reaching child readers, and the filter is often used to 'correct' aspects of the original text that are not deemed pedagogically acceptable for them. An example here is the episode in the German transla-tion of *Pippi Longstocking* in which the anarchic Pippi – instead of handing two pistols to her friends Thomas and Anneke – is made to proclaim in a most unlikely manner that children shouldn't play with pistols that she is going to put them back in the chest.[4]

It is also at the stage of translation where decisions are made as to how much a child can understand, how much can be left unsaid, how many of the 'gaps' (Iser, 1984) in the text that are filled in the reception process can be left unfilled in the translation for children. An extreme example of the extent to which an attempt to make something understandable to children can be brought, is to be found in the German translation of *Alice in Wonder-land*, by Franz Sester, published in 1949. Not only is Alice presented in Sester's translation as a well-behaved, somewhat boring English-learning German schoolgirl, but in the course of the explanation of what a Mock Turtle is, the reader also gets the bonus of being told about Alice's teacher and her relatives, and he or she is also given a recipe for Mock Turtle soup. [Editorial note: For the full text of this example and further discussion, see O'Sullivan in Part 2 of this Reader.]

We have seen from our look at some translations of children's literature that the areas in which the target culture prescribes the norms of accept-ability of translations cover much more than those elements which we might assume (and which often are) the first to be changed, the elements which Göte Klingberg (1986) summed up in his study on the translation of children's literature as candidates for cultural context adaptation. These include names, appearances, habits which transcend the idiosyncratic, locations – descriptions of landscapes or cityscapes – flora and fauna, the food eaten, references to historical or cultural contexts, currency, weights and measures, etc. They are the aspects which make a text – at least superficially – recognizably foreign, and are those which are most readily changed, especially in the translation of children's literature. While all texts are unquestionably culturally specific in terms of their origin, some reveal themselves to be more so than others – especially when the culture is made explicit in the book. It is rare that such books gain an international readership, and the exceptions which go to prove this particular rule are Johanna Spyri's very Swiss *Heidi* and Selma Lagerlöf's very Swedish *Wonderful Adventures of Nils Holgersson* – both of which have greatly influenced the perception of their countries abroad.

The fate of Pinocchio in some of the examples I have given here, or the admittedly rather extreme explanatory translation of the 'Mock Turtle' in *Alice in Wonderland* would seem to support the claim that the assumption that international children's classics are an example of how an understanding of and exchange between cultures can take place, is not valid. The practice of translation often involves either a universalizing or a localizing of the texts. What this means is that we cannot automatically assume that just because a book is the product of one culture that, first of all any of its specific features will have been retained in translation or adaptation and, even if they have been, that the translation will be realized as the product of another culture by its readers.

'Every country gives and every country receives – innumerable are the exchanges', that was what Paul Hazard (1944) wrote about the internationalism of children's books in the passage quoted at the beginning of my paper. Anyone who has ever actively worked with children's literature on an international level will know that this statement is little more than a Utopian fantasy. Up until recently, 70% of all the books produced in the world were originated in four languages: English, French, Russian, and German. As is well known, countries whose national languages rank as world languages publish a far smaller proportion of translations than small countries whose national boundaries also constitute language ones. The US and the United Kingdom, for example, belong to the countries which translate least of all: the percentage of translations in their output of fiction is only 3 to 4%[5] (the comparative figure for small European countries with a high level of literacy and well-developed publishing enterprises – Norway, Denmark, Sweden, Finland, the Netherlands and Switzerland – is around

55%). But it is not the exchange of current children's literature that is the topic I am addressing, it is that of the coming into being and continued existence of a body of children's classics which are regarded as international.

Once again naming some of the most common titles of such classics – *Don Quixote, Robinson Crusoe, Gulliver's Travels, Baron Munchausen,* Grimms' fairy tales, the fairy tales of Hans Christian Andersen, *Struwwelpeter, Alice in Wonderland, Tom Sawyer, Huckleberry Finn, Heidi, Pinocchio, Treasure Island, The Jungle Book, Peter Pan, Emil and the Detectives, Mary Poppins, Pippi Longstocking* – it is apparent that not every country is represented on the list. Those involved are the countries of Europe – north western Europe mainly, and the USA. When we talk about a World Literature for children, we actually mean books produced in the Western Tradition,[6] with a significant proportion of books in English. The reasons for this dominance are two-fold. The first has to do with the development of children's literature. The second has to do with the development of a world market for children's books.

When we look at the historical development of children's literature, it is at once evident that certain attitudes and conditions had to prevail before it could emerge on any sort of scale. An awareness of childhood as being intrinsically different from adulthood and thus requiring special treatment was the first precondition. Another was the emergence of a social class whose children had the time and possibility of learning to read, in other words, children who were released from the cycle of work to enjoy an education. This precondition was an economic one. Both of these were fulfilled in the countries of Northern Europe – England, the Netherlands, parts of Germany and France – towards the middle of the 18th century, and so it was in these countries that children's literature was developed on any mentionable scale. This headstart, so to speak, is doubtlessly one of the main explanations of the dominance of England and Germany amongst the 'classics' of children's literature.

The production of books written intentionally for children and their exchange between countries in Northern Europe up until and during the time of the Enlightenment was, mainly, in the hands of educationalists. But the 18th century also saw the start of the purely commercial exploitation of children's literature. One of the key names in this development – as is well known – is that of the English publisher John Newbery. Although he has long since been dethroned as the patron saint of children's literature, his position in the history of this literature is significant. An alert businessman, he discovered and shrewdly exploited the new market of middle class children, or rather their parents. The English were, therefore, not only one of the first nations in history to develop a self-conscious, independent children's literature, but they also developed the commercial institutions capable of supporting and furthering it.

The exchange of children's books between cultures has, we can safely claim, nearly always been determined by questions of economics, the status of the literature of one language is often tied to commercial and cultural links. Not a lot is known about the history of translation of children's literature into various languages – Sweden is exceptional here in having produced excellent studies, led initially by the comparative scholar, Göte Klingberg. In a subsequent survey of the history of translations in Sweden, Lars Furuland (1978) traces the point from which the predominance of English was established amongst the languages from which children's books are translated to, amongst other things, a general shift in orientation of trade and commerce. Its replacement of German as the dominant import, so to speak, on the children's market coincided around the middle of the 19th century with the development of Swedish children's publishing into an industry catering for a wider and growing market borne up by the middle classes around that time. A major factor which influenced the change was the fact that 'trade and the flow of foreign exchange were tending more and more to pass through England. As well as being the foremost customer of the Swedish timber industry, England was now playing a part in the industrialization of agrarian Sweden' (Furuland, 1978: 65). Added to that was the increase in output of children's literature in English from the 1850s and 60s, providing publishers in other countries with an abundance of material. The English publishing and literary sectors became a growing export area in the mid-19th century. The book industry behind English literature, as Furuland (1978) writes, was a force with which German and French publishers, who were also trading on the international market, could only seriously compete for short, intermittent periods.

This is an extremely brief and necessarily incomplete sketch of conditions within Europe in the 19th century, between countries who were competing in a free market. The situation on a world scale was characterized by totally different positions of power: the colonized and exploited were hardly in a position to 'compete' with a politically, militarily and economically over-powerful Europe. Bearing in mind that the economic and military conquest of countries is usually followed by a cultural colonization, we can see clearly the conditions which supported the canonization of an almost exclusively Northern European and dominantly English language children's literature in the world.

When speaking critically in Osaka in 1986 about the conditions of an international network of children's literature, Klaus Doderer (1986) reported on the UNESCO study according to which the European fairy tale (the genre usually held up as the model of international children's literature) was suppressing indigenous ideals in South American countries. In a storytelling competition amongst Ecuadorian children, over 80% of the stories told were variations of European fairy tales or Wild West films, not Ecuadorian tales. Evidence of the European, or more specifically, the Grimms' model influencing the way South American fairy tales were recorded was to be seen where princesses in the fairy tales of the Mapuche Indians in Chile were described as having white skin. Everything that was rich and fine was given European features. Klaus Doderer also mentioned reports in the newspaper in the 1960s, that in the Congo Grimms' fairy tales were the most widespread children's books while in China this honor was conferred upon Heidi. Examples of this variety of questionable internationalism, which amounts to little else than cultural colonization, are legion.

I would like to say a final word about the diversity of cultural origins or identities of children's classics. In Western Europe cultural differences are accurately perceived between Italy and Germany, between France and England, but when we look at the classics that are the object of our investigation then we must ask whether a certain cultural affiliation between them can be observed. Isabelle Nières (1992), in her contribution to a catalogue accompanying the exhibition '*Livres d'enfants en Europe*,' talks about the common heritage that unites Europe: the culture of ancient Greece and Rome, and the Christian religion. She also mentions the oral folklore tradition. The history of children's literature in Europe is also a history of the formulation of images of childhood. Many of the classics of children's literature discussed here are not only originally specific to their cultures but they are also specific in the sense of a shared tradition of images of childhood, the use of collective Christian Myths – that of the divine child, for example – and in what can be seen as the step by step development in European literature of childhood towards the – gradual and mutually influenced – portrayal of the autonomous child. The story of the European classics of children's literature is ultimately the story of this development.

Studies that concern themselves with differences and similarities of classics, with continuation and breaks in traditions, reconstruct the original conditions of reception in the cultures in which these classics originated, study the conditions of their popularity, their potential for providing new impetus and new direction in their own literature and for influencing the development of children's literature in general. At the centre of my concern here has not been a historical, interpretative approach. Rather I have focused on cultural transfer, on the idea of a genuine exchange between cultures which is generally held to be a feature of the simultaneously national and international character of children's classics.

Returning to the question of the systematic changes that can be observed in the texts after they cross cultural and linguistic borders, the transformations undergone by children's classics through different cultures and times, I would now like to ask how the status of these texts, how their relationship to their originals is to be defined and classified.

The classification and categorization of the classics of children's literature does not have much in common with the rules which apply to classics of general literature, which always clearly refer to specific texts, produced by one author, whose composition is sacrosanct. Taking the most common categories cited in general debates on classics – the normative, the qualitatively excellent and the exemplary – we can see that they cannot apply to a work such as *Don Quixote* or others adapted for young readers, because if those are the categories that apply as a general maxim, which version of *Don Quixote* do we take to see if it fulfils this requirement?

If we try to assess the position or status of classical figures and titles of children's books in relation to the original work which bore their name or their tale – Don Quixote, Robinson Crusoe, Alice in Wonderland, Pinocchio, Heidi, Peter Pan, etc. – if we look at the tradition of handing down these works in translations, adaptations in print, in comic, in film, television series, cartoon form, then the category with which we have to describe the status of these figures and constellations cannot be that of literature.

How, then, can we describe the status of Alice when she is claimed as being an international household name for children? What is meant is not the work of literature *Alice in Wonderland* by Lewis Carroll, but the figure of a little girl in a strange, fantastic land, who is confronted with a medley of peculiar creatures. That which, apart from the creation of the figure Alice, characterized the text by Lewis Carroll – the constant undermining of Alice's frames of reference including the communicative nature of language itself, the arbitrariness of behaviour of the irrational Wonderland creatures, the games and tricks which constantly push the understanding of language and logic beyond their conventional borders, the elements of satire and parody in the text, the obscuring of the distinction between fantasy and reality – just to mention a few elements which are an intrinsic and important part of the literary text that we call *Alice in Wonderland,* not a lot of this remains in current media versions of the story. Their common denominator is a little girl in a fantastic but not even necessarily overwhelmingly threatening world. So how, to return to the question in hand, can the status of the chopped up, rewritten, reinterpreted texts or other media in which these classical figures continue to appear be described, what is the relationship of the famous classical children's figures to the works which originally bore their name?

I would like to suggest that there are two modes simultaneously involved in the transmission of the classics of children's literature. These modes are not to be seen as absolute: there is a sliding scale between them, upon which some translation/adaptations can be seen to be closer to one mode than the other. The first is an ideal mode, that of 'literary' translations of literary originals, that is, what, within a traditional concept of translation, is regarded as being a 'good' translation. I again insist that this is an ideal that puts itself outside the realities of the determining factors of translation. This mode can apply to only one of our three sources of children's literature, literature written intentionally for children and, while a literary translation will still necessarily reveal much about the target culture into which it is translated, it represents a serious attempt to recreate the original text on its own terms. It tries not to add, subtract or alter the narrative. It tries to reproduce the communication situation of the source text and it tries to find the closest approximation for the constitution of the aesthetic and linguistic idiosyncrasies and is carried out by translators who have an ideal of trying to remain true to the spirit of the work. As two examples of translations from English into German which could be generally ascribed to this mode are Christian Enzensberger's translation of *Alice in Wonderland* (1963) and Harry Rowohlt's of *Winnie-the-Pooh* (1989).

This mode, as I said, can only apply to literature composed specifically for children. The other two sources – adaptations from the sphere of general literature and literature originating from the oral tradition – fairy tales, legends, etc. cannot be adequately described using its terms. Taking literary translation as a yardstick with which to measure these other two sources and, indeed, as we have seen, many of the translations and adaptations of literature written specifically for children, too, results in having to classify them as second-rate. Because most of the texts we are talking about do not qualify on the terms of this prescriptive model, another framework is needed with which we can characterize the mode of transmission of the majority of children's classics.

As an alternative mode of transmission that we could attempt to describe how the figures of children's literature are handed down through generations of print and other media, I would like to suggest using the category of folklore. By that I do not mean redefining them all as some sort of fairy tale. What I mean is that we have to look for a different explanation of their continuing tradition other than that of our ideal concept of literature. To do this I would briefly like to present a theoretical framework.

The well-known structuralist folklore theory of Roman Jakobson was based on a theory of opposition of 'literature' and 'folklore' as two different traditions determining the passing on or handing down of texts. For

Jakobson, 'folklore' was the means of transmission of texts within oral cultures, 'literature' was that within written ones. This binary concept has been enhanced in recent years to take account of the fact that there can be such a thing as written folklore, a form of written material which conforms, not to the transmissional norms of 'literature' but to that of 'folklore'. Alieda Assmann (1983), who coined the phrase 'written folklore', concentrates on five areas of difference between written folklore and literature, which I believe can help us to explore what is actually going on in most of the cases of transmission of children's literature into other cultures and media. Hans-Heino Ewers (1990: 86) was the scholar who discovered the value of the mode of written folklore for describing different forms of children's literature. He does, however, explicitly exclude what he calls the small number of children's classics from this mode.

The first of the five areas of difference is in the openness of the work: whereas 'literature' is defined as being composed, complete, finished, written folklore has the character of a compilation, a collection of materials, it is like a quarry, from which pieces can be taken and put together. We could think here of collections of sagas and legends, or of an episodic work like *Gulliver's Travels* from which different episodes are taken and combined and new ones are added.

The second characteristic is the variant status of the texts: what applied to the openness of the compilation on the level of the whole work, applies also to the text itself, to the words, sentences, paragraphs, etc. There is no canonized adhesion to the order of the words here as there is in 'literature', where the impeachability of the wording of the text as a unique expression is a central tenet.

The third area in which the difference can be identified is the question of author and authority. Whereas in the 'literature' mode, the author, and only he or she is the originator of the text, the folklore and written folklore modes display an obliteration of the author: what is transmitted is general property, merely given different form in a new version or a compilation. The names of those involved are interchangeable.

The fourth point is that, whereas the continued existence of a literary text is linked with its being conserved as a unique work, that of written folklore is guaranteed by a series of versions which replace one another. The final characteristic is that of the use of the texts. Whereas one of the main features of 'literature' is its autonomous status, its lack of practical function in life, folklore is to be found bang in the middle of it. The texts have a use, often a didactic or a social one in initiation, instruction, illustration of skills, knowledge, rituals relevant for everyday life, in other words, they are orientated towards the needs of their readers – also in terms of entertainment.

A case which conforms in almost ideal fashion to all the characteristics of written folklore is that of *Robinson Crusoe*. Out of a work of literature, a synthesis of economic adventure and an individual story of religious salvation, elements were taken to suit the purposes of the adaptors: it became, shortly after publication in 1719, a model for a series of amazingly popular adventure stories on the continent of Europe: Silesian, Saxon, Islandic, Danish, Austrian, etc. Robinsons were produced in almost epidemic style. Robinson was a household name, his story was varied, compiled from bits of other Robinsonades and later, as we all know, found its way – by means of a recommendation by Rousseau taken up by the German educationalist Joachim Heinrich Campe – into the world of children's literature. In this sphere its usefulness for educational purposes, its character of being constantly rewritten to suit those purposes, the replacement of one version by another – as Elke Liebs (1977) showed in her comprehensive study of Robinson Crusoe in Germany, every generation rewrites their own Robinson – and the lack of importance of the names of the adaptors, the non-sanctity of the original – both in terms of content as well as of style – all these elements show the history of the transmission of Robinson Crusoe to belong to the tradition of written folklore rather than that of literature.

The mode of transmission of the classics of children's literature that is the most dominant one and indeed the only one that applies to adaptations of literature for adults for children – the adaptors and their adaptations replacing one another and disappearing into the fog of history – is the mode of written folklore. It also applies, needless to say, to works of children's literature which themselves have their origin in oral folklore: legends, myths and fairy tales. But it also applies to books written specifically for children when they are translated, edited or adapted in such a way that all that is left is a recognizable character, situation or plot that can be seen as the marketable aspect synonymous with the general idea of what that work is. These transmitted elements, these fictions of fictions that have been removed from their context to become free-floating images or myths can be a type of character: Pippi, the totally autonomous, empowered, independent, superhuman child; it can be a situation: a man alone on a island, faced with the sole task of survival – the only element which various adaptations of Robinson Crusoe have in common; it can be the exciting contrast of a tiny person in a world of huge beings and vice versa, that is what the reduction of *Gulliver's Travels* has become or it can be a myth of eternal childhood, Peter Pan, or the child in nature who is Heidi and so on. I could go on to name what has become the only common denominator of other classics, but I think it should be clear by now what I mean. This folklore mode is, so I believe, the most dominant one, ensuring the continued presence of these figures in the 'world republic of childhood'. That the versions in which they appear will differ greatly in terms of composition, content and interpretation has been shown by some examples listed here. They were all, once upon a time, Italian, Swedish, English, Danish or German, the figures who populate what is taken to constitute the international classics of children's literature with the not-so international origins. But, as I have tried to illustrate, they are subject to transformations through which they are supplied with other cultural identities than those of their origin – cultural identity being taken to mean more than the superficialities of what they eat and how they look to include the literary tradition to which they belong and the cultural, ideological and pedagogical norms to which they conform. In this sense we can say that these figures are truly international because they are not fixed. But it should be realized that the international Gulliver, Pinocchio, Alice and the others are the common denominators of every cultural or national version of themselves and that they cannot simultaneously be seen to carry the passport of the land of their origin.

Notes

1. Later generations of German translators – and indeed translators into other languages – some naturally more successful than others, have, of course, proven the lie of the 'untranslatable' claim.
2. The first English translation was undertaken by Mary Alice Murray: *The Story of a Puppet or the Adventures of Pinocchio*. London: Fisher Unwin, 1891.
3. They are the play Pinocchio by Yasha Frank which premiered in 1937 and a 'retelling' in book form by Roselle Ross (1939) *Pinocchio: A Story for Children*. Akron, OH: Saalfield.
4. Astrid Lindgren (1969) *Pippi Langstrumpf*. Deutsch von Cäcilie Heinig. Hamburg. This 'correction' is removed in the revised edition of the translation published in 1987. See O'Sullivan, 'Narratology meets Translation Studies' in Part 2 of this Reader for further discussion if this example.
5. cf. Mary Ørvig (1981: 229).
6. Such is the accurate subtitle of the book by Charles Frey and John Griffith (1987) *The Literary Heritage of Childhood. An Appraisal of Children's Classics in the Western Tradition*. Of the 29 authors selected for presentation and discussion in the book, only nine did not write in English: Charles Perrault, Marie le Prince de Beaumont, the Brothers Grimm, Hans Christian Andersen, Heinrich Hoffmann, Peter Asbjörnsen and Jörgen Moe, Carlo Collodi and Johanna Spyri.

David Blamires

The Early Reception of the Grimms' Kinder- und Hausmärchen *in England*

When the two volumes of what turned out to be the first edition of Jacob and Wilhelm Grimms' *Kinder- und Hausmärchen* (KHM) were published by the Realschulbuchhandlung in Berlin in 1812 and 1815, the two brothers can hardly have suspected that the product of their scholarly collecting would turn out to be the most widely disseminated and translated work of German literature.[1] In the English language alone the *British Library Catalogue of Works Printed up to 1975* lists over 300 separate publications (excluding adaptations) ranging from translations of the complete collection to printings of a single story. Even that is not a complete account of everything that was printed during the period.

The Grimms, it is well known, embarked on their collecting of *Märchen* in the wake of Arnim and Brentano's *Des Knaben Wunderhorn* (Heidelberg: Mohr und Zimmer, 1806–08). Their sources were many and various. Originally they had wanted to confine themselves to contemporary oral versions, but in order to make their collection comprehensive, they eventually extended their interest to older, printed tales and even made adaptations from medieval Latin poems. They scoured recent publications of *Märchen* in Germany, but were largely dismissive of what they found, though they mentioned them in the preface to their 1812 volume. Fairy tales were far from unknown to German readers of the previous half-century, but they were diverse in mood and form and were more self-consciously literary than the Grimms wanted. [...][2]

The *Kinder- und Hausmärchen*, therefore, need to be seen in a fourfold context: (1) the transmission of fashionable fairy tales from France (Perrault and Mme d'Aulnoy) and the Middle East (via Antoine Galland's *Mille et une Nuits*); (2) the development of a narrative literature for children, which includes the occasional adaptation of traditional oral tales such as Otmar's *Volcks-Sagen* (Bremen, 1800) and Johann Gustav Gottlieb Büsching's *Volks-Sagen, Märchen und Legenden* (Leipzig, 1812); (3) the antiquarian and scholarly collection of traditional tales and songs, represented by such works as Macpherson's *Ossian* (1760–63), Percy's *Reliques of Ancient English Poetry* (1765), Herder's *Volkslieder* (1778–79), and Arnim and Brentano's *Des Knaben Wunderhorn* (1806–08); (4) the imaginative use of fairy tale themes and structure in contemporary literature, for example Goethe's 'Das Märchen' in *Unterhaltung deutscher Ausgewanderten* (1795). Alongside all this there was a political dimension to the Grimms' enterprise: the recording of folktales, folksongs and folk traditions proved to be a powerful element in the development of national consciousness. This can be seen not only in a fragmented Germany seeking to free itself from the shackles of France, but also later in Norway and Ireland, for example.

The Grimms worked at the KHM from about 1806 right through to the end of their lives, the seventh edition of 1857 being the final product of Wilhelm's continual reshaping and (as he saw it) improvement of the collection. When people nowadays talk of the KHM, it is the 1857 edition that they usually mean, with its deliberately numbered 200 items, plus the ten *Kinderlegenden*. However, it is important to remember that each of the seven editions of the KHM differs in some measure, smaller or greater, from the rest. Tales were added and subtracted, texts were altered as new versions flowed in, and stylistic changes were made all the time, sometimes for reasons that were entirely subjective and cannot be accounted for by the normal criteria of scholarship. The first edition was published in two volumes, dated 1812 and 1815, with 86 and 70 items respectively in each volume, making a total of 156. A second edition appeared in two volumes in 1819, with a third volume consisting of notes in 1822. This made drastic changes in every respect to the first edition. Much smaller alterations were made between the succeeding editions – the third in 1837, the fourth in 1840, the fifth in 1843, the sixth in 1850 and the seventh in 1857.

The first translation of the KHM into English appeared in 1823 with the title *German Popular Stories, translated from the Kinder und Haus Märchen, collected by M.M. Grimm, from Oral Tradition* (London: C. Baldwyn). The first copies of this volume omitted the umlaut sign from 'Märchen'. It was reprinted in 1823, 1824, and 1825. Its success led to a second volume, published in 1826, but with different publishers – James Robins & Co., London, and Joseph Robins Jr and Co., Dublin – though the format was identical. This second volume was reprinted in 1827 with no date on the title-page.[3] The anonymous translators were Edgar Taylor (1793–1839) and, presumably, others in his immediate circle of family and acquaintances. Edgar Taylor had set up, in 1817, the firm of Taylor and Roscoe, solicitors, in partnership with Robert Roscoe,[4] for whom as a boy the famous children's book *The Butterfly's Ball* (London: J. Harris, 1807) had been written by his father, the highly successful and cultivated Liverpool merchant and MP,

William Roscoe.[5] Edgar Taylor's interests were not confined to children's literature. He deserves considerable credit for his pioneering efforts to introduce medieval German lyric poetry to the English public, in his translations entitled *Lays of the Minne-singers* (London: Longman, Hurst, Rees, Orme, Brown and Green, 1825). Taylor's translations, as represented by these two books, should be seen as part of the growing English interest in German literature and culture.[6]

Over the previous 30 or so years a considerable number of contemporary works of German literature had been translated into English. Goethe's *Werther* had appeared even earlier, in 1779, though it is symptomatic of English unfamiliarity with the German language that it was translated from the French; new translations directly from the German came from 1801 onwards. [...] Among children's books J.D.Wyss's *Der schweizerische Robinson*, first published in Zürich in 1812–13, made its debut in English as *The Family Robinson Crusoe* in 1814, a second edition following in 1818, when it received its better-known title *The Swiss Family Robinson*. [...] But what was the situation with regard to fairy tales? Perrault and Madame d'Aulnoy had long been made available in English, and individual tales by them circulated, usually anonymously, in chapbook form for children. The latest reprint of Madame d'Aulnoy was the 1817 *Fairy Tales and Novels* (London: Walker and Edwards). Sections of the *Arabian Nights* had circulated in English throughout the 18th century,[7] but in 1811 Jonathan Scott produced a new six-volume edition based mainly on Galland. There were also chapbooks of English fairy tales such as 'Tom Thumb' and 'Whittington and his Cat'. In 1804 Benjamin Tabart brought out a *Collection of Popular Stories for the Nursery* in four volumes, containing some thirty-four stories taken from French, Italian, and English writers. This included tales from Perrault, Madame d'Aulnoy, and the English chapbooks, but also others such as 'Fortunatus', 'Griselda', and 'The Children in the Wood'. The material all came from printed sources, but it is probably the nearest thing to the KHM existing in England at the time, and the Grimms refer to it in their notes.[8] [...] The systematic collection of English fairy tales, however, did not come until towards the end of the 19th century.

This, then, was the context for Edgar Taylor's translation of the KHM into English. Despite the fact that it was made long before the KHM reached its final form and despite its various inadequacies from the scholarly point of view, the time was certainly ripe. It has been constantly reprinted in some shape or form ever since it was first published. A vital factor in this was George Cruikshank's engravings, to which I shall return later. The text and illustrations were republished as a Puffin Book by Penguin Books in 1948, and this edition is, I believe, still in print. A facsimile of the original two volumes of 1823 and 1826 was published by Scolar Press in 1977 and reprinted in 1979. With all its faults, Taylor's translation has achieved a sort of classic status of its own. If modern readers were aware that it is a period piece, that would not much matter, but most do not realize just how skewed a picture of the Grimms' collection they get through reading Taylor. Not that Taylor attempted to camouflage what he was doing in adapting, combining and expurgating his originals – on the contrary, he signalled his changes very frankly in the notes he appended to the tales. But what he presents is not what a modern reader would be entitled to expect.

Let us look first at the contents of the two volumes. Taylor's principal source, the 1819 edition of the KHM, contains 161 fairy tales and 19 *Kinder-Legenden*, from which Taylor took 57 plus one further tale ('The Nose') that he extracted from the notes in the third volume of 1822. That is about a third of the total then available. Most of these correspond to single tales in the translation, but he combined '*Das Lumpengesindel*', '*Herr Korbes*' and '*Von dem Tod des Hühnchens*' into the one story 'Chanticleer and Partlet' (incidentally taking the names from Chaucer), and '*Der junge Riese*' and '*Das tapfere Schneiderlein*' were joined to make 'The Young Giant and the Tailor'. Similarly, '*Das kluge Grethel*', '*Der gescheidte Hans*', and '*Die faule Spinnerin*' were turned into 'Hans and his Wife', while '*Vom Fundevogel*', '*Der Liebste Roland*', and 'Hänsel und Grethel' were transformed into the one story 'Roland and Maybird'. The first volume contained 'The Grateful Beasts', a translation of a story that retained its place in the KHM up to the sixth edition of 1850, but was then relegated to the appendix as no. 18 in the 1857 edition. In the same volume only one of the three tales that form '*Die Wichtelmänner*' is retained in 'The Elves and the Shoemaker'.

The second volume is distinguished from the first in that it contains four tales that do not belong to the Grimms' collection at all. Two of these were taken from Johann Büsching's *Volks-Sagen, Märchen und Legenden* (Leipzig, 1812), namely, 'Pee-wit' ('*Kibitz*') and 'Cherry, or the Frog-bride' ('*Das Märchen von der Padde*'). 'Peter and the Goatherd' is taken from Otmar's *Volcks-Sagen* (Bremen, 1800), probably prompted by the recent publication of Washington Irving's *Rip van Winkle* (1819), which Taylor refers to in his notes and which is a version of the same tale-type. Finally, with 'The Elfin-Grove' Taylor provided a much abridged adaptation of Ludwig Tieck's *Die Elfen*.

It is noticeable that Taylor zealously avoided using any of the tales with a religious dimension, so there is no '*Marienkind*', no '*Der Schneider im Himmel*', no '*Der Gevatter Tod*', no '*Bruder Lustig*' – the list could be extended. The prevalence of the Devil in the German tales caused Taylor worry, so these tales also were omitted, or the Devil was converted into a giant, as in 'The Giant with the Three Golden Hairs'. '*Von dem Fischer und siine Fru*' (The Fisherman and his Wife), one of the two Low German tales submitted by Philipp Otto Runge to the Grimms, had to be slightly modified in the end. Where the fisherman's wife declares finally that she wants to be '*as de lewe Gott*' (like our dear God), Taylor 'soften[ed] the boldness of the lady's ambition'[9] by saying that she wants to be 'lord of the sun and moon'. Taylor tended also to avoid stories that contained too much of a frightening character, so there is no '*Märchen von einem, der auszog, das Fürchten zu lernen*' (The man who set out to learn fear), and '*Der singende Knochen*' (The singing bone) with its sorrowful ending probably did not commend itself to him for that very reason. It is surprising that he actually included 'The Robber Bridegroom' in his selection, though he eliminated the cannibalistic intentions of the robbers, their deliberate murder of the captured maiden, and their chopping off of her finger. These horrifying details are some of the most memorable features of the KHM, and similar ones are to be found in several other tales. '*Aschenputtel*' (Cinderella), for example, ends with the doves picking out the eyes of the wicked stepsisters as the heroine goes to her wedding, but this final paragraph of the German version is excised from Taylor's translation so that the story ends on a happier note. His second volume ends with 'The Juniper Tree', the Low German '*Van den Machandel-Boom*', the second of Runge's tales. Taylor translated this rather freely, perhaps because the Low German was difficult for him, but again he cut out the cannibalistic episode in which the father is served up the flesh of his murdered son in a stew. Taylor simply has the father given 'a large dish of black soup' with no implication as to its content. Furthermore, he had then to alter the second line of the famous song of the bird – the song that Gretchen sings in Goethe's *Faust* – so that instead of

Min Moder de mi slacht't
Min Vader de mi att
(My mother slew me, my father ate me)

we have the much milder

My mother slew her little son
My father thought me lost and gone.

There is still plenty of violence left in the tale, especially at the end where the bird drops the millstone on the stepmother's head and crushes her to pieces, but it is clear that Taylor took pains to reduce the elements of terror and cruelty that he found in the KHM.

This first of the translators of the Grimms into English is very concerned about the impact of the stories on his readers. In his introduction he alludes to 'many stories of great merit, and tending highly to the elucidation of ancient mythology, customs and opinions, which the scrupulous fastidiousness of modern taste, especially in works likely to attract the attention of youth, warned [the translators] to pass by.' This 'scrupulous fastidiousness of modern taste', an expression which may be linked with the growth of Evangelicism and of prudery that is characteristic of the end of the 18th and beginning of the 19th century, accounts for Taylor's alterations of religious and other features mentioned earlier, but there are a few others that should be noted too. The original of 'The Fisherman and his Wife' has the couple initially living in a 'Pispott', which Taylor changed to a 'ditch', while in his 1839 revision of the text (which I shall come to in due course) he altered it again to a 'pig-stye'.

But there were other places where sexuality was the issue. 'Rapunzel', with its unavoidable implication that the girl and the prince have made love in the tower, was not translated at all. Then there was the 'Frog-Prince', the ending of which Taylor drastically altered. Exceptionally here, Taylor was translating from the 1812 text of the story, not the 1819 edition that was the source for all his other tales. This is the opening tale in all seven editions of the KHM, and it seems likely that Taylor first encountered the Grimms' collection in the first edition and made at that time a translation of the first tale. When he later got down to serious work on the tales, he then followed the more recent second edition.

In the German original the frog is supposed to sleep with the princess in her bed, but she cannot bring herself to do this, despite the king's insistence that she must fulfil her promise to the frog:

> *Es half nichts, si musste tun, wie ihr Vater wollte, aber sie war bitterböse in ihrem Herzen. Sie packte den Frosch mit zwei Fingern und trug ihn hinaus in ihre Kammer, legte sich ins Bett und statt ihn neben sich zu legen, warf sie ihn bratsch! an die Wand; 'da, nun wirst du mich in Ruh lassen, du garstiger Frosch!'*

> *Aber der Frosch fiel nicht tot herunter, sondern wie er herab auf das Bett kam, da war's ein schöner junger Prinz. Der war nun ihr lieber Geselle, und sie hielt ihn wert, wie sie versprochen hatte, und sie schliefen vergnügt zusammen ein.*

(It was no good, she had to do what her father wanted, but there was bitter anger in her heart..She took hold of the frog with two fingers and carried him to her room where she got into bed but, instead of placing him next to her, she threw him thump! against the wall 'There, now you'll leave me alone you nasty frog!'

But the frog did not fall down dead; when he came down onto the bed he was a handsome young prince. He was now her dear companion and she admired him as she had promised and they fell happily asleep together.) [Literal translation by the editor G.L.]

Taylor's version – it cannot be called a translation – tells a different set of events:

... the princess took him up in her hand and put him upon the pillow of her own little bed, where he slept all night long. As soon as it was light he jumped up, hopped down stairs, and went out of the house. 'Now', thought the princess, 'he is gone, and I shall be troubled with him no more.'

But she was mistaken; for when night came again, she heard the same tapping at the door, and when she opened it, the frog came in and slept upon her pillow as before till the morning broke; and the third night he did the same: but when the princess awoke on the following morning, she was astonished to see, instead of the frog, a handsome prince gazing on her with the most beautiful eyes that ever were seen, and standing at the head of her bed.

He told her that he had been enchanted by a malicious fairy, who had changed him into the form of a frog, in which he was fated to remain till some princess should take him out of the spring and let him sleep upon her bed for three nights.

There is nothing in Taylor's adaptation of the prince and princess sleeping together in human form, though he allows the frog to sleep on the princess's pillow for three nights running. He obviously cannot countenance the princess's attempt to kill the frog by hurling it against the wall. The transformation takes place as it were unconsciously, while the princess is asleep. The transformed frog is not in her bed, as one might have expected from its lying on her pillow, but is 'standing at the head of the bed'. One detail Taylor may have taken from the 1819 text of the story, and that is the emphasis on the fact that the prince has the 'most beautiful eyes that ever were seen'. The 1812 edition has no comparable comment here, but the 1819 version says: '*Was aber herunterfiel, war nicht ein todter Frosch, sondern ein lebendiger, junger Königssohn mit schönen und freundlichen Augen*' (but what fell down was not a dead frog, but a living, young prince with beautiful, friendly eyes). In making his alterations Taylor has rendered the princess passive and obedient to her father's commands and thus deprived her of taking her own initiative and responsibility for what follows. In the German original she confronts her own distaste and causes, however unwittingly, the prince's transformation; she does not simply submit to male authority as embodied in the king, her father.

Taylor was an inveterate softener of harsh details that he found in the Grimms' tales. In the story of 'Rumpelstilzchen' the 1819 edition has a disturbing conclusion:

> 'Das hat dir der Teufel gesagt! Das hat dir der Teufel gesagt!' schrie das Männlein und stiess mit dem rechten Fuss vor Zorn so tief in die Erde, dass es bis an den Leib hineinfuhr, dann packet es in einer Wuth den linken Fuss mit beiden Händen und riss sich mitten entzwei.

('The devil told you that! The devil told you that!' shouted the little man and in his fury stamped his right foot and leg into the ground right up to his crotch, then in a rage he took hold of his left leg with both hands and tore himself in two.) [Editor's translation with advice from Anthea Bell.]

With Taylor it has become a childish temper tantrum, whereas the German ending can be seen as an act of self-destruction that removes the threat of Rumpelstilzchen for ever from the queen's life.

Taylor's interferences with the German texts are too extensive to deal with *in toto* here, but they can be characterized as tending to make the stories more reassuring and less disturbing to the children whom he envisaged as readers. This first English translation thus has a markedly different tone from that of the Grimms' text. Yet we must remember that this is a commonplace occurrence in the transmission of fairy tales, whether oral or in printed form. Every storyteller puts his or her own mark on the tale told. There is no perfect, uncontaminated process, as a comparison of the summaries in their manuscript collection with the printed forms of the seven editions readily demonstrates. Where they used printed texts from the 16th to the early 19th centuries, the same kind of adaptation and homogenisation is also to be seen.

Of crucial consequence for the popularity of Taylor's translation is the fact that he secured the collaboration of the greatest illustrator of the day to provide twelve etchings for the first volume and a further ten for the second volume. George Cruikshank (1792–1878) was an extraordinarily prolific artist and caricaturist, and his illustrations have elicited the highest praise. John Ruskin declared that the original etchings done for *German Popular Stories* were 'unrivalled in masterfulness of touch since Rembrandt; (in some qualities of delineation unrivalled even by him).'[10]

In addition to frontispieces depicting scenes of listening to stories round a fire, Cruikshank provided illustrations for the following tales: 'Hans in Luck', 'The Travelling Musicians, or the Waits of Bremen', 'The Golden

Bird', 'Jorinda and Jorindel', 'The Waggish Musician', 'The Elves and the Shoemaker', 'The Turnip', 'The Jew in the Bush', 'The King of the Golden Mountain', 'The Golden Goose', and 'Rumpel-stilts-kin' (volume 1); 'The Goose Girl', 'The Blue Light', 'Pee-wit', 'Cherry, or the Frog-Bride', 'The Elfin-Grove', and 'The Nose'. Cruikshank's delight in the comic and the grotesque has proved enduringly attractive to English-speaking readers, though the Germans tend to prefer the more gentle, somewhat sentimental approach of their own 19th-century artists.

The immediate success of Taylor's translation in terms of the new impressions during the 1820s has already been noted. [...]More than a dozen years elapsed before Edgar Taylor's translation, together with preface and notes, made a second appearance in 1839 with the new title *Gammer Grethel; or German Fairy Tales, and Popular Stories, from the collection of MM. Grimm, and Other Sources* (London: John Green). This was quite a new book, as the translation was heavily revised and recast and contained a lot of additions in the nature of asides specifically addressed to a child audience. A number of the originally anonymous protagonists of the stories were given names, and some of the titles of the stories were changed. 'The Grateful Beasts', for example, becomes 'Fritz and his Friends', while Otmar's 'Peter the Goatherd' is renamed 'Karl Katz'. Eighteen of the originally translated stories were omitted, and one new one was added – 'The Bear and the Skrattel'. [...] The tales in *Gammer Grethel* were arranged in a completely different sequence from *German Popular Stories* and designed to be read over a dozen evenings, with three or four tales per evening. Cruikshank's etchings were replaced by wood-engravings by John Byfield after Cruikshank's designs. The revised text was reprinted in 1849 (Bohn's Illustrated Library), 1888 and 1897 (George Bell and Sons) and possibly at other times as well.

Meanwhile, the original translation continued to be reprinted. It appeared with stereotype reproductions of Cruikshank's illustrations, issued by John Camden Hotten in 1869, the original two volumes being printed together as one. This contained a ten-page introduction by John Ruskin. Chatto and Windus, who purchased Hotten's business on his death in 1873,[11] did another edition in 1884. Taylor's original translation continued to be used for a large number of subsequent editions, right into the 20th century, though almost always without any indication of his name. The translation is, however, easily recognizable by the occurrence of certain characteristic titles of individual tales, for example, 'Rose-bud' ('*Dornröschen*'), 'Snow-drop' ('*Sneewittchen*'), 'Roland and Maybird' ('*Der Liebste Roland*', '*Fundevogel*', and '*Hänsel und Grethel*' combined), and by the presence of the four tales not from the KHM.

Edgar Taylor's translation was made in the early stages of the development of the KHM, before it had reached its full growth. The second English
translation had the advantage of some additional growth to the collection,
though it was still not complete. In 1846 John Edward Taylor published a
translation of an additional selection of tales under the title of *The Fairy
Ring: A New Collection of Tales, translated from the German of Jacob and Wilhelm
Grimm* (London: John Murray). It contained twelve illustrations by the
up-and-coming artist Richard Doyle (1824–83). Doyle later illustrated
Ruskin's *King of the Golden River* (London: Smith, Elder and Co., 1851). John
Edward Taylor used the Grimms' fifth edition of 1843 for his translation,
including a number of tales that made their first appearance in print in that
edition, namely, 'The Nix in the Millpond', 'The Hedgehog and the Hare',
'The Goose-girl at the Well', 'The Spindle, the Shuttle and the Needle', 'The
Drummer', 'The True Bride', and 'The Giant and the Tailor'. He made the
first translation of 'Rapunzel', though he gave the heroine the name Violet,
with the consequent alteration in the type of plant that the pregnant mother
longs for.

John Edward Taylor referred to Edgar Taylor in the introduction to *The
Fairy Ring* as being his kinsman (Taylor, 1846: iv), and he was indeed a
cousin. He was a printer in Little Queen Street, London, and he is credited
in the *British Library Catalogue* with eight other translations over the period
1840–55. Most important in the context of *The Fairy Ring* is the fact that he
translated thirty tales from Basile's *Pentamerone*, first published in 1848, a
couple of years after Felix Liebrecht had made the first German translation.
The Fairy Ring proved popular, a third edition being published in Philadelphia in 1854, while Murray in London produced a new edition in 1857.

At this point in the mid-century new editions began to pour from
various publishing houses. The two Taylors had established the Grimms as
a favourite with the reading public, and it was now possible to produce a
much more comprehensive translation of the KHM. In this the new
two-volume edition entitled *Household Stories*, published by Addey and Co.
in 1853, led the way. Despite the fact that it provided translations of 191
tales and five children's legends and was thus much more wide-ranging
than anything previously attempted, it still found it prudent to omit a
certain number. These were '*Der Schneider im Himmel*', '*Des Teufels russiger
Bruder*', '*Das eigensinnige Kind*', '*Das junggeglühte Männlein*', '*Das Herrn und
des Teufels Getier*', '*Das Bürle im Himmel*', '*Die ungleichen Kinder Evas*', '*Die
Brosamen auf dem Tisch*' and five of the *Kinderlegenden* '*Die zwölf Apostel*',
'*Gottes Speise*', '*Muttergottesgläschen*', '*Die himmlische Hochzeit*', and '*Die
Haselrute*'. They are all religious tales. Yet it was not the religious element as
such that caused any given tale to be excluded, since five children's legends

are incorporated in the translation. It seems to be the element of religious superstition or perceived contravention of Biblical teaching that leads to the omission. The preface in fact states quite baldly: 'The mixture of sacred subjects with profane, though frequent in Germany, would not meet with favour in an English book.'

In 1853 the preface to Addey and Co.'s edition could refer quite simply to KHM as 'a world-renowned book', though it was somewhat prematurely hyperbolic in claiming that 'hundreds of Artists have illustrated' the fairy tales. Their edition contained 240 pictures by Edward H.Wehnert, of which 36 were full-page illustrations. These are agreeable period pieces and typical of the Victorian predilection for sentimentality and reassurance. With the addition of colour-printing they reappeared in later collections of the tales published by George Routledge & Co.

Addey and Co.'s edition was translated from the Grimms' sixth edition of 1850, still not quite the final form of the KHM. Nonetheless, it is so markedly different from the selections of the two Taylors that it is no longer part of the pioneering world that they represent. The first complete translation of the KHM only came with Margaret Hunt in 1884, published by Bohn and with an introduction by the eminent folklorist Andrew Lang. Every few years since then has seen new editions of the Grimms' fairy tales in English. Publishers, translators and especially illustrators have collaborated in presenting the tales afresh to every generation of children. The most remarkable feature in this never-ending enterprise has been the durability of Edgar Taylor's translation, usually, but not always, accompanied by Cruikshank's illustrations. The product of the English Romantic fascination with German folktales and folklore is still with us.

Notes

1. Heinz Rölleke (ed.) (1982) *Brüder Grimm, Kinder- und Hausmärchen; Nach der zweiten vermehrten und verbesserten Auflage von 1819, textkritisch revidiert und mit einer Biographie der Grimmschen Märchen versehen* (pp. 523–4) (2 vols). Köln: Diederichs.
2. [...] indicates points where David Blamires' original article has been edited.
3. Percy Muir (1979) *English Children's Books, 1600–1900* (p. 51). London: Batsford, 1979, 51.
4. *Dictionary of National Biography.*
5. See F.J. Harvey Darton (1958) *Children's Books in England* (pp. 205–6). Cambridge: Cambridge University Press.
6. For a literary-historical and folklore background, see Katharine M. Briggs (1963) The influence of the Brothers Grimm in England. In Gerhard Heilfurth, Ludwig Denecke and Ina-Maria Greverus (eds) *Brüder Grimm Gedenken* (pp. 511–24). Marburg: Elwert.
7. See Harvey Darton (1982) *Children's Books in England*, 90.

8. See Rölleke, KHM: Ausgabe letzter Hand, iii (326–7).
9. *German Popular Stories,* i, 221 (notes).
10.Edgar Taylor (ed.) (1869) *German Popular Stories, with Illustrations after the Original Designs of George Cruikshank.* Introduction by John Ruskin. London: John Camden Hotten.
11.The Osborne Collection. See *The Osborne Collection of Early Children's Books: A Catalogue* (1958–75). Prepared by Judith St John. Toronto: Toronto Public Library, 479.

Karen Seago

Nursery Politics: Sleeping Beauty or the Acculturation of a Tale

The 'classic fairy tales' are still a staple of English childhood and seem to be enjoying a renaissance in recent years, which is all the more remarkable for the fact that perhaps for the first time in the fairy tale's long march into the nursery, surprisingly few doubts are voiced about its suitability as children's literature. Critical attention has also been intense and, unlike the initially hostile reaction of feminist criticism in the seventies, and the somewhat defensive vindication of Bettelheim's (1976) famous *The Uses of Enchantment*, both of which concentrated on the influence that fairy tales exert on their readers, the emphasis has shifted towards an examination of the factors which shaped the tale itself.

Jack Zipes (1979, 1983a, 1983b, 1988) and Marina Warner (1994) have drawn attention to the reality of historical and social conditions portrayed in the tales. Seeing the fairy tale embedded in social context also draws attention to the role it has always played, whether in book format, as a film or orally transmitted. Though the core of the story stays more or less the same, the details change, depending on the expectations of the target audience as they are perceived by its mediator. Rather than being an age-old form, residing in untouched purity in an 'other-world', fairy tales are intensely topical. Disney's independent, intellectual 'Belle' in *Beauty and the Beast* bears witness to this fact, as do James Finn Garner's (1995) cheeky *Politically Correct Bedtime Stories, Modern Tales for Our Life and Times.*

Fairy tales have a message, and this depends on the life and times of the 'authors' and how they see the tale and its function. In this, the fairy tale is didactic and, of course, highly political. However, although there are any number of new translations, adaptations, rewritings and new tales inspired by the old ones, they by no means make up the lion's share of the market. The formulaic opening of the fairy tale, the 'once upon a time', seems to appeal to a yearning for nostalgia, perhaps it is 'the good old times' of another age or of childhood, supposedly portrayed in the tales, which spills over into the choice of books.

Many of our best-known fairy tales are a product of the 19th century; they were translated from French and German sources which had been

175

introduced into England in the 18th and early 19th centuries. In a process of adaptation and assimilation a recognisably English tradition was created, bearing witness to political and social change, but also bound by didactic constraints. Situating the tale in the intersecting field of tensions between individual and national political identity acted out in the nursery, this paper examines how, in the course of the 19th century, the German tale *'Dornröschen'* became *'Sleeping Beauty'*, a 'classic' English fairy tale for children. Before engaging in a detailed analysis of this process, it is necessary to contextualise our understanding of the fairy tale by looking at its historical and political background and the genre's slow evolution as children's literature.

The explicit connection between folk tales and the political has always been apparent: 'The rising nationalisms of the 19th century made much use of folklore to typify and thus create new national identities around new national boundaries' (Fernandez, 1986: 135). One of the most famous fairy tale collections, the German *Kinder- und Hausmärchen* of the Brothers Grimm, grew out of a strong sense of German patriotism in opposition to the political oppression of French occupation. Jakob and Wilhelm Grimm's deliberate 'excavation' of *'that long forgotten literature'* was undertaken in a spirit of resistance and as a means of political change.

Man suchte nicht bloß in der Vergangenheit einen Trost, auch die Hoffnung war natürlich, daß diese Richtung zu der Rückkehr einer anderen Zeit beitragen könne. (Quoted in Seitz, 1984: 123)

(One did not only look for solace in the past, also there was naturally the hope that this direction might contribute to the return of another time.)

In their understanding, the nation state was defined by a shared language and a shared cultural heritage, and in this context the traces of a German literature as found in the songs and tales of the peasants were seen to be essential in the attempt to forge a German national identity.

However, the fairy tales also functioned as a clearly understood means of escaping the realities of life under Napoleonic rule. And it is this escapist role of the fairy tale that Jack Zipes recognised in the English context towards the middle of the 19th century. Although England had a rather more clearly established national identity than many of the other European states, the country was undergoing great changes in the wake of the Industrial Revolution, radically altering the fabric of English society. Writers turned to the fairy tale as a medium to express their discontent with an increasingly alienated society attempting to come to terms with urbanisation, the creation of slums, exploitation and dramatic poverty. For them, fairy tales offered a utopian otherworld in which the effects of industrialisation could be dealt with, and in this they made their contribution to the Condition of England Debate. It is important, though, to keep in mind that this subversive function applies primarily to the authored, literary tale, while the traditional tale, as we shall see, endorsed and actively promoted the establishment values of the middle class.

While this explicitly political role of the fairy tale is obviously important, and particularly so where the German tradition is concerned, I wish to point out the less obvious impression that the political, ideological and socio-economic context has on the translation of a tale:

In each country the tales function differently, and the way they are used and received in each country indicates something about the national character of that country. (Zipes, 1986: 281)

This cultural specificity and the expression of the Zeitgeist shape the content and meaning of a tale not only where conscious adaptations are concerned, but also in the case of translations. The specific time and culture in which a translator works will influence the resulting text, and the prevailing political concerns can be traced in the language used. The acculturation of the tale thus concerns firstly, the process of translation from the German into the English cultural context, and secondly, the reception of the tale in the course of the 19th century as it responds to and engages with a rapidly changing society in a time of social and political upheaval.

Furthermore, the reception of the tale in England was also heavily influenced by its uncertain status as a genre, precariously balanced on the margins of propriety in its proximity to adult ribald jesting on the one hand, and suspect, infantile escapism into the realms of the wonderful on the other. Today, fairy tales are the domain of childhood but this has, of course, not always been so. Traditional tales were orally transmitted, told to a mixed audience of adults and children, often in the work environment of the '*Spinnstube*' (spinning room) in Germany or the '*veillée*' (communal evening) in France. It was only at the end of the 17th century in France, when these peasant tales were taken up by the educated and became fixed in book format that the firm association with the nursery was created. Charles Perrault published the now famous *Contes de ma mere l'oye* (1697), but, as a member of the Académie Française, it appeared to be difficult for him to admit to absolute authorship of such simple tales, however polished their style and sophisticated the irony. So radical was this departure from the learned wit and tortuous elegance of the salons and court that he distanced himself by claiming that the stories were not original creations but had been told to his son by their nurse, and that it was this son who had then recounted them in book format.

It was a double denial then, which identified childhood, for the first time, as the exclusive arena in which the fairy tale's meaning could be constituted, and it took over a century before the tales were indeed established in the nursery. With childhood emerging as a distinct concept, the question of how to educate children increasingly gained importance; as a consequence, the subject of suitably edifying and enlightening reading became a matter of public debate. In England, books for children were characterised by a highly didactic and utilitarian strain, teaching quantifiable and measurable facts about the 'real' world on the one hand, while spiritual needs were subsumed under moral and religious instruction. The imagination and the fanciful were regarded with deep distrust and had, indeed, been suppressed since the 17th century, first by the Puritans for religious reasons, then by Enlightenment thinkers in their efforts to overcome superstitious beliefs with rationality.

Perrault's tales had been translated into English by Robert Samber in 1729 and were so popular that they were available as separate chapbooks throughout the 18th century. These crude editions with their rough woodcut illustrations, however, militated against the tales finding a place in the libraries of the emerging middle class. Despite their beautifully rhymed morals, they were regarded with misgivings by educators intent on socialising children into responsible citizens. This was partly due to the mistrust that all French ways inspired in the English,[1] but even more so to what was perceived as the fairy tales' unorthodox and frivolous subject matter.

As fairy tales were not primarily didactic, did not instil moral values and diverted children from their duties, they were not considered appropriate reading matter for children. The real world contained enough wonders, such as the discoveries in science and technology, to waste time on the study of the wonders of fairyland. As late as 1851, R.H. Horne wrote an article in Dickens' highly influential *Household Words*, severely criticising fairy tales for their cruelty and immorality which seemed to be intentionally aimed at: 'perverting, if not destroying, the generosity, innocence, pure imagination and tender feelings of childhood'. And he goes on to ask:

> will children be interested in this purity – this innocence: Is it not too much like themselves, and do they not crave for more exciting aliment? Do they not delight in horrors, and such things? Not a doubt of it. In like manner, children of a larger growth delight in gin, and take other stimulating things to excess. If a child cries for a nice mixture of poisoned

plums and sweetmeats, are we to give them because of the pleasure they excite at the moment? (Horne, 1851: 70 and 78)

With the conception of domestic ideology, centred around the family which was seen as the core of the nation state, the education of children as future citizens and representatives of the empire became an increasingly political matter in the course of the 19th century. It was a slow process in which the fairy tale became acceptable as an educational tool, struggling to overcome the opprobrious reputation it had acquired and obliged to prove again and again that it was morally sound and taught a valuable lesson:

Wise men are recognising that it is not always wasted labour that is spent on building castles in the air, and that that which stimulates the imagination has its part in education as well as that which stores the mind with hard, prosaic facts, and strengthens the more critical faculties. (Miles, 18: 92, preface to *Fifty-two Fairy Tales*)

Fairies were introduced, around the turn of the century, in entirely moral stories as personifications of the virtues and vices which it was the story's express intention to demonstrate and teach. Although they prepared the ground for a more receptive atmosphere in which 'real' fairy stories could be presented as children's literature, these still had to be adapted to conform to moral principles. It is in the resulting censorship of the content and format of fairy tales, that they acquire the clear didactic dimension for which they have been criticised in the second half of this century. In becoming the carriers of morals, fairy tales also become an expression of the dominant modes of conduct and in this, too, they are intimately linked with politics.

The following analysis takes account of conscious changes which are introduced for didactic and moral reasons to make '*Sleeping Beauty*' acceptable as children's literature, but concentrates on the unconscious shifts in meaning as an expression of the social and political environment which has shaped the translator. Rather than looking in detail at any one translation, I am presenting an overview of consistent trends that have emerged out of the close examination of thirteen translations of the Grimms' '*Dornröschen*' published between 1823 and 1888.

The tale is generally known today as *Sleeping Beauty*, partly, no doubt, a reaction to its name *Dornröschen* (*Little Thornrose*) which is poetic in the German but difficult to render elegantly in English. However, the fact that this title, which is an abbreviated version of Perrault's *Sleeping Beauty in the Woods*, established itself, points to one of the most important features of the tale's reception in England, namely the way in which the two very different traditions from the French and German background are merged as the century progresses.

Briefly, the main points where the German and the French diverge are as follows: the German tale emphasises its close links with Nordic myth in its insistence on a timeless unfolding of fate, which is dealt, not by fairies but by wise women – recognisably the Norns of Nordic mythology. It stresses its peasant origins by adopting a simple narrative voice and structure and its world-view is characterised by a strong sense of oneness with nature. This is particularly apparent in the opening scene of the story, where the barren queen receives the prophecy of her pregnancy from a frog while bathing in a pond. Because of a lack of golden plates, only twelve of the thirteen wise women are invited to the celebration of the birth of the child. The curse of death by the uninvited thirteenth fairy is mitigated to a simple 100-year sleep, which extends to all the inhabitants of the castle, including the king and queen when the curse is fulfilled. A thorny hedge grows up and in their attempts to penetrate this, a number of princes die, impaled on its resisting thorns. At the approach of the last prince, however, the hedge turns into flowers, and he wakes the princess with a kiss.

The French tale, on the other hand, is a polished and ironic story, robustly contemporary, pragmatically Christian and firmly anchored in the fashionable aristocratic environment of the late 17th century. In their attempt to overcome their barrenness, the royal couple take the waters at fashionable spas, and when the child is born, six fairies are invited as powerful patron godmothers to the christening ceremony. The neglected invitation to the seventh fairy is an oversight, partly due to her unsociable withdrawal from society, and to some extent, she curses the child because she is old and spiteful. The youngest fairy's mitigation clearly states that the princess will be awakened by a prince, which may explain why the king goes to great trouble to have her displayed in an advantageous manner when the curse is fulfilled. Called by a dwarf in seven-league boots, the good fairy arrives in a chariot drawn by dragons, and approving the king's arrangements, it is she who puts the castle to sleep and causes the tangled woods to grow. The king and queen are not included in the sleep, their removal from the scene necessary for the sequel to the story, usually omitted in editions aimed at children. When the right prince arrives, the overgrown woods open up for him, excluding his retinue. Overcome by adoration, he sinks to his knees in front of the princess who wakes up because the time has come for her to do so. Their marriage is kept secret from the prince's parents out of his fear of his mother's cannibalistic urges. When the old king dies, the prince brings his wife and two children to court, entrusting them to his mother while away in battle. The old queen duly persecutes the young family, ordering the butler to cook first the children and then their mother. This cannibalism is, however, thwarted by the butler by serving animals instead, and when the old queen finds out, she prepares a gruesome death for all involved. However, it is she who ends up in the vat of vipers, since the prince arrives at the last moment to save his family.

It is interesting to see which motifs were chosen from the French and which ones from the German as appropriate for the emerging English tradition. While the French is essentially a Romantic tale of courtship which centres on the prince and princess outside the context of the family, with the curse and one-hundred year sleep as necessary tragic obstacles to be overcome before consummation, the German tale revolves much more around the patriarchal family. The position of the paterfamilias and his caring relationship with his dependents both as father and as king play a central role. The princess sleeps embedded in a familial context and her protection against any unsuitable husbands, successors to her father's role as guardian, is foregrounded in the episodes of the unsuccessful princes who die impaled on the thorns of the hedge surrounding the castle. It is also this protective environment which allows the prince to waken the princess with a kiss, an overtly sexual gesture, which the French, with its barely suppressed erotic subtext, is careful to avoid.

The English tale takes over the element of romantic courtship by strengthening those motifs which deal with the creation, manifestation and the removal of the obstacle to love (curse and disenchantment) but preserves the pronounced family interest of the German tale by keeping the parents in the castle. Retaining the strong protection against unapproved romantic interests and containing the sexual safely within the confines of marriage and parental supervision, it is able to foreground the erotic and retain the kiss. In addition, the English versions prefer the more bourgeois setting of the German where the king cannot afford enough golden plates to invite all the wise women in the country, and where the queen does not indulge in fashionable trips to spas in order to overcome her barrenness. In the English tale's firm allegiance with middle class values of economy and moderation, there is a hint here of bourgeois disapproval of the aristocracy's sexual and financial excesses (Weeks, 1990).

The clear separation of good and evil fairies and the explicit link between evil and old age, however, is an element that is taken over from the French from 1839 onwards and becomes ever more clearly established as the century progresses. As the witch emerges as an increasingly powerful figure, so the good fairies lose in stature and are often portrayed in a way that ridicules them. In his revised edition of 1839, Edgar Taylor, for example, has them dressed in ridiculous clothes while an anonymous edition in 1872, illustrated beautifully by Doré, shows the fairies quarrelling like silly children (or indeed, silly women) over the invitation to court. While the fairies in the German are mythically impartial 'wise women', a repository of knowledge and powerful magic outside human considerations of good and evil, in the English they are clearly divided into the good and bad woman.

With the good fairies diminished and humanized, and the witch growing in threatening and evil control, the clear message in the English versions is that power invested in a woman is sinister, unnatural and therefore cannot be other than wrong and evil. This is particularly so when the woman is a spinster, threatening with her ambiguous status the social roles available within the domestic ideal of the bourgeois family. Neither a wife nor mother, she cannot be a good woman, nor does she fit into the role of the fallen woman, since she is a virgin (or a widow). From 1839 the English versions develop the connection between the evil fairy and the spinster, and by 1872 the identity of the old woman, spinning in the tower, is explicitly that of the witch. This feature is not present in either the French or the German tradition and may give an indication of the unease felt about the high percentage of unmarried women established by the 1851 census.[2] How keenly the existence of great numbers of 'superfluous', single women was considered to be a threat to the social order can be seen both in the vigorous public debate of the 'Woman Question', and the vicious treatment they were subjected to in the Music Hall and other outlets of popular culture.

Similarly, contemporary concerns, intent on upholding respectability specific to the cultural context, seem to have shaped the representation of the queen. Where the German queen's bathing signifies her mythical identification with nature, the English tale rejects this as a possible indication of lower class habits. Nude, mixed sex, bathing in rivers and the sea was a common practice, shared by working class men and women, and in 1857, the Marquis of Westmeath attempted and failed to introduce a bill into Parliament barring women from the practice.[3] Furthermore, drowning was understood to be the inevitable outcome to prostitution, which in itself was often seen as the result of adultery, and as the queen receives news of her pregnancy from an animal sharing the bath with her, uncomfortable overtones must have been raised by this conflation of a number of signs all indicating the queen's possible sexual deviancy. And as if this were not enough, in the original German version on which the first translation of the tale by Taylor was based, the animal was a crab, awkwardly similar to 'crabs', a term widely used to denote sexual disease, which in itself was considered a certain sign of promiscuity. So, although the motif of the prophecy is retained, the queen is rarely shown to be bathing but takes a walk to receive the news from a little innocuous fish or even from a fairy who comes to court.

In addition, none of the English versions show the German tale's time-lessness and mythic detachment but evoke a sense of the contemporary, of existing in the here and now of the reader. They involve the reader by dramatising the action and creating a strong sense of suspense. This is further strengthened by addressing the reader directly. Where the German describes the quiet in the sleeping castle impersonally, creating distance, the English invites the reader to participate in the story by identifying with the prince's experience: 'he could hear every breath he drew' (Taylor, 1823) or 'he almost heard the beatings of his own heart' (Gillies, 1855) are two examples. This focus on the prince and what he feels also means that the omniscient perspective of the German is abandoned, primarily in the second half of the story, in favour of a subjective perception of events through the eyes of the prince.

This introduction of the male point of view, and in particular, the young male's point of view, as the dominant voice goes hand in hand with the overall perspective that is introduced into the stories. They are told from the position of power invested in the male, with all other positions seen in relation to the masculine and defined as its Other, which needs to be controlled and is regarded with suspicion. The issue of social control and strong mistrust of the lower classes appears again and again in upstairs–downstairs scenarios where servants are portrayed as lazy, untrustworthy, stealing food and drink, and with lax sexual mores. In some stories this serves as a comic interlude, for example in H.W. Dulcken's 1869 *Sleeping Beauty*, the main intention of which seems to be to describe the various misdemeanours of the servants who are caught in the act at the moment that sleep overcomes them and displays them in their shame. These descriptions, however, serve to reinforce generally held ideas about clearly distinguished class boundaries, in which middle-class identity established itself around the domestic ideal and evangelical virtues in opposition to the other classes.

> The moral decay of the working class was seen above all in terms of its deficient pattern of family life, the apparently absent values of domes-ticity, family responsibility, thrift and accumulation ... [their] sexual rampancy and immorality. (Weeks, 1990, 32–3)

A more disturbing perception of the people as a threat to the authorities emerges in many stories where the king's command to destroy all spindles has to be explicitly enforced by the introduction of officers supervising the burning. In Dulcken's translation of 1869, the death penalty is introduced as a punishment for disobeying the order and in the 1872 version illustrated by Gustave Doré the suppressed anxieties are made explicit: the order (again on pain of death) to destroy the spindles causes riots. The introduction of machine looms, a concentration of work in the mills and the attendant reduction of outwork in the home provides a context in which the destruction of the spindles has risen above being a fairy tale metaphor and has become a social comment in its description of the sequence of industrialisation and its effect on the workforce.

Similarly, in many stories it is the neglect of servants that causes the fulfilment of the curse. In1855 (Gillies), for example, the parents have left their daughter in the care of the servants who are incapable of exercising the necessary control to keep the girl from harm. Twenty years later, antagonistic class positions have become entrenched and the king's trust is betrayed by servants who actively disobey his orders. While this escalation of mistrust may be seen to reflect the fears of the adherents of the old order around the extension of democratic power to wider sectors of the population in the wake of the Second Reform Bill of 1867, it is also clear that the role and function of the family both as a constituent element of the state, and as a mainstay of individual control against increasing state intervention, are at issue.

It is evident that the English versions have a problem with the description of neglectful parents; practically without exception they alter the circumstances in which the king and queen are absent on the fateful day and can be held responsible for the fulfilment of the curse. This concern can be so pressing that the actual content of the story is changed; in an 1859 version (*The Home Treasury*), the birthday passes and it is only afterwards that the parents leave their child alone, hoping that the danger is over. In other stories they are unavailable because of matters of state, their duties in the public domain overriding all responsibilities in the private and excusing the parental omission. With the introduction of a number of important Acts throughout the 19th century, the role of a centralised state in relation to areas that traditionally had been privately regulated remained an area of discussion. By overriding parents' rights to decide on their children's education in enforcing attendance at elementary schools, the Education Act of 1870 contributed to latent resentment against the state intruding into the individual's sphere (Weeks, 1990). It is hardly surprising then that a motif hinting at parental irresponsibility and neglect is so consistently changed in a story aimed at children and thus situated at the precise site of contested authority.

The exoneration of the parents goes hand in hand with another trend that is also present in the German editions but is expressed even more clearly in the English. It is the representation of the king as blameless, fully in control and discharging his duties without fault. While in the early German versions, neglecting to invite the thirteenth wise woman to the celebrations was presented in such a way that it was clearly the king's responsibility, in English versions the decision to leave out one fairy is either forced on him as an impersonal, that is, state obligation, or it is determined by the queen. Taylor's second, revised edition, for example, has the queen insist that the fairies be invited as well, and in an edition of the seventies she is approached to intercede with the king for an invitation. What emerges is a startlingly clear picture of a middle-class identity, based on the central axiom of separate spheres of action for men and women. 'Class coherence was established through the formation of shared notions of morality and respectability – domestic ideology and the production of clearly demarcated gender roles were central features' (Nead, 1990: 5).

The king occupies the role of paterfamilias, he is the site of authority and objectivity and is governed by rational factors, while the queen represents the gentler emotions and is perceived as a softening influence. In line with these gendered expectations, the English tale's representation of the masculine consistently stresses the king's control over his emotions where the German shows him overcome by his feelings at the birth of his daughter to the point that he does not know what to do. This loss of rational faculties is further balanced in the English by accentuating the authority he exerts over others, giving orders or commands where the German king organises the celebration himself.

In addition, the English texts take care to present the emotional attachment which the father feels for his daughter as not exceeding what is right and proper. Several versions stress that his precautions, which in the German become more and more loaded with feeling, are only 'natural'. This distancing can go so far that the king's reaction to the threat is entirely logical and controlled. Rather than ordering precautions immediately after the curse, the king in Mrs. H.B. Paull's 1872 version waits 15 years until the dangerous time draws near, and only then arranges for suitable measures to be taken. While this insistence on appropriate emotional restraint is a further facet in the construction of the king's manliness and self-reliance, the urgent need to stress that the father's love for his daughter is natural could also be seem to indicate the opposite, an excessive, unnatural love. Incest was an issue that was emerging as one of great social concern in the second half of the 19th century,[4] but it was the incest of the working classes, perceived to be an almost inevitable result of overcrowding in slum tenements, which was seem as the problem.

As Jeffrey Weeks observes, this perception of widespread lower class perversion should probably be seen more as an expression of middle-class tensions and anxieties about sexuality and the sanctity of the family rather than as a reflection of the actual incidence of incest (Weeks, 1990: 31). Certainly, the princess is persistently portrayed in a sexualised way contrasting strongly with the innocent childish girl that the German insists on.[5] The father's reaction to his newborn daughter's beauty prefigures the prince's possessive gaze. A sense of male helplessness in the face of female beauty applies to father and suitor who both lose (or fear to lose) control of their senses. Indeed, in three versions in 1869 and 1872, the text states explicitly that the princess's beauty is so great that the prince cannot resist it but must give in to his urges and kiss her, as 'ninety-nine out of a hundred young men would have done' (Dulcken, 1869).

This quotation from Dr Dulcken's 1869 version demonstrates particularly clearly the 19th-century understanding of male sexuality as a forceful drive which cannot be denied and the attendant move towards naturalising its aggressive components as part of a healthy, thrusting virility. Since male passion could not be controlled, a safe outlet had to be found for it outside the middle-class family whose respectability rested on the construction of the desexualised, chaste wife and daughter. In this sense, prostitution, though described as a social evil, was also seen as a necessity, and the prostitute became, paradoxically, the guardian of the patriarchal family. While the double standard apparently allowed men to have their cake and eat it as well, the obverse of this ideology of male sexual needs must have created in men a sense of dependency, of being out of control and consequently at the mercy of the prostitute specifically and women in general.

This spills over into the story in the way that the princess is described from the fifties onwards. In one version, she exerts an irresistible pull on the prince, who at the same time is also quite repelled by her, but this is the only story where the push–pull of sexual attraction is so clearly spelled out. Generally, the princess, though portrayed as a passive victim, is shown to be irresponsibly giddy, in need of supervision and as a flirt in order to counteract and explain this compulsive sexual allure that undercuts the active self-determination and the increasingly forceful character of the prince. In 1855, Matilda Louisa Davis has her pretend to be asleep so as to be kissed awake, and in line with this element of dangerous coquetry, reminiscent of the 'girl of the period' (Nead, 1990: 179–88) paternal guidance and direction is increased.

Reflecting the move towards state regulation of marriage in the second half of the century, all versions from 1855 onwards show increasing detail around the courtship and marriage motif, with the king consenting to the match or even giving his daughter as a reward for the disenchantment.

There is an increased observance of the formalities: several stories explicitly state that there are no causes preventing the union. This may partly be a throwback to the French tradition, which insistently declares that the prince is from another ruling family, but it may also express tensions caused by the necessity of ensuring an appropriate alliance. These apprehensions surface very clearly in Mrs H.B. Paull's 1872 version which re-writes the episode of the unsuccessful princes in such a way that only those who persist in attempting to overcome the obstacle of the thorny hedge die. While this serves to tone down the violence in the tale, a persistent trend due to didactic considerations of making the tale suitable for children, it also highlights an awareness of the need for rigorously protecting the daughter of a respectable family from undesirable attention.

A similar awareness of dynastic exigencies is articulated in expansions of the opening motif of the story, again in the versions of the latter half of the century. The royal couple's long expressed wish for a child is embedded in tense contemplation of who would inherit their possessions and the crown if they were to die without issue. While these additions are obviously related to bourgeois preoccupations with property as an indication of status, they also play on subconscious fears around the identity of the middle class and its preservation as a group. Uncertainly sandwiched between the aristocracy on the one hand and the lower orders on the other, the middle class strove to establish and maintain its status as a separate category. And in this context the 'underbreeding' of the respectable, which is always seen in relation to the 'overbreeding' of the poor, expresses anxieties of being invaded from below. Translated into Malthusian terms, these versions give an indication of the hysteria over what was perceived as the hyperbreeding of the working class on the one hand, and the infertility of the dominant class on the other (Weeks, 1990: 19, 122–5). Considering the on-going debate about over-population, the anxieties that are expressed are presumably aimed at the consequences of the educated classes putting into practice the increasingly freely available advice on birth control leading to a stagnation in their birth rate, while the unchecked fertility of the working class would lead to an imbalance in the representation of the social classes in the population overall.

The fascination which the Sleeping Beauty exerted on the 19th century imagination is evident in the exceptional success of an animated waxwork of the fairy tale princess in Madame Tussaud's exhibition in 1851. The figure of the prone woman, on display like an objet d'art, patiently waiting to be energised by the stimulating presence of (the right) man could be seen as the iconic representation of Victorian womanhood (Auerbach, 1982: 34 and 41–3). Put to sleep at the first hint of awakening sexuality she is the ultimate good woman, firmly protected from straying off the path of chastity and locked in innocence both in body and in mind. She is the personification of the child-bride of the period. With a separation of the private from the public sphere, enforced by the practically impenetrable barrier of the hedge of thorns, and the deferred gratification of a 100-year sleep, her story embodies to perfection the values central to the emerging middle-class. The construction of the patriarchal family and the representation of the masculine and feminine are an illustration of the concept of respectability and the double standard. The less striking examples of self-help, self-reliance, hard work and thrift, are also features which the tale in its process of assimilation into the English context in the course of the 19th century develops in a highly gender and class specific way. Thus the tale actively participates in and contributes to the articulation of domestic ideology, but, as we have seen, in its gaps, protestations and tensions the story also bears witness to the anxieties produced by a class uncertain of its boundaries and based on an ideology of separation.

Translations of the Grimms' 'Dornröschen'

1823 Edgar Taylor, *German Popular Stories*, Collected by M.M. Grimm from Oral Tradition. London: C. Baldwyn.

1839 Edgar Taylor, *German Popular Stories and Fairy Tales as told by Gammer Grethel.* London: George Bell & Sons.

1853 Edward Wehnert, *Household Stories*, Collected by the Brothers Grimm, Newly translated. London: Addey & Co.

1855 Matilda Louisa Davis, *Home Stories:* Collected by the Brothers Grimm, Newly translated. London: Routledge & Co.

1855 Robert Pierce Gillies, *German Stories: Being Tales and Traditions Chiefly Selected from the Literature of Germany.* Edinburgh: Fullerton & Co. This Gillies version must be assumed to be a translation by G.G. Cunningham. Cunningham had published – in 1828 – a two-volume edition of literary and traditional tales and legends that contained five Grimm stories, among them 'Thornrose' (*Dornröschen*), in the second volume. This second volume was re-printed anonymously in 1855 as *German Stories: Being Tales and Traditions chiefly selected from the Literature of Germany*, a title which is very similar to Robert Pearse Gillies's *German Stories: Selected from the Works of Hoffmann, de la Motte Fouque, Pichler, Kruse,* published in 1826 in three volumes. Because of this similarity in titles, the anonymous 1855 edition has long been attributed to Gillies. However, the texts in the anonymous German Stories (1855) are identical with those in Cunningham's edition and must therefore be assumed to be his.

1859 *The Home Treasury of Old Story Books*. London: n.p.

1869   H.W. Dulcken Phd, The Child's Popular Fairy Tales, told for the hundredth time. London: Ward, Lock & Tyler.

1872? (n.d.) Mrs H.B. Paull, *Grimms' Fairy Tales*, A New Translation. London: Warne. (anonymous) *Fairy Tales told again, by the author of 'Little Red Shoes', ill. by Gustave Doré*. London, Paris and New York: Cassell, Petter & Galpin.

1878   Anon., *Grimms Tales, Selected and Translated for use in Schools*, Bells Reading Books. London: George Bell & Sons.

1882   Lucy Crane, *Household Stories*, from the Collection of the Bros. Grimm. London: Macmillan & Co.

1884   Margaret Hunt, *Grimm's Household Tales*. London: Bell.

1888   Alfonzo Gardiner, *Household Tales*, John Heywood's Literary Readers. Manchester: John Heywood.

Notes

1. 'French society was regarded as unstable and dangerous, its literature was believed to be a source of corruption and immorality, and many contemporaries were concerned about the harmful reverberations of French morality in England', Lynda Nead (1990) *Myths of Sexuality* (p. 73). Oxford: Blackwell.
2. According to Joan Perkins (1989), it was found in the census that 30% of women between the ages of 20 and 40 were unmarried. She also points out that as many men were unmarried without giving rise to concern over their status (Perkins, 1989: 226)
3. Perkins (1989: 141)
4. Awareness of incest was growing, although legally it was not recognised as an offence in England before the 1857 Matrimonial Causes Act, which cited it as one of the grounds for divorce, and it was as late as 1908 that it became a criminal offence.
5. Although the early German editions recognise the mature princess, referring to her as *'das Fräulein'*, the title appropriate to her age and status, later versions revert to the childish application of 'girl' at age 15. Furthermore, Wilhelm Grimm's instructions to his brother Emil, who was doing the illustrations, clearly demand that he portray her in a much more childlike way, although the draft drawing has her sleeping like a small child, curled up on a couch with not a hint of sexual maturity about her.

Nancy K. Jentsch

Harry Potter and the Tower of Babel: Translating the Magic

Since their appearance in 1997, the Harry Potter books in English have spread their charms to readers across the globe. It follows that persons not able to understand the original English version make up a large enough market for publishers to consider producing translations. In fact, according to the *Christian Science Monitor* of July 6, 2000, J.K. Rowling's Harry Potter books have been translated into 40 languages. The stage and state of Pottermania, though, vary greatly by country. Whereas German readers counted the days until the publication of the fourth book on October 14, 2000, and could already order book five as early as August 2000, readers in the People's Republic of China were not officially introduced to the young sorcerer until October 12, 2000. Thailand welcomed the first Harry Potter book in its native language in July 2000, and the Czech Republic awaited the printing of the second book in Czech in fall 2000.

Each translator involved with these books has been faced with the normal challenges of the occupation, but also with a number of unique situations. For example, the Harry Potter series contains many words newly coined for the books by their author. Though this is not uncommon in children's fantasy literature, translating such words does present unusual difficulties. Elizabeth Devereux is reported to have said that the Harry Potter books in general are easier to translate than other children's literature that is much more concerned with language, such as Lewis Carroll's *Alice's Adventures in Wonderland*.[1] I would argue, nonetheless, that the translator of the Harry Potter series has a unique challenge in the genre, that is, to portray a setting and its people that are a world apart from ours, and at the same time located due north of London. This prompted Hilal Sezgin of the *Frankfurter Rundschau* to write:

> *Manche zählen Harry Potter nicht zum Abenteuer-sondern zum Fantasy-Roman. Doch Rowling erzählt nicht von Trollen und Elfen, die in einem fernen Gebirge umherziehen, nicht von Helden, die nie gelebt haben und nie leben werden. Harry Potters Welt ist eine Welt mitten in der unseren, der der Muggel, im Modus des Was wäre wenn ...*

(Some say Harry Potter is not of the adventure genre, but rather the fantasy genre. But Rowling doesn't tell a tale of trolls and elves that come and go in faraway mountains, or a tale of heroes who have never lived and never will. Harry Potter's world is a world within our own, our Muggle world, in the manner of 'What if ...')[2]

This juxtaposition of magical and Muggle worlds is integral to the original text and must be a serious consideration to its translators. The translator thus has to decide not only how to translate, but when to translate and when to leave words in the original. Certainly, names readily understood by the target audience and those that have no further significance can and should be left in the original. After all, English names for people and places can help create the sense of place, integral to a novel whose setting is in large part a boarding school in Britain. Further, it is obvious that J.K. Rowling chooses her characters' names carefully. They often have a meaning, be it in French, the language and literature she studied at the University of Exeter, or otherwise. Malfoy (bad faith), Voldemort (flight from death) and Sirius (the Dog Star) are examples of this. The decision of how much should be left in the original language, and how to translate such significant words (when necessary to promote these meanings) is a subjective one, but also one that will affect the overall success of the translation.

A further challenge to the translator of these works is one that occurs any time an English text is translated into a language that has more than one form of the word 'you'. The translation should appropriately render the universal 'you' of English to specific forms, which in the target language not only denote the relationship of the speakers to each other but also contribute to the readers' sense of characterization. Other more general issues for translators involve the translation of word plays and the age-old dichotomy between faithfulness and freedom in translation.

Publishers in France, Germany and Spain had come out with the first three books in the series in translation by April 2000, and these volumes are the subject of this study. The French translator of the Harry Potter books is Jean-François Ménard, who was the favourite translator of Roald Dahl. The publisher, Gallimard Jeunesse, changed the title of the first book to *Harry Potter à l'école des sorciers (Harry Potter at the Sorcerers' School)*, but the succeeding books retain titles that are translations of the originals. By July 2000, 580,000 copies of the first three books had been sold in France, with the publication date of the fourth book in the series publicized as November 29, 2000. Carlsen Verlag in Hamburg, Germany, publishes Klaus Fritz's translation of the works. The title of the first book in German mirrors the British title, *The Philosopher's Stone,*[3] the German equivalent of which is

Der Stein der Weisen, but the second book's title, *Harry Potter und die Kammer des Schreckens (Harry Potter and the Chamber of Terror),* deviates from the original, though it certainly accurately describes the chamber in question. As of August 10, 2000, *Der Spiegel* reported that 2.3 million copies of the first three books in the Harry Potter series had been sold in Germany. Earlier it had been reported that Harry Potter books had topped *Der Spiegel's* list of best-selling books for most of the year, and, according to the publisher's website at http://www.carlsen-harrypotter.de, those top billings lasted into 2002. The first edition of book four, which came out on October 14, 2000, was originally set for 350,000 copies, but in September 2000 *Der Spiegel* reported that the first printing of that book, which had already been available for sale and in German libraries in English, would be a record one million. Alicia Dellepiano translated the Spanish version of the first book in the series (and the only Spanish translation quoted in this essay) for the Emecé Editores in Barcelona, which maintained direct translations of the first three titles. The first two books in the series had sold 120,000 copies by June 2000, and Emecé's branch in Argentina reported light sales, amounting to fewer than 40,000 copies of the first two books sold by May 2000. (Book three was not published until April 2000, but was in its sixth edition by October 2000.) Despite relatively low numbers, Emecé reported that book four was scheduled to appear in March or April of 2001. In comparison, according to *AP Worldstream,* 30,000 copies of the Thai translation of book one were sold within two weeks of its appearance, bringing it quickly to first place on at least one bestsellers' list.[4]

At more than three million copies, the French, Spanish, and German translations of the Harry Potter books combined represent a good 10% of sales of the first three books of the series, which was estimated at 30 million in July 2000.[5] These three translations offer an opportunity to examine the choices translators face and make and the influence their solutions have on such elements as character development, the sense of place, and, in the end, on the relative merit and success of the translation as a whole. While translators of any work face many common challenges and the Harry Potter books present peculiarities such as the presentation of a magical place not far removed from reality and the use of many newly coined but contextually significant terms, it is also unusual to have many translations published soon after the appearance of the original. The situation lends itself well to a comparative study of the translator's art.

The relationships among characters are important aspects of their portrayal and development. One way to determine this relationship is to look at how the characters address one another. French, German and Spanish share with many other European languages the use of two or more forms for the word 'you'. Distinctions are thus made between formal and informal relationships as well as between words addressed to either one or more than one person. Since these differentiations are lacking in the original English text, translators must make their own decisions about the use of words such as *'du'*, *'Sie'*, *'tú'*, *'tu'*, *'usted'*, *'ustedes'*, *'vosotros'*, and *'vous'*, and all their related forms.

The pupils at Hogwarts would all very naturally use the informal forms when conversing among themselves, and all three translators have consistently employed these forms in such situations. In none of the books does a student use the informal form of 'you' with a teacher, save in the case of Hagrid. In the Spanish version of the book, Harry's special relationship with Hagrid is marked by his use of the informal *'tú'* with the gigantic gamekeeper beginning in the fifth chapter of book one of the series, after originally addressing the giant Keeper of the Keys with *'usted'*. He is soon joined by his friends Ron and Hermione. In the German books, these four characters also share an unambiguous friendship, marked by their use of the informal form of 'you' with one another. Their relationship in the French version is not set so much apart from those of other adults with pupils; while Hagrid uses the informal form with the three central characters, they address him with the formal *'vous'*. Gilderoy Lockhart, for example, as he tries to make Harry his ally, also uses the informal *'tu'* with him. His motivation for this is obviously quite different from that of Hagrid, a true friend, yet because of the parallel uses of the forms, that difference is masked. Furthermore, elsewhere in the French books this same degree of relationship, where the adult uses the informal *'tu'* and Harry addresses the adult with *'vous'*, exists between Harry and Cornelius Fudge and Harry and Mr Weasley. In the German and Spanish books, on the other hand, the closeness of Hagrid's relationship with the three friends is unique. The subtlety of the difference between formal and informal address and what it has to say about the state of a relationship can be apparent only in a translation into a language with more than one form of address, and the Spanish and German versions have been successful in conveying the specialness of this particular mixed-age clique.

Whenever Harry Potter visits the Leaky Cauldron, he is treated with deference by the bartender/landlord Tom, and with awe by the pub guests. In the original English, this is signalled by Harry's being addressed as Mr Potter, even at the age of eleven. The French translator takes the cue well and has Tom not only call Harry 'Mr Potter' but also use the formal *'vous'* with him. This is in contrast to the adults who use the informal *'tu'* when addressing Harry. In addition, the level of language used by Tom in the French version is one of distinct formality. The German translation is identical in style and mechanics to the French, with 'Mr Potter' being addressed formally as *'Sie'*, despite his age, and the unmistakable formality of Tom's words, *'Würden Sie mir bitte folgen'* (would you please follow me) and *'Wenn Sie irgendetwas brauchen, Mr Potter, zögern sie nicht zu fragen'* (If you need anything at all, don't hesitate to ask) (*Harry Potter und der Gefangene von Askaban*, 52–53). In contrast, the Spanish translation fails to give its readers an idea of the impression Harry's appearance at the Leaky Cauldron makes on its owners and customers. Here, Harry is addressed by all with the informal *'tú'* and with all the 'Mr Potters' of the original becoming 'Harrys'. The French version of Tom's original words of welcome to Harry in book one are, *'Soyez le bienvenu, Mr Potter. Bienvenue parmi nous.'* (Be most welcome, Mr Potter, welcome in our midst) (*Harry Potter à l'école des sorciers*, 80). In comparison, the Spanish *'Bienvenido, Harry, bienvenido'* (welcome, Harry, welcome) (*Harry Potter y la piedra filosofal*, 64) certainly fails to alert the reader to the respect of the magical public for the young boy who has loosed them from the grip of the evil Lord Voldemort.

In the German versions of the Harry Potter books, there is unfortunately much inconsistency in the forms of address used by teachers to pupils. This detracts from the translation, as the reader continually wonders if he or she has missed some important relational shift. For example, Professor McGonagall uses the formal form of address with students, while Professor Flitwick uses the informal *'du'*. Common practice in German schools indicates that the informal form is used by teachers with their students until approximately the age of fifteen. In *Harry Potter und der Gefangene von Askaban* (178–79), there is a passage where Professor Snape uses the informal form with a female student, the informal form with Harry, and then the formal form with the entire class, all within one page of text, illustrating well the inconsistencies found throughout the book.

One very poignant moment occurs in book three of the German series, where Harry realises at last that Sirius Black is his friend and not the arch-enemy he had thought him to be. Black asks Harry if he might want to live with him once he is cleared of charges, and Harry responds, using the familiar form for the first time with the man he had been living in terror of for so long. '"Are you insane?" said Harry, his voice easily as croaky as Black's. "Of course I want to leave the Dursleys! Have you got a house? When can I move in?"' (*Prisoner of Azkaban*, 379). In German it appears as *'"Du bist wohl verrückt," sagte Harry und seine Stimme krächzte längst genauso wie die von Black. "Natürlich will ich von den Dursleys weg! Hast Du ein Haus? Wann Kann ich einziehen?"'* (*Gefangene von Askaban*, 392). The bond thus formed between Harry and Black remains constant, and the two consistently use *'du'* with one another from then on.

Voldemort's nickname, 'You-Know-Who', was treated as an unchangeable formal form by the German translator, becoming *'Du-weisst-schon -wer'*, the *'wer'* (who) being declined as necessary by the grammatical context. The *'schon'* in this translation is an emphatic particle, typical of the German language, which indicates that the speaker does expect the person addressed to be fully aware of who is being talked about. The French and Spanish translators switch from formal to informal forms, as appropriate in the context. For example, Professors McGonagall and Dumbledore discuss *'Quien-usted-sabe'* at the beginning of the Spanish book one, but in chapter 4 of the same book, Hagrid says, *'Quien-tú-sabes los mató'* (You-Know -Who-killed them) as he explains Harry's parents' death to him (*Piedra filosofal*, 53).

In addition to forms of address, the level of language that is used in dialogue is an important aspect of characterization. In the Harry Potter books, for example, one of the most interesting and well-drawn figures is Hagrid, the gamekeeper and sometime teacher at Hogwarts. He has a mysterious past that is revealed to the reader in increments, but his rough exterior and softhearted interior are what make him most appealing. An important part of this rough exterior is his manner of speech, which is consistent with his wild clothing and ungroomed appearance. He speaks in an undistinguishable accent that, by seeming uncouth, belies the emotional and good-hearted man that he is. Unfortunately, none of the translators in this study has chosen to render his speech with anything but normal vocabulary and syntax. Perhaps the translators were concerned that using a particular dialect for the character of Hagrid would be demeaning to the speakers of that dialect, as Hagrid's speech is obviously that of a less-educated and uncultured person. In the interest of character development and also of playfulness, though, the translators surely could have come up with an inoffensive solution.

As discussed by Philip Nel in *J.K. Rowling's Harry Potter Novels*, class issues play a significant role in the novels (2001a: 43). A skilled translator can portray the important aspect of social class by level of language. The German translator, though hesitant to modify Hagrid's language, demonstrates his ability to do this in book three, where Harry boards the Knight bus and is greeted by its driver and conductor in very standard and convincing German colloquial speech. Here, *'Wen suchst du denn?'* (who are you looking for?) becomes *'Wen suchste denn?'* and *'Und jetzt ist er raus'* (Now he's out) is rendered as *'Und jetzt isser raus'* (*Gefangene von Askaban*, 39, 45). These modifications of standard language do not belong to a single dialect area in Germany, but they do imply a certain social milieu. Surely the translator could similarly modify Hagrid's lines to show the gruffness of his speech without offending anyone in Germany.

In the French version, the translator shows an occasional use of colloquial language, but not in the context of Hagrid's speech. The driver and conductor of the Knight bus let go of an occasional 'Ouais' (yeah) and Fred Weasley leaves off an occasional *'ne'* as in *'T'inquiète pas'* (Don't worry), which in written French should read *'Ne t'inquiète pas.'* Convincing modifications of speech are Harry's words *'Qu'essquiya?'* (What's going on?) (*Harry Potter et la Chambre des Secrets*, 117) when woken abruptly by Oliver Wood, which corresponds to *'Qu'est-ce qu'il ya?'* in written language. Similarly, the translator renders the gnome's scream 'Geroff me! Geroff me!' (*Chamber of Secrets*, 37) in book two as *'Fishmoilapaix! Fishmoilapaix!'* (Leave me be! Leave me be!) (*Chambre des Secrets*, 44). In written French this should read *'Fiche-moi la paix! Fiche-moi la paix!'* Similarly, the speech of Hagrid could be written as spoken language, for example using *'jensérien'* (I don't know anything) for *'je ne sais rien'* or *'tuveupas'* (you don't want) for *'tu ne veux pas.'*

The Spanish translator limits Hagrid's colloquial speech to an occasional *'buen día'* (Hello) instead of *'buenos días'.* Otherwise, his language is rendered without a trace of difference from that of the others. Colloquialisms occur in the book, but always on the level of vocabulary, never syntax or accent. Draco Malfoy, for example, refers to Neville Longbottom as a *'gran zoquete'* (great fat and ugly little runt) (*Piedra filosofal*, 126) where Rowling uses 'great lump' (*Sorcerer's Stone*, 147). The translator shows finesse, though, in her translation of the often recurring references to a 'great lump.' In the description of Dudley in the opening pages of book one, Rowling has Hagrid refer to him also as a 'great lump' (47). This is rendered in Spanish as *'bola de grasa'* (ball of fat) (*Piedra filosofal*, 46). The translator has captured the difference between these two references to 'great lump', and used specific and colourful translations to convey that difference.

One significant aspect of language in the Harry Potter books is J.K. Rowling's sense of playfulness. Who can doubt this important element, when even in the opening pages of book one she wrote these words of Professor McGonagall that describe Harry Potter: 'He'll be famous – a legend – I wouldn't be surprised if today was known as Harry Potter day in the future – there will be books written about Harry – every child in our world will know his name!' (*Sorcerer's Stone*, 13). These words and the subsequent references to Harry's celebrity stature throughout book two have, of course, become a prophecy fulfilled, though their original intent was surely a playful one. In names, in the coining of new words, and in Rowling's descriptions of the magical place the reader enters upon opening the covers of her books, she displays a keen sense of language's ability to amuse. Who can leave the world of Harry Potter without fond memories of Diagon Alley, or without a smile for Cornelius Fudge in his pin-striped robes? The playful titles of magical ministries are easily translated, and sound just as comically pompous in any target language. Likewise, the pin-striped robes, the acid green pen, and the tartan dressing gown that make their appearances in the books are easily rendered in other languages.

The word plays are, of course, another matter. While it is impossible to translate most word plays as such, an attempt to capture the tone of the words involved is often feasible. For example, the Spanish translation of Diagon Alley, *'callejón Diagon'* captures a degree of playfulness, with the shortening of the word 'diagonal' to make it match in ending the word *'callejón'*. Similarly, the German translation of the broom called 'Clean-sweep Seven' mirrors at least some of the author's intent. Though 'Clean-sweep' has overtones of a winning streak that the German *'sauberwisch Sieben'* does not, the German retains not only the allusion to cleaning by broom (*'wischen'*) but also an alliteration, which gives the line of brooms the flashy image inherent not only in the brand name 'Cleansweep Seven', but in the names of all the broom models used by Hogwarts pupils. A further example of playfulness expressed in a translation occurs in the first two chapter headings in the Spanish version of book one. *'El niño que vivió'* (The Boy Who Lived) and *'El vidrio que desvaneció'* (The Glass That Vanished) are parallel forms grammatically, both using relative pronouns. The second is not a direct translation of the English 'the Vanishing Glass', and obviously represents a conscious decision on the part of the translator to show playfulness. The French translation for the 'Sorting Hat', which itself is not a playful term, shows the translator's attention to the role of word play in the books. He chose the brilliant *'Choixpeau magique'*, *'Choixpeau'* being a play on the words *'chapeau'* (hat) and *'choix'* (choice). The French solution to the problem of translating 'Tom Marvolo Riddle' so that its letters can be arranged to spell 'I am Lord Voldemort' is worth noting. Tom Marvolo Riddle becomes Tom Elvis Jedusor. The French last name has a double meaning, as does the English original: the French is phonetically identical to *'jeu du sort'* (game of the curse). If this meaning isn't clear to the French reader, it is spelled out in book two when Jedusor explains his identity to Harry in the Chamber of Secrets. Rearranged, the letters spell, of course, *'je suis Voldemort'* (*Chambre des Secrets*, 331).

Each translator has come up with a different solution for the translation of such newly coined words as Hogwarts (Table 1), and for the insertion of explanatory material. In the French version, most people's and place names

Table 1 Words common to the Harry Potter books that are translated in at least one language

English	French	German	Spanish
Muggle	Moldu/moldu	Muggel	*muggle*
4 Privet Drive	4, Privet Drive	Ligusterweg, 4	Privet Drive, 4
Leaky Cauldron	Chaudron baveur	*Tropfender Kessel*	Caldero chorreante
Diagon Alley	Chemin de Traverse	Winkelgasse	callejûn Daigon
Knut	Noise	Knut	*knut*
Sickle	Mornille	Sickel	*sickle*
Galleon	Gallion	Galleon	galleon
Flourish and Blotts	Fleury et Bott	*Flouris &Blotts*	Fourish y Blotts
Hogwarts	Poudlard	Hogwarts	Hogwarts
Sorting Hat	Choixpeau magique	Sprechender Hut	sombrero Seleccionador
Gryffindor	Gryffondor	Gryffindor	Gryffindor
Ravenclaw	Serdaigle	Ravenclaw	Ravenclaw
Hufflepuff	Poufsouffle	Hufflepuff	Hufflepuff
Slytherin	Serpentard	Slytherin	Slytherin
Snape	le professeur Rouge	Professor Snape	el profesor Snape
Madam Hooch	Madame Bibine	Madam Hooch	la señora Hooch
Professor Sprout	le professeur Chourave	Professor Sprout	la profesora Sprout
Madam Pomfrey	Madame Pomfresh	Madam Pomfrey	la señora Pomfrey
Mr Filch	Mr rusard	Mr Filch	el señor Filch
You-Know-Who	Tu-Sias-qui	Du-weisst–schon-wer	Quien-tu-sabes
Quidditch	Quidditch	Quidditch	*quidditch*
Golden Snitch	Vif díor	Goldener Schnatz	snitch dorada
Quaffle	Souafle	Quaffel	quaffle
Bludger	Cognard	Klatscher	bludger
Beater	Batteur	Treiber	golpeador
Chaser	Poursuiveur	Jäger	cazador
Seeker	Attrapeur	Sucher	buscador

Table 1 - *continued*

English	French	German	Spanish
Keeper	Gardien/gardien de but	Hüter	guardiùn
Cleansweep Seven	Astiqueur/ Brossdur 7	Sauberwisch Sieben	Cleansweep 7
Scabbers	Croátard	Krätze	Scabbers
Fang	Crockdur	Fang	Fang
Mrs Norris	MisTeigne	Mrs Norris	Señora Norris

are reinvented in French. Thus, 'Squib' becomes 'Cracmol' and 'Hogwarts' is called 'Poudlard'. Many of the characters are given French names as well. Longbottom becomes Londubat and Snape is renamed Rogue. These translations are of questionable value, as they do not add to the reader's understanding of the text and they undermine the important sense of place in the novels. They also prove awkward in book four, where Madame Maxime and the pupils from Beauzbatons visit Hogwarts. With the proliferation of French names in the French version of Hogwarts, there is much less of the desired contrast between the visitors and the British pupils and teachers than there would have been had more English names been retained for the Hogwarts contingent. Even in the first three books, the excessive use of translated proper names detracts from the translation's ability to convey a sense of place, particularly the translation of the names of Hogwarts' four houses. With such an abundance of French names used, the reader has much less the sense of being at a British boarding school.

For instance, while Professor McGonagall's tartan dressing gown seems incongruous in the halls of Poudlard, its appearance is most natural in the original text. An example of a successful rendering of a name in French is that of Draco Malfoy, which becomes Drago Malefoy. Here the translator is getting across an intended meaning, and unobtrusively aiding the French reader in pronunciation. It could be argued that readers in other countries find words such as 'Slytherin' too hard to read and pronounce, and that such words should therefore be translated, even when the translation is not necessary to convey meaning. The flaw in this argument is that many of Rowling's newly coined words are so unusual that even English speakers disagree on their pronunciation. The author even attempts to put an end to the question of how to pronounce 'Hermione' in book four of the series, where she renders the name phonetically, ostensibly for the benefit of

Hermione's newfound friend, Viktor Krum (*Goblet of Fire*, p. 419). The questions about pronunciation among English-speaking readers abound to the point that Scholastic even offers its readers a pronunciation guide on its website. The French translator occasionally finds explanation necessary, as in Justin Finch-Fletchley's mention of Eton in book two, where he explains that Eton is the best private school in England: '*Normalement, je devais aller à Eton, le meilleur collège d'Angleterre, mais je préfère être ici*' (Normally I should have gone to Eton, the best private school in England, but I'd rather be here) (*Chamber of Secrets*, p. 94).

The Spanish translator has approached words that can't easily be translated by using the English words in italics (see Table 1), which is a widely used method of treating foreign words in contemporary Spanish texts. Thus 'Mimblewimble' is 'mimblewimble' and 'Snitch' is 'snitch'. Because of this approach, though, there is no consistency in instances where some magical vocabulary is translated into standard Spanish and other words are left in the original. For example, the names of the magical currency types are 'knuts', 'sickles' and 'galeónes', the last being a standard Spanish word. Proper names and place names tend not to be translated in the Spanish version of the books, which lends more consistency to the sense of place felt by the reader. There is, however, something disorienting about the fact that the italicization of words occurs without a clear system. Untranslated words are usually italicized, with the exception of people's names and the names of the four houses, which are untranslated but not in italics. Though the Spanish translator does not translate the name Draco Malfoy, she does add an explanation of it to aid the Spanish reader in seeing the relationship between 'Draco' and 'dragon'. In book one, after Malfoy introduces himself to Ron and Harry, the translator writes, '*Draco (dragón) lo miró*'. (Draco [dragon] looked at him) (*Piedra filosofal:* 94). A further example of an added explanation comes with the first mention of Peeves, the poltergeist. There is no Spanish equivalent for 'poltergeist', and Percy explains the phenomenon as '*Es un duende, lo que en las películas llaman poltergeist*' (It's a ghost – the one that they call a poltergeist in the movies) (p. 111). While the name 'Peeves' never appears in italics, in his first appearance, the reader encounters him as 'Peeves el Duende' (Peeves the ghost) (p. 114), again with the rare occurrence of a Spanish word in italics.

The German translator has the advantage of working with two Germanic languages. 'Muggle' is simply rewritten to correspond to German orthography as '*Muggel*', and 'Sickle' easily becomes '*Sickel*'. In book three, Draco Malfoy's taunting 'Potty and the Weasel' (*Prisoner of Azkaban*, 80) can be rendered as 'Potty and das Wiesel' (*Gefangene von Askaban:* 86), with the expectation that the German reader will make a connection between 'Wiesel' and 'Weasley'. Most people's and place names are not translated into German, except when they have a significance that would otherwise be lost on the German reader. Therefore, Professor Kettleburn becomes 'Professor *Kesselbrand*' (Kettleburn), Crookshanks is '*Krummbein*' (crooked leg), and Scabbers is called '*Krätze*' (scabies), but Snape remains Snape and Pomfrey stays Pomfrey. It is curious, therefore, why the translator chose to render 'Privet Drive' as '*Ligusterweg*'. Though the words 'privet' and '*Liguster*' denote a shrub commonly used in hedges, the translation of the street name does not seem to be integral to the story. Even the French translator, who translated 'Hogwarts', '*Hogsmeade*', and the names of the school's four houses, didn't touch 'Privet Drive'. The unnecessary translation of this place designation in the German text detracts from the all-important sense of the story being set in Britain.

Translation requires the use of precise words, lest subtle meanings become blurred. In the German version, for example, the translator renders 'cauldron' with the German word '*Kessel*', which can mean either 'cauldron' or 'kettle'. Although '*Kessel*' is a word widely used in German fairy tales for a witch's cauldron, '*Hexenkessel*' (witch's cauldron) would unambiguously represent the English 'cauldron' and prevent confusion, especially since the word '*Kessel*' is used at other times in the books to refer to a tea kettle. Reading the word '*Kesselkuchen*' (kettle cakes) as it appears in the German translation will not necessarily lead the German reader to the same mental image as would, for example, '*Hexenkessel Hörnchen*' (cauldron croissants).

Translators can be aided or hampered by specific characteristics of the language they are translating into. The word 'Muggle' provides interesting examples in French, German, and Spanish. It is used in the original text both as a noun and as an adjective and is capitalized by Rowling in both instances. The French language does not provide for nouns to be used as adjectives. Though both nouns and adjectives often take appropriate endings (masculine, feminine, and plural), they remain separate parts of speech. Therefore a Muggle can be a '*Moldu*', or in the case of a woman a '*Moldue*' and Muggles can be '*Moldus*' or '*Moldues*'. But as an adjective, as in '*côté moldu*' (Muggle side) and '*parents moldus*' (Muggle parents), the word is no longer capitalized, takes the appropriate endings, and follows the noun it modifies, making it without doubt an adjective. Thus the solution for a newly coined word that doubles as a noun, '*Moldu*', and an adjective, '*moldu*', is appropriate for the French language. In German, there is a propensity toward building compounds to accommodate new words, and this technique works also for nouns turned adjectives. Therefore a '*Muggel*' is a Muggle, and '*Muggeleltern*' are Muggle parents. Normally, nouns that refer to people have a masculine form and a feminine form. Therefore, one would expect a female Muggle to be a *'Muggelin'* in German. The translator chose, though, to show gender through the definite article, making *'der Muggel'* a male and *'die Muggel'* a female. Spanish, like the other languages, cannot easily make adjectives from nouns. In the Spanish translation, we encounter the noun forms 'muggle' and 'muggles', and also two ways of using 'muggle' as an adjective. *'Familia de muggles'* (family of muggles) and *'familias muggles'* (Muggle families) are examples of the translator's solutions. The use of a foreign word and its italic appearance disturbs the flow of the text more than the French translator's approach, though the Spanish translator retains the placement of adjective following noun and of appropriate singular and plural adjective endings.

In these translations, there are other examples of language-specific solutions, which, when appropriately made, result in a more natural-sounding text. For example, the French translator uses the French verb and its predilection for prefixed forms to his advantage. In book two, he translates 'de-gnome' (*Chamber of Secrets:* 35) simply as *'dégnomer'* with the noun form *'dégnomage'* (*Chambre des Secrets,* pp. 43, 45). The result is even more idiomatic than the original, since there is no hyphen in the translation.

In German, nouns are capitalized, but adjectives related to them are not. Therefore the German rendition *'undursleyhaft'* (J.K. Rowling, *Harry Potter und der Stein der Weisen:* 5) in book one is even more idiomatic than the original 'unDursleyish' (*Sorcerer's Stone:* 2), with its internal capital letter. The German translator frequently uses nouns, and often compound nouns, to translate phrases and even clauses of the original. For example, he renders 'As you're all in my house' (*Prisoner of Askaban:* 149) as *'Als Ihre Hauslehrerin'* (As your house-teacher) (*Gefangene von Askaban:* 157) and 'that I am up to no good' (*Prisoner of Askaban:* 192) as *'dass ich ein Tunichtsgut bin'* (that I am a do-no-gooder) (*Gefangene von Askaban:* 202). These and other examples of noun substitutions for the original add to the idiomatic nature of the German translation.

The Spanish translator makes good use of the Spanish language's affection for diminutive forms. The endings *'-ito'*, *'-ita'*, *'-illo'*, and *'-illa'* added to a noun make it smaller, dearer or sweeter than without the ending. The wands that the young magicians carry with them are *'varitas'*, Draco Malfoy's 'little friends' are *'amiguitos'* and Peeves's 'annoying singsong voice' (*Sorcerer's Stone:* 160) is his *'molesta vocecita'* (annoying little voice) (*Piedra filosofal:* 136). Peeves's words in book one, 'Naughty, naughty, you'll get caughty' (*Sorcerer's Stone:* 159) become *'Malitos, malitos, os agarrarán del cuellecito'* (Little bad ones, little bad ones, they'll grab you by your little necks) (*Piedra filosofal:* 135). Also in the first book in the series, one of the twins says, 'Aaah, has ickle Ronnie got somefink on his nose?' (*Sorcerer's Stone:* 95). The Spanish translation reads, '*Ah, el pequeñito Ronnie tiene algo en su naricita?*' (Ah, does the little little Ronnie have something on his little nose?) (*Piedra filosofal:* 84). Compound words made up of a verb followed by an object are also characteristic of Spanish. Therefore, Hagrid is a '*guardabosque*' (one who keeps/guards the forest). In book one, where Neville tries to help Harry by telling Professor McGonagall about Malfoy's threats, Rowling has Harry thinking of him as 'Poor, blundering Neville' (*Sorcerer's Stone:* 243). The Spanish translator chooses to use the verb phrase '*meter la pata*' (to butt in, to upset everything) to form the compound '*metepatas*', resulting in '*Pobre mete-patas Neville*' (Poor butter-in Neville) (*Piedra filosofal:* 202). The compound, which so aptly describes Neville, is an accepted word in the Spanish language, making the translator's hyphen unnecessary and awkward.

Each of the translations discussed here demonstrates at least one situation that could have been more accurately or more convincingly portrayed in the target language. The French translator, for example, avoids the use of exact colour names that so appeal to the visually oriented reader of the Harry Potter books. On one occasion in book two, Lockhart wears a robe of 'deep plum' (*Chamber of Secrets:* 189). The French refers to it as nothing more than '*violette*' (*Chambre des Secrets:* 202) rather than '*prune foncé*'. He appears later in a robe of 'palest mauve' (*Chamber of Secrets:* 113), which in the French is rendered simply as '*mauve*' (*Chambre des Secrets:* 125). The robes of the Gryffindor Quidditch team are not scarlet, but rather '*rouge*' (red), which led a French journalist to come to political conclusions not intended in the original.[6] Also in book two, Rowling tells us, 'Ron went as brightly pink as Lockhart's Valentine flowers' (*Chamber of Secrets:* 331), which the French translation renders as 'Le visage de Ron prit une teinte rose vif' (Ron's face took on a bright pink colour) (*Chambre des Secrets:* 349), making it impossible for the reader to smell the flowers of the original. The French translator often leaves out other details, both in description and in the portrayal of actions. At the beginning of Chapter 10 in book two, for example, Rowling describes how Lockhart has Harry help him re-enact scenes from his past, and she mentions the cure of a Babbling Curse, a sick yeti, and a vampire that Lockhart had cured of his bloodthirstiness (*Chamber of Secrets:* 161). The French translator, on the other hand, describes the sketches without details: '*Souvent, il demandait à Harry de jouer le rôle d'une créature féroce qu'il avait terrassée, délivrant ainsi tout un village d'une menace mortelle*' (Often he asked Harry to play the part of a ferocious creature whom he had brought down, thus delivering an entire village from mortal danger) (*Chambre des Secrets:* 173). In the same book, Professor Binns shows his absentmindedness by calling students by the wrong names, O'Flaherty for Finnigan and Pennyfeather for Patil (*Chamber of Secrets:* 151–2). The French text leaves out any indication of equivocation (*Chambre des Secrets:* 163), and this detracts from the characterization of Professor Binns. Many other examples of the omission of particulars in the French translation occur, weakening the books' ability to transport the reader to Rowling's fantasy world, full of fascinating details, some merely entertaining and others integral to the story. There are also examples of inconsistency in the translation of terms. In book one, the Cleansweep brooms are called '*Astiqueurs*' (polishers) (*A l'école des sorciers:* 155), but in book two they are '*Brossdurs*' (stiff brushes) (*Chambre des Secrets:* 123). And in book three their mention is avoided, as the translator has left out the sentences where 'Cleansweep' occurred in the original.

In the German translation, two of Hagrid's beasts receive less than perfect treatment. Hagrid's dog Fang is also called 'Fang' in the German translation. The word 'fang' in German is one of the imperative forms of the verb 'to catch'. Thus, the German rendition, while it makes sense as the name of a dog, does not at all convey the original ironic intent of the author. Hagrid's hippogriff Buckbeak becomes the German '*Hippogreif Seidenschnabel*'. While '*Hippogreif*' is an even more exact word than 'hippogriff' ('*Greif*' means 'griffin'), '*Seidenschnabel*' (Silk-Beak) unsatisfactorily represents 'Buckbeak'. In German, the word '*Schnabel*' can be either a beak or a bill. Therefore it does not necessarily portray the sharpness of the English 'beak', and Buckbeak, no matter how helpful he is in book three, has, as a hippogriff, a sharp side to his personality. Added to the ambiguity of '*Schnabel*' is the modifier of 'silk'. These two elements combined result in an inaccurate translation.

Another interesting error in the German translation occurs in the naming of the card game Exploding Snap. In Britain, Snap is a common children's card game that comes in numerous variations: Number Snap, Alphabet Snap, etc. the German translator, though, mistakenly renders the name of this game as '*Snape explodiert*' (Snape exploding). This makes perfect sense to the reader, as who among the Hogwarts pupils (Slytherins excepted) wouldn't have a good time seeing Snape explode? German readers have found this idea so appealing that a fan website even has an animated demo of '*Snape explodiert!*'

The Spanish translation is hampered mostly by the appearance of so many words in English (sometimes in italics) whose meanings are important enough that they should be translated in order to convey the author's intent. Examples are '*Norberto, el ridgeback noruego*', '*Fanf*', '*Fluffy*', and '*Cleansweep 7*'. A good use of the diminutive would have been with the name 'Fluffy', Hagrid's three-headed dog. As 'Fluffy', there is no indication of the ironic nature of the name Hagrid has given this ferocious creature. *'Fofito'* or even *'Fluffito'* would better relay the author's intent to the Spanish reader. A specific problem with the Spanish translation occurs with the rendition of the name of the Mirror of Erised. 'Erised' is, of course, a mirror-image of the word 'desire'. The Spanish translator uses the word 'Erised', though a cognate of the word 'desire' does not exist in the Spanish language, thus preventing the Spanish reader from knowing the origin of the name and relating it to its mirror image. If the Spanish translator had named the mirror 'Oesed' (*'deseo'*), as the German translator did with 'Nerhegeb' (*'Begehren'*) and the French translator with 'Riséd' (*'désir'*), the meaning would become clear to the reader. Further, the 'gibberish' inscription above the mirror is rendered in the Spanish translation in its original English form, thereby masking its mirror-image meaning (*Piedra filosofal:* 174).

As to the overall success of the translations, much will depend on the personal reactions of the reader, but there are many areas over which the translators do have control. Their overriding concern is to convey the sense of the original text in the words of the target language. An examination of the French translation, for example, shows that it suffers from the lack of vivid detail that abounds in Rowling's original and enchants young imaginative minds. On the other hand, there are some ingenious translations of both slang and newly coined words that delight the reader with a linguistic bent. Although nouns specific to the magical world are usually capitalized in this translation, thus setting them off in the text, the flow of the text is not disturbed, as the capitalization is consistent. This means that not only the newly coined word *'Souafle'* (Quaffle) is capitalized but also *'Guardien'* (Keeper), which is a French word. This mirrors Rowling's capitalizations of words with meanings unique to the magical world, be they accepted English words or not.

The German version of the books, with its almost perfect mix of retained English words and imaginative German translations, reads very smoothly. Fortunately, the translator avoids the current trend of inserting English words into German texts whenever possible, even when a perfectly good German word exists, though he does occasionally use words like 'Dad' and 'Mum' in his translation. While book sales do not necessarily correspond to the literary merit of a book, it is clear that the German version of the Harry Potter books has sold better than the French and Spanish translations combined. Undoubtedly, the German publisher, Carlsen, has marketed the books much more aggressively than the French and Spanish publishers. Carlsen has a website dedicated to the Harry Potter series (http://www.

carlsen-harrypotter.de), complete with excerpts from the books, information about the author, and a chat room. In August 2000, the German
publisher announced a '*Cover-Wahl*' (book cover vote) and gave viewers of
the website the opportunity to choose between the two cover designs. More
than 38, 000 participants voted, and the overwhelming majority chose a
cover similar to the British cover of book four. (*Goblet of Fire* had been available for purchase in Germany in English since July 8, 2000, and was a
number one seller in at least one German online bookstore.) The German
publisher is also alone among the three in this study to have allowed its
customers to order the fourth and fifth Harry Potter books prior to publication.

The Spanish translation suffers mostly from the lack of integration of
newly coined words into the text. Many are in italics, disturbing the flow of
the text, and often words that should be translated to afford the reader the
author's original intent are not. The inconsistency in the use of italics and
translations disorients the reader. For example, in the Spanish version of
Quidditch, the words '*buscador*' (Seeker), '*cazador*' (Chaser), '*golpeador*'
(Beater), and '*guardián*' (Keeper), which exist in the Spanish language, are
used and not set apart by capitalization as in the English original. On the
other hand, Rowling's words such as Snitch, Quaffle, etc. are interspersed
with them but italicized in the text, serving to disorient the reader, who is
seeking to understand the already chaotic rules of Quidditch. There are,
however, some very fine translations of descriptions, and the personalities
of many characters are well portrayed, mostly by use of very specific adjectives. In coining new words, the translator may have been hampered by the
relative rigidity of the Spanish language with respect to the new terminology.

The magical world of Harry Potter continues to grow, with readers of the
books in all hemispheres, thanks in part to the easy access to merchandise
the global market place has produced. The sales success of the books in
some countries seems to be linked to the success of the books in English,
which always arrive before the translations. Despite the shortcomings
inherent in these later arrivals, translations continue to be written,
published, sold, read, and cherished the world over. For readers with a
knowledge of English, the choice will remain whether to read a translation
in their native language or the original in a language foreign to them. For
others, there is no choice but to enter the magical world through the door
opened to them by a translator. Thus translators of the Harry Potter books
are faced with numerous unusual situations, and must weigh the options
carefully, in order not to compromise J.K. Rowling's characterizations, her

novels' sense of place, and her careful use of language, be it in the realm of nomenclature, satire, or playfulness.

Notes

1. See Kim Campbell (2000) The whole world is wild about Harry. *Christian Science Monitor*, July 6, 1.
2. Hilal Sezgin (2000) Alle Menschen werden Muggel. *Frankfurter Rundschau*, July 8, 22.
3. *Harry Potter and the Sorcerer's Stone* is the US title of *Harry Potter and the Philosopher's Stone*
4. Helen M. Jerome (2000) Welcome back, Potter. *Book,* May/June, 40-45.
5. Malcolm Jones (2000) The return of Harry Potter. *Newsweek*, July 10, 57.
6. Pierre Bruno (2001) Moldus, poufsouffles et stéréotypes. *Libération.com* February 2. On WWW at http://www.liberation.fr/quotidien/debats/janvier01/20010120a.html.

Part 5

The Translator's Voice

It has become a commonplace to comment on the invisibility of translators, to refer to them as 'unsung heroes' or 'shadowy figures'. Moreover, thanks to the low status of children's books, an accreditation of the translated work has always been less likely in translations of children's than adult literature, so that many translators of children's books belong to the great disappeared of literary history. When searching in vain for the translator's name in some children's picture books, for example the British version of Jean de Brunhoff's *The Story of Babar* (see Part 3), it would be easy to imagine that the text had switched languages by some kind of literary osmosis, with no human agent involved. Yet there is, of course, evidence of the translator's existence in prefaces and other peritextual material and, as Emer O'Sullivan argues in Part 2 of this Reader, as a discursive presence within the translated text. There are, too, odd moments in literary history where the translator assumes an uncharacteristically prominent role in the consciousness of readers. Mark Twain's translation from German of Heinrich Hoffmann's early and controversial picture book, *Struwwelpeter*, has remained a literary curiosity precisely because Twain was the translator. Twain's English translation is available in Germany to this day in a small pocket book edition, no doubt to the amusement of students of English, and to German adults who remember the book from childhood with mixed emotions.

J.D. Stahl identifies what drew Twain to Hoffmann: the ambiguity of the text and the subversion of a tradition from within. Although many children – and adults – take *Struwwelpeter's* gruesome moral lessons at face value, Stahl argues that Twain and Hoffmann shared an ironic stance towards the excesses of Puritan and mid-19th-century German manners respectively. During his travels in Germany, Twain immersed himself in German culture, but confessed to a poor command of German: his translation of *Struwwelpeter* is an intriguing case study both of the translator's motivation and of an interpretive and inventive translation.

Two pieces written by experienced translators focus on linguistic features that express cultural difference. The issue of forms of address raised by Nancy Jentsch in discussing French, German and Spanish translations of the Harry Potter series in Part 4, reaches new levels of complexity in the article in this section by Cathy Hirano, an American translator of Young

Adult fiction from Japanese into English. Hirano indicates the subtleties of matching pronoun to social status to conform to a tight and intricate politeness structure in Japanese. She writes of the 'strenuous cultural and mental gymnastics' of translating from Japanese; this is surely a worthy addition to the store of descriptions and metaphors for the translation process. And in a rare insight into motivation beyond the professional and economic, Hirano expresses personal reasons for becoming a translator: the aim of sharing her experience of living in Japan with fellow Americans, and, like Mark Twain, the desire to translate a text for her own children.

Anthea Bell, distinguished British translator and winner of many translation prizes including the Marsh Award for the Translation of Children's Literature (twice) enjoys translating for children whenever possible. She is, together with Derek Hockridge, translator into English of the Astérix series: her account of the wit, breadth of knowledge and precision necessary for this task is a delightful contribution to literature on the translation process (Bell, 1980). Bell's list of delicate matters in the *Signal* article reprinted here illustrates the difference made to the overall tone, style and mood of a translation by the use of the present tense, the translation of gendered nouns, and changes of attitude that echo Marisa Fernández López' discussion of ideological issues affecting translation in Part 1 of this Reader.

J.D. Stahl

Mark Twain's 'Slovenly Peter' in the Context of Twain and German Culture

Both Germany and the United States have moralistic traditions of childhood instruction reaching back to the formative periods of their cultural origins. The interest Mark Twain showed in Heinrich Hoffmann's *Struwwelpeter*, and his editorial and creative decisions in translating the popular German original, represent revealing intersections of two related but distinctly different cultural traditions. Mark Twain was drawn to the orderliness of German culture, but his interpretation of violence in the anecdotes of Hoffmann's ironically cautionary work is more indebted to the American experiences of the frontier than to the German *'Kultur der Zurückhaltung'* or 'culture of restraint.' Hoffmann's *Struwwelpeter* embodies a German cultural theme of conflict over 'Zucht des Körpers' or 'discipline of the body,' which clearly fascinated Mark Twain, but which in his translation he shifted to emphasize social domination and control.

Punishment made vivid by its violence is a didactic theme that spans the centuries. In the volume titled *Poetische Bilderschatz der vornehmsten Biblischen Geschichten des alten und neuen Testamentes, zum erbaulichen Vergnügen der Jugend ans Licht gestellet* (Poetic Image Treasury of the most noble Biblical stories of the Old and New Testament, brought to light for the instructive pleasure of youth, Doderer & Müller, 1973: 7), published in 1758 in Leipzig by an anonymous author, the illustrations include the following:

Adonibesek werden die Daumen und Zehen abgehackt,
Gericht der Sündfluth,
Isaacs Opferung
Pharaoh ersäuft im Rothen Meer,
Der gestrafte Flucher,
Die Rotte Korah wird verschlungen,
Der Tod der fünf Könige,
Sauls Söhne gefangen,
Die Bären fressen die spottenden Knaben, u.a.

(Adonibesek's thumbs and toes are hacked off,
the judgment of the flood,
the sacrifice of Isaac,
Pharaoh drowns in the Red Sea,
the punishment of the one who curses,
the band of Korah is devoured,
the death of the five kings,
Saul's sons captured,
the bears eat the mocking boys, etc.)

The verses in this work were accompanied by moral lessons that drew pointed conclusions for young readers about the application of the stories to their life and conduct.

Similarly, in the American Puritan tradition, James Janeway illustrated the need for children's spiritual repentance and moral vigilance through his horrific 'Happy Death' stories, which invariably ended with the death of his young protagonists. Janeway, Isaac Watts, and other Puritan writers shared a moral passion for the reform and redemption of the young that issued in such frightful warnings as the one contained in a stanza of Watts' poem 'Obedience to Parents': 'and ravens shall pick out his eyes/ and eagles eat the same' (Demers & Moyles, 1982: 70).

In the German tradition, this moralistic and religious strain was counter-balanced somewhat in the 19th century by a more scientifically-oriented informational genre, the 'Sachbuch,' which originated in the works of Johann Amos Comenius (*Orbis Pictus*) and Johann Bernhard Basedow (*ein Vorrath der besten Erkenntnisse* ...). It was this factual tradition, though, in a particularly pedantic and unimaginative form, that, at least according to one of Hoffmann's accounts, provided the impetus for his critical and creative departure.

As he told the story,

> *Ich hatte in den Buchläden allerlei Zeug gesehen, trefflich gezeichnet, glänzend bemalt, Märchen, Geschichten, Indianer- und Räuberszenen; als ich nun gar einen Folio-Band entdeckte, mit den Abbildungen von Pferden, Hunden, Vögeln, von Tischen, Bänken, Töpfen und Kesseln, alle mit der Bemerkung 1/3, 1/8, 1/10 der Lebensgröße, da hatte ich genug. Was soll damit ein Kind, dem man einen Tisch und einen Stuhl abbildet? Was es in dem Buche sieht, das ist ihm ein Stuhl und ein Tisch, größer oder kleiner, es ist ihm nun einmal ein Tisch, ob es daran oder darauf sitzen kann oder nicht, und von Original oder Kopie ist nicht die Rede, von größer oder kleiner vollends gar nicht ...* (Hoffmann, 1985: 106).

(I saw all sorts of things in the bookstores, expertly drawn, glowingly painted, fairy tales, stories, scenes of life among Indians and robbers. When I finally saw a folio volume with reproductions of horses, dogs, birds, and of tables, benches, pots and kettles, all with the remark 1/3, 1/8, 1/10 of life size, I had had enough. What is a child supposed to do with the reproduction of a table or a chair? What the child sees in the book is a table and a chair, whether it is larger or smaller; it just is a table, whether the child can sit at it or on it or not. And to talk of original or copy, greater or smaller, is simply out of the question ...) [my translation, J.D.S]

Hoffmann's dissatisfaction with the slickly-produced children's books of his day, coupled with his disgust at the dry scientific approach, unsuited to children, in his opinion, of a particular type of Sachbuch, culminated in his determination to make a better effort himself. What his brief critique of the folio volume reveals is his imaginative capacity to envision how a child is likely to perceive objects represented in a book. Perhaps the most revealing phrase of Hoffmann's is *'was es in dem Buche sieht, das ist ihm ein Stuhl und ein Tisch ... ob es daran oder darauf sitzen kann oder nicht'* (What the child sees in the book is a table and a chair ... whether the child can sit at it or on it or not). His interpretation of the child's consciousness focuses on the child's imaginative relationship to the object pictured, whether that relationship be physical or mental. He insists that, to the child, the object is not an abstraction or a concept, but rather a real object: *'es ist ihm nun einmal ein Tisch'* (it just is a table).

Mark Twain's dissatisfaction with the prevalent juvenile literature of his time bears some similarities to Hoffmann's. Twain objected to the sentimental and didactic abstraction of much literature available to or aimed at young audiences in the American republic. In the 'Ode to Stephen Dowling Bots, Dec'd,' in *The Adventures of Huckleberry Finn* (1985), he juxtaposed the mundane, physical reality of death with the high-flying ethereal rhetoric of sentimental religious poetry:

They got him out and emptied him,
Alas, it was too late;
His spirit was gone for to sport aloft
In the realms of the good and great. (Twain, 1985: 139)

By doing so, he deflated the pretentiousness of a didactic tradition that ignored the concrete realities of children's lives in favor of a kind of transcendental nonsense, or hogwash, as he termed it.

Mark Twain's relationship to the moralistic tradition was, like Hoffmann's, a highly paradoxical one. He cannot be said to have been free from it so much as to have made a radical departure within it. In savagely humorous parodies such as 'The Story of the Good Little Boy' and 'The Story of the Bad Little Boy,' Twain inverted the pieties of Sunday School fiction. The good little boy is Jacob Blivens, and he is destroyed by a nitro-glycerine explosion. Mark Twain's counter-moral (or anti-moral) is directed against the tradition that taught Jacob Blivens that 'the good little boys always died. He loved to live, you know, and this was the most unpleasant feature about being a Sunday-School book boy. He knew it was not healthy to be good' (quoted in Stone, 1961/70: 35).

Mark Twain was contemptuous about most of the genteel children's literature of his time, and his goal in writing was always to write for adults and young people simultaneously, or for adults who could remember what it was like to have been a child. Like Hoffmann, he was somewhat embarrassed by the enormous success of some of his works and would have preferred to have acquired a more serious reputation for the work he considered his best and most important.

Certainly, when Mark Twain chose to devote time and energy to the project of translating Hoffmann's *Struwwelpeter* in Berlin in October of 1891, he had some commercial goals in mind and was keenly aware of the popularity of the book. As he wrote, '*Struwwelpeter* is the best known book in Germany, and has the largest sale known to the book trade, and the widest circulation' (Twain, 1935: 9). In a time when the members of the Clemens family, as his daughter Clara later wrote, 'were compelled to spend every German mark as if it were an American dollar,' 'owing to financial losses,' any scheme to turn a quick profit was appealing. However, at least two further motivations for Twain's efforts are easily discernible. One was the prospect of giving pleasure to his children, which he succeeded in, as Clara's account reveals. She tells how she and her sisters shared in their father's dramatic rendition of *Slovenly Peter* that Christmas morning in 1891. Samuel Clemens placed his translation of *Struwwelpeter*, carefully wrapped and adorned with a huge red ribbon, beneath the Christmas tree. Clara recounts:

> He seated himself near the tree and read the verses aloud in his inimitable, dramatic manner. He was a good actor! He knew the verses by heart and required only the uncertain light of the candles to prevent his getting off the rhythmical path. Jean and Susie and I were very youthful and susceptible. We responded almost with tears to Father's graphic gestures in describing Pauline's conflagration. And how we laughed when he eloquently pictured the careless Hans walking straight into the

pond among all the little fishes! All because the poor boy could not remove his eyes from the sky! (Twain, 1935: 45)

Clara's adult analysis of why the verses appealed to Clemens reveal the other evident facet of his attraction to Hoffmann's work:

There is an impious spirit of contrariness in the verses of this work that appealed to Father, suffering as he was from the blue Berlin mood of those first few weeks. He could sympathize with Kaspar, who wouldn't take his soup, because Father did not care for German soup either. The man who dipped the recalcitrant boy into the ink-bottle was after his own heart. How often had Father wanted to dip interrupting intruders into his own ink-bottle and watch them slink away in a black garb of shining fluid! (Twain, 1935: 3)

Significantly, Clara finds the 'impious spirit of contrariness' in both a child and in an adult in Slovenly Peter. This accords with Mark Twain's powerful insistence that children and adults are subject to the same temperamental impulses, hypocrisies, and contradictions. In a pivotal scene in *The Adventures of Tom Sawyer*, Tom doses Peter the cat with the Pain-killer his Aunt Polly has been dosing him with. The Pain-killer 'was simply fire in liquid form,' but Aunt Polly is convinced that it is good for Tom, until Peter goes on a wild rampage after receiving a treatment of it.

Peter sprang a couple of yards in the air, and then delivered a war-whoop and set off round and round the room, banging against furniture, upsetting flower pots, and making general havoc. Next he rose on his hind feet and pranced around, in a frenzy of enjoyment, with his head over his shoulder and his voice proclaiming his unappeasable happiness. Then he went tearing around the house, again spreading chaos and destruction in his path. Aunt Polly entered in time to see him throw a few double somersets, deliver a final mighty hurrah, and sail through the open window, carrying the rest of the flower-pots with him. (Twain, 1993: 95)

Aunt Polly interrogates the boy about what he has been doing:

'Now, sir, what did you want to treat that poor dumb beast so for?'
I done it out of pity for him – because he hadn't any aunt.'
Hadn't any aunt! – You numskull. What has that got to do with it?'
Heaps. Because if he'd a had one she'd a burnt him out herself! She'd a roasted his bowels out of him 'thout any more feeling than if he was a human!
Aunt Polly felt a sudden pang of remorse. This was putting the thing in a

new light; what was cruelty to a cat might be cruelty to a boy too. (Twain, 1993: 96)

Here Mark Twain has reversed the customary didactic relationship. The child teaches the adult a lesson, but unlike most instruction of children by adults, Tom's lesson is humorous, ironic, and mischievously pragmatic. Lewis Carroll achieved a similar purpose in Alice in Wonderland when he satirized stories in which 'friends,' which was the Rationalist euphemism for adult authority figures, taught children lessons such as that 'if you cut your finger very deeply with a knife, it usually bleeds' (Carroll, 1992: 11). However, Mark Twain dramatized the conflict, not merely as a battle between pedagogical styles, but as a question of perspective and values. Tom's prank raises the question of who should have the inherent right to teach whom.

Similarly, Hoffmann in 'Die Geschichte vom Wilden Jäger,' or 'The Story of the Wild Hunter,' reversed a relationship of power and oppression. The hunter is near-sighted, like Aunt Polly. He goes out 'to have some fun,' as the Tuttle translation glosses his intention. Hoffmann was more blunt: 'Er ... wollte schießen tot den Has' (1984: 56) – he wanted to shoot the hare to kill, or, as Evan K. Gibson translates it in Der Struwwelpeter Polyglott (Hoffman, 1984), 'to see the hare and shoot him dead.' But the hare mischievously 'sits in his house of leaves and mocks' the hunter. The hunter succumbs to his weaknesses as a human being: under the influence of the heat of the sun and the weight of his gun, he falls asleep.

What follows is a carnivalesque comedy: the hare becomes the hunter, the hunter becomes the hare. In an absurd sequence of events, the hunter plunges down a well, foreshadowing Alice's plunge down the rabbit-hole, the hunter's wife's cup of coffee is shot out of her hand and the hare's child's nose is burned by the hot coffee. (Incidentally, perhaps the figure of the hare with the spectacles and gun also foreshadows and perhaps even inspired the character of the imperious White Rabbit with his white kid-gloves, coat, and watch on a chain in Alice in Wonderland).

Here, as elsewhere in Struwwelpeter, the density and intensity of physical sensations is noteworthy: a nose being burnt by coffee, a shattering cup, the explosion of the gun, the cries of the hunter fleeing for his life, and before that, the drowsiness induced by the heat, the hopping of the hare – all vivid sensations children can readily imagine, unlike, perhaps, the abstraction of proportionate sizes. The theme of Hoffmann's stories is frequently the comedy of simple sensations. This comedy of simple sensations 'Am Brunnen stand ein großer Hund, trank Wasser dort mit seinem Mund' (Hoffman, 1984: 18) ('At the fountain stood a large dog, drinking water with his mouth') is linked to the inversions and distortions of ordinary relationships: the boy beats the maid, cats warn of disaster, the hare hunts the hunter, a boy flies away in a storm, carried by an umbrella, which is ordinarily an object of protection from storms. The tailor, who ordinarily sews clothes to protect human bodies, snips off thumbs with giant scissors. Hoffmann extrapolates familiar sensations and figures into grotesque exaggerations that are still linked to the familiar through elements of the mundane.

Though many of Hoffmann's stories appear to teach clearly defined lessons, their didactic stance is not easily defined. Some critics have recoiled from the violence of these tales, as Thomas Freeman does in an essay in the *Journal of Popular Culture*, in which he states, 'I do not agree that these poems can be justified as suitable reading material for small children. Both the stories of Conrad and Paulina play upon some of the worst fears which can torment a child' (Freeman, 1977: 813). Freeman attacks the lessons of the stories as he sees them: 'We are not told to be moral for morality's sake. Instead we are told to behave–or else' (Freeman, 1977: 813). Other critics, such as Dyrenfurth (1942: 814), have defended the stories as reflecting 'the child's simple desire for justice,' while still others have regarded the book primarily as satire or comedy and have pointed out that the exaggeration of the stories is readily recognizable as such by children.

My own assessment of the didactic purpose and method of Hoffmann's enduringly popular work is as follows. While the stories – verses and pictures – have undoubted cautionary and instructional content, they are also suffused with a wry combination of humor, extravagance, and pragmatism. The world of Hoffmann's imagination as revealed in this book is a harsh and abrupt one, but it is also vigorous and fascinating. There is an undercurrent of anarchic energy running through this work that is not entirely contained by the moralistic frame. Thus, while some of the stories have obvious morals such as 'eat your soup,' 'don't play with matches,' 'look where you're going,' and 'don't rock back on your chair at table,' other stories and scenes, such as 'The Wild Hunter,' 'Flying Robert,' and the eponymous Struwwelpeter himself, immortalized upon a pedestal, are less transparent and univocal. Even the stories with the clear, unquestionable morals have an odd, distinct quality that transcends their teaching purpose.

One way of examining this odd quality is to say that there are two conflicting, yet equally valid ways of regarding this book. The first is that Hoffmann evokes, through a vivid exploration of its opposite, a comfortable childhood world in which children do not burn to death, are not dipped in ink or bitten by a dog until they bleed, do not have their thumbs cut off, do not starve to death, or even normally pull tablecloths on to the floor, fall into canals, or fly away in storms – except in their imaginations.

The other, perhaps complementary way of regarding this book is to see it as a work in which children are the central actors. This is not a realm of dry, factual information, but neither is it a realm in which adults are in the foreground. It is an active stage, with energetic, assertive figures, starkly outlined, sometimes surprisingly alone. In existential isolation, boldly disobedient characters defy authority and suffer the consequences. Whatever else one may say about Hoffmann's characters, what they do matters. If one were to imagine the improbable fiction of a child reared entirely upon a diet of Struwwelpeter and nothing else, it would be more likely to say, as an adult, 'Here I stand, I can do no other,' or 'Give me liberty or give me death' than 'Life has no meaning' or 'Hell is other people.'

Putting these two somewhat incompatible descriptions of Hoffmann's work together, namely its indirect evocation, through its opposite, of the normal, less violent, less threatening world many bourgeois children inhabit, and its representation of bold if bad existential martyrs of childhood self-assertion, we arrive at a paradoxical vision of a work in which the instincts of self-preservation and the allure of rebellion do battle. The drama of this battle is given sensory shape in the bodily inflictions and pleasures endured and enjoyed by characters in this book – and we should not forget that Hoffmann emphasizes physical pleasures as well as the punishments that are so often the cause of unsympathetic critics' revulsion.

Children are promised the pleasure of *'Gut's genug, und ein schönes Bilderbuch'* if they behave, but more vivid is the dog's pleasure in the *'große Kuchen, gute Leberwurst,'* and the *'Wein für seinen Durst'* in the story of Cruel Fredrick, the spectator's voyeuristic pleasure, redeemed by participating in moral instruction, in seeing the child burning 'lichterloh,' (with a blazing light) the boys *'viel schwärzer als das Mohrenkind,'* (much blacker than the Moorish child) and the humorous pleasure of the visual joke of a soup tureen adorning Kaspar's grave.

If German culture is indeed the *'Kultur der Zurückhaltung,'* Struwwelpeter is its psychomachia as much as *Faust* or *Magister Ludi* might be said to be.

What, then, does Mark Twain, the archetypal American author, do with this very German set of stories? Mark Twain's relations with Germany and the Germans of his time were generally cordial. The tone of the relationship was set by Baron von Tauchnitz's voluntary payment of royalties to Samuel Clemens for the German translations of his works at a time when international copyright laws did not yet exist or were entirely ineffective. Mark Twain's writings were well received in Germany, and his popularity made him a literary lion by the 1890s, as Clara's comment about her father's steady stream of visitors indicates. Samuel Clemens devoted considerable energy to learning the German language and chronicled some of his frustration with the complexities of German grammar in his essay 'The Awful German Language,' published as an appendix to *A Tramp Abroad* in 1880. He was confounded by the many cases and difficult declinations, but he turned his frustration into comedy, coining some of the most hilarious descriptions of German linguistic practices ever.

> In German a young lady has no sex, while a turnip has. Think what overwrought reverence that shows for the turnip and what callous disrespect for the girl. ... I translate this from a conversation in one of the best German Sunday-school books:
>
> 'Gretchen: Wilhelm, where is the turnip?
> Wilhelm: She has gone to the kitchen.
> Gretchen: Where is the accomplished and beautiful English maiden?
> Wilhelm: It has gone to the opera.'
>
> To continue with the German genders: a tree is male, its buds are female, its leaves are neuter. Horses are sexless, dogs are male, cats are female – tomcats included, of course. A person's mouth, neck, bosom, elbows, fingers, nails, feet and body are of the male sex, and his head is male or neuter according to the word selected to signify it and not according to the sex of the individual who wears it – for in Germany all the women wear either male heads or sexless ones. A person's nose, lips, shoulders, breast, hands and toes are of the female sex and his hair, ears, eyes, chin, legs, knees, heart and conscience haven't any sex at all. The inventor of the language probably got what he knew about a conscience from hearsay (Twain, 1977: 70).

Twain was one of the great cultural interpreters of his time, writing widely-circulated books that influenced how Americans saw Europe and Europeans. In *A Tramp Abroad* and elsewhere, he represented German culture with a mixture of reverence, irreverent comedy, satire, and frustration. He described romantic scenes such as the Lorelei and the castle at Heidelberg with relish, but he was particularly fascinated by the elaborate rituals of the Burschenschaften (student fraternities) at the university, and described their duels in great detail. He pretended to raft down the Neckar as one would raft down the Mississippi River, and he wrote a brief burlesque of a Black Forest novel, which turns on the question of whose manure pile is the largest.

The great difficulty that Twain faced in translating *Struwwelpeter* was to retain some of the idiomatic flavor of the original while still writing rhyming verse. Translating poetry is a notoriously difficult enterprise, and it is no surprise that translation is often equated with betrayal. One can think of the effort of translation as a scale of choices, from literal on the one side to highly interpretive and inventive on the other. The dangers of the literal approach include woodenness, incomprehensibility or awkwardness because of idioms, metaphors, or phrases that are not used in the target language, lifelessness, and artificiality. The perils at the other end of the scale are obvious: departure from the meanings and stylistic qualities of the original, betrayal of the spirit of the source work.

Mark Twain's *Slovenly Peter* is far more interpretive and inventive than faithful. As Susanna Ashton and Amy Jean Petersen (1995: 36) have emphasized in their excellent article in *Children's Literature Association Quarterly*, Twain attempted to 'fetch the jingle [of the original] along' in his interpretation. As Mark Twain himself stated, 'Poetry is a sandy road to travel, and the only way to pull through at all is to lay your grammar down and take hold with both hands.' This he does, with a vengeance, in *Slovenly Peter*. Twain loved to dramatize intellectual labor as struggle and conflict, as is evident in his violent metaphors throughout his humorous essays and speeches about the German language.

Ashton and Petersen make a largely positive assessment of Twain's interpretation of *Struwwelpeter*:

Although full of awkward rhymes and structures, Twain's renditions may be seen as far more faithful to the spirit of the original illustrations and text than the previous translations had been; his difference from the standard English version will strike many readers as all to the good. The language of Twain's work, however, often differs dramatically from the German. He elaborates extensively on scenes that receive little, if any, treatment in the original German version, presumably a reason for his decision to describe his version of Hoffmann's poems as 'freely translated.' (Ashton & Petersen, 1995: 37)

This thoughtful judgment has much truth in it, but it perhaps underemphasizes the degree of Mark Twain's interpretation in the process. As in his writings about Germany in *A Tramp Abroad* and elsewhere, Twain puts a selective and distinctly American spin on the material. By intensifying certain elements that are present in the original, he estranges them from their culture of origin and puts a specifically American and Twainian stamp on them.

In particular, Twain uses a range of American references, intensifies the violence, makes himself as translator/interpreter a subject of his writing, and shifts the morals idiosyncratically. Ashton and Petersen point out

Twain's use of American slang, such as when the hare 'stole his gun and smooched his specs/And hied him hence with these effects.' They do not mention that Twain calls the hare 'Brer Rabbit,' a name that immediately invokes the wealth of American stories dealing with the trickster rabbit who has connections to Anansi, the trickster god of West Africa, and who was popularized for white readers by Joel Chandler Harris. They also do not mention that Twain does not mitigate the implicit racism of 'The Story of the Black Boys,' which represents the Moor's darkness as something to be pitied. Twain translated the description of the *'kohlpechrabenschwarzer Moor'* rather literally as the 'coal-pitch-raven-black young Moor'. If anything, Twain increases the racism of the episode, for he refers to the Moor as 'that poor Missing Link,' making an obvious reference to the Darwinian controversy of his time. He also calls the boy 'that poor pitch-black piteous Moor,' and, most offensively, 'that Niggerkin.' Where Hoffmann wrote, *'Du siehst sie hier, wie schwarz sie sind, viel schwärzer als das Mohrenkind,'* ('You see them here, how black they are, much blacker than the Moorish child' – editor's translation) Twain wrote: 'You see them here, all black as sin – Much blacker than that Niggerkin.'

Similarly, Twain intensifies the violence of the story in American frontier fashion. Whereas Hoffman's Friederich *'schlug den Hund, der heulte sehr, und trat und schlug ihn immer mehr,'* (he 'beat the dog, which howled greatly, and kicked and beat it more and more'), Twain's Fred'rick 'whacked him here, he whacked him there, He whacked with all his might and main, He made him howl and dance with pain.' Where Hoffmann stated that wicked Friedrich *'peitschte seine Gretchen gar'*—'even whipped his Gretchen,' Twain uses the vastly more suggestive 'He banged the housemaid black and blue.' When the hare chases the hunter across the landscape, in German he *'läuft davon und springt und schreit: 'Zu Hilf', ihr Leut'! Zu Hilf', ihr Leut!'* (He 'ran away, and leaped and cried, 'Help, People, Help, People!') In Twain's burlesque, Brer Rabbit:

> drew a bead, the hunter fled, And fled, and fled! and FLED! and **FLED!** And howled for help as on he sped, howled as if to raise the dead; O'er marsh and moor, through glade and dell, the awful clamor rose and fell, And in its course where passed this flight, All life lay smitten dead with fright. (Twain, 1935)

Twain does well with some of the onomatopoeic qualities of Hoffmann's original, as in the story of the thumb-sucker: 'Bang! here goes the door ker-slam! Whoop! the tailor lands ker-blam! Waves his shears, the heartless grub, And calls for Dawmen-lutscher-bub. Claps his weapon to the thumb, Snips it square as head of drum,' and, as Ashton and Peterson note, he intensifies the boy's cry of pain: 'While that lad his tongue unfurled And fired a yell heard "round the world."' Some of Hoffmann's bizarre details become more bizarre in Twain's interpretation: the little fishes that laugh at Hans Guck-in-die-Luft *'lachen, daß man's hören tut, lachen fort noch lange Zeit; und die Mappe schwimmt schon weit'*–they 'laugh audibly, continue laughing a long time, and the satchel swims far away already.' But for Twain,

> Those little fish go swimming by
> And up at him they cock their eye,
> And stick their heads out full a-span,
> And laugh as only fishes can;
> Laugh and giggle, jeer and snort –
> How strange to see them thus cavort!
> Meantime the atlas, gone astray,
> Has drifted many yards away.

What I am suggesting is that Twain adds a strong flavor of fascination with the absurd, grotesque, and violent to his rendition, going considerably beyond the 'spirit of the original.' This tendency is rooted, I believe, in the frontier tradition of the tall tale, the brag, the burlesque, of the kind that surfaces in his writings again and again, and that reflects the American experience of conflict, isolation, and overwhelming forces on the frontier. Furthermore, an undercurrent of Puritan theology is visible in certain details, such as the already mentioned phrase 'black as sin,' and, in reaction, in the glee with which Twain dwells on the drunkenness of the dog at Fred'rick's table:

> He sips the wine, so rich and red,
> And feels it swimming in his head,
> He munches grateful at the cake,
> And wishes he might never wake
> From this debauch; while think by think
> His thoughts dream on, and link by link
> The liver-sausage disappears,
> And his hurt soul relents in tears.

This is clearly a Presbyterian, not a Lutheran dog.

Hoffmann mentions the wine as a matter of course; Twain, coming from a society in which alcohol was a subject of religious controversy, emphasizes it with libertine pleasure in the violation of taboo. In *A Tramp Abroad*, he pursued a similar theme when he wrote about German professors' relations with their students:

There seems to be no chilly distance existing between the German students and the professor but, on the contrary, a companionable intercourse, the opposite of chilliness and reserve. When the professor enters a beer-hall in the evening where students are gathered these rise up and take off their caps and invite the old gentleman to sit with them and partake. He accepts and the pleasant talk and the beer flow for an hour or two, and by and by the professor, properly charged and comfortable, gives a cordial good night, while the students stand bowing and uncovered. And then he moves on his happy way homeward with all his vast cargo of learning afloat in his hold. Nobody finds fault or feels outraged. No harm has been done (Twain, 1977: 24).

Twain's final comments here suggest that he is writing pointedly to an American audience that would not take professors drinking with their students, or perhaps any form of drinking of alcoholic beverages, for granted, or approve at all.

Ashton and Petersen have emphasized the friendliness and personableness of Twain's persona as he makes himself visible as translator and narrator in the story, addressing an individual reader: 'You see them here ...' But I wish to add that his asides to the reader seem to me either condescending to the child or meant as jokes aimed at adults. When he writes 'The dog's his heir, and this estate That dog inherits, and will ate,*' he adds in the footnote: '*My child, never use an expression like that. It is utterly unprincipled and outrageous to say ate when you mean eat, and you must never do it except when crowded for a rhyme.' Similarly when he comments about the phrase 'He took his game-bag, powder, gun, And fiercely to the fields he spun,*' he notes: '*Baby, you must take notice of this awkward form of speech and never use it. Except in translating.'

In a curious way, the American quality of Slovenly Peter contrasts with the communal or collective German quality of Struwwelpeter. Hoffmann's classic work is a complex instruction book, not so much in the manners as in the 'Sichtweise' or social perspective of German society, with its conflicts about control of the body and of its impulses: issues of Mäßigung, Zucht, Anstand (moderation, breeding and decency), all common words in German childrearing that have few or no equivalents in American English, at least in idiomatic conversation about children. Mark Twain emphasizes himself as the interpreter and teller of the tales, which he embellishes with themes that are preoccupations of the frontier. He succeeds in making vivid renditions, particularly of the stories of the girl with the matches and 'Cruel Fred'rick'.

Yet Mark Twain misses something essentially German in the original, and substitutes something quintessentially American in the process. Perhaps his subtly eccentric interpretation of the 'story of Flying Robert' provides an aptly epigrammatic conclusion symbolic of this transposition. Hoffmann concludes with the cryptic image of an unknowable fate that befalls boy, umbrella, and hat as they are carried away:

> Schirm und Robert fliegen dort
> durch die Wolken immer fort.
> Und der Hut fliegt weit voran,
> stößt zuletzt am Himmel an.
> Wo der Wind sie hingetragen,
> ja! das weiß kein Mensch zu sagen. (Hoffman 1984)

In Evan Gibson's translation:

> Robert and umbrella there
> still upon the gusty air,
> while his hat blows far ahead;
> from the earth it now has fled.
> where the wind blew them away
> no one here below can say.

Though Hoffmann emphasizes universal limits: the hat finally hits heaven, and no human being can tell where the three were carried to. But Twain describes it thus:

> And so he sails and sails and sails,
> Through banks of murky clouds, and wails,
> And weeps and mourns, poor draggled rat,
> Because he can't o'ertake his hat.
> Oh, where on high can that hat be?
> When you find out, pray come tell me. (Twain 1935)

Both Hoffmann's and Twain's poems are images of human fate in the universe; but Hoffmann's has a stoic agnosticism, a recognition of limits to human knowledge. Twain's 'poor draggled rat' is a pitiful soul, absurdly grieving for a lost hat while flying through the vast unknown, and the question Twain wants to have his listeners answer him is not what becomes of the boy, but where the hat has gone. Just as he misses the subtly melancholic yet resigned tone of Hoffmann's flight, the thing he should have been 'auf der Hut' (on the watch) for, Twain misses something of the German quality of Struwwelpeter, and substitutes for it a new hat, though not old hat, to be sure.

Cathy Hirano
Eight Ways to Say You: The Challenges of Translation

Last year I had the honor of attending the Boston Globe-Horn Book awards ceremony in Massachusetts, not as an award recipient but as an accompanist – as the translator for Kazumi Yumoto's *The Friends* (1996), which won the fiction award.[1] It was exhilarating to meet so many people who had actually read the book. Not only had they read it, but they had been touched by it, moved by it, as I was every time I read it during the translation process – which must have been at least ten times. These people shared the insights it had given them into their own lives, the encouragement it had brought them in a time of grief, the laughter it had sparked. And I thought, 'Yes! This is why I translate!' It's my way of sharing what I (a Canadian woman married to a Japanese man, with two children who speak primarily Japanese) have experienced here in Japan, both the universal and the unique; experiences that have forced me to think in new ways and look at life with new eyes.

People who have never translated often assume that it is a purely mechanical process. The translator, proficient in both languages, simply has to substitute one word in the source language for an equivalent word in the target language. To some extent this is true, particularly for texts with specific and frequently repeated terminology such as machine manuals, and especially if those texts are being translated into a language related to one's own. If you have ever read some of the incomprehensible manuals that have come out of Japan for VCRs or electrical appliances, however, you will realize that there is more to translation than owning a good foreign language dictionary. Translation of literature is far from mechanical, and translating between languages that, like Japanese and English, are very different from each other requires fairly strenuous cultural and mental gymnastics. A cursory glance at Japanese sentence structure and some of the idiosyncrasies of Japanese composition will give you an idea of what a Japanese-to-English translator is really required to do.

Japanese sentences do begin with a subject, but it is often unstated and must be inferred from the context. There is no plural, either – or rather, there can be but it is rarely used, again requiring the reader to guess from the context whether there is only one of the subject or more. The subject is followed by the object, and then finally the verb. Suffixes on the end of the verb establish the tense and make the sentence a positive or negative statement while an additional suffix makes it into a question. The first task of a translator, then, is to unravel the sentence and rearrange the appropriate pieces in English order. When the sentences are embellished with extra clauses, this is rather like piecing together a jigsaw puzzle, trying to find where each piece fits into place. Here is a sentence randomly selected from a Japanese magazine I happen to have on my desk. In Japanese, the order would be as follows: 'International cooperation, when said, country or government or local administrative body do something is, we direct relation is not.' Rearranged in English order and with the addition of implied nuances and unstated information, the sentence becomes: 'When we talk about international cooperation, we usually assume that it is the domain of the country, the government, or the local administrative body, not something that directly concerns us.'

More than grammar, however, it is the differences in writing style that are a challenge for the translator, because these reflect differences in cultural perspective and ways of thought. The most obvious differences between Japanese and English writing styles are organization and tone. My English composition classes in high school taught me that English is supposed to flow in a linear fashion, from introduction to body to conclusion, and that statements should be supported by logical explanations. Even in literature, a book works towards a climax and then a conclusion. In contrast, Japanese composition appears almost circular, and although it has its own logic and organization, it is very different from how I learned to write in school. Whereas in English we stress clarity, in Japanese subtlety is preferred. The Japanese writer dances around his theme, implying rather than directly stating what he wants to say, leaving it up to readers to discern that for themselves. He or she appeals to the reader's emotions rather than to the intellect, and tries to create a rapport rather than to convince. The Japanese reader, in turn, is quite capable of taking great leaps of imagination to follow the story line. Direct translations of English into Japanese, therefore, often appear crude and abrasive, insulting the reader's intelligence with their bluntness, while direct translations of Japanese into English are often frustrating to read because they come across as emotional, even childish, and without any point or conclusive ending. Although they may be faithful to what is actually written, this type of translation fails to achieve its purpose because it does not convey the author's intended meaning. It is worth noting that there is considerable controversy about this issue amongst translators themselves and among authors being translated. Although translation should convey the meaning, and not necessarily in precisely the same words, there is a very fine line between translating and tampering with or rewriting the original text.

The first thing I need to know before I even start translating is the intended readership and the purpose of the translation. That information determines how I deal with implied but unstated content and foreign cultural assumptions. For example, when I am translating academic works or articles for publication in the West, if the purpose is to make an impact on the author's Western peers, I will, with the author's permission, occasionally go so far as to reorganize and even rewrite some sections to present the author's point more clearly to the intended audience, overstepping the bounds of strict translation. I also routinely weed out inconsistencies and repetition that are unobtrusive and, in the case of repetition, even effective in Japanese, but very distracting and annoying in English.

Literature, however, is another matter, because to both the reader and the author the form is as important as the content. I must strive to remain true not only to the essence, but also to the style and tone of the writer in the source language while at the same time render it in a way that is understandable to someone from a very different culture and way of thinking. It is a balancing act, requiring sensitivity and intuition, a combination of humility, vigilance, and arrogance. I say humility because as a translator I must be willing to accept that the author comes first, and that even if I don't agree, or think that I can say it better, the author is always right. Moreover, it is dangerous to assume that I understand, and thus I must be constantly vigilant. In Kazumi Yamoto's second book, *The Spring Tone* (1999, original Japanese title *Haru no orugan*), she uses the word *jersey*, a term borrowed from English. The Japanese dictionary defined it as a garment made of jersey cloth and the English dictionary as a close-knit upper garment. A sweater, I assumed, and translated it as such, but it was one of the many small points that continued to niggle at me. When I mentioned it to Kazumi, she hastily informed me that she had meant a sweat suit or tracksuit, with pants and top, and not a sweater at all.

Arrogance and humility may appear to be contradictory, but I need a certain amount of arrogance to believe that I have the ability to become the author in another language. If, for example, you give ten excellent translators the exact same passage to translate, you will invariably end up with ten excellent, but very different translations. Which one of those is 'right'? I am terrified of reading my translation after it has been published because I know that I will find errors, omissions, or things that I would now say differently. I need that arrogance during the translation process to sustain me to the finish. Otherwise I would be paralysed by doubts.

The target audience of the Japanese literature I translate is young adults. The objective is to bring the world of Japanese children and adolescents closer to them, to help them feel what Japanese kids feel, view the world through their eyes, while still appreciating the differences. Ideally, the translation should make them laugh where a Japanese reader would laugh, cry where a Japanese reader would cry, etc. Although I may be underestimating them, I do not expect this audience to have much prior knowledge of the daily life of an ordinary Japanese child or much tolerance for assumptions that are foreign to their culture.

Here's an example. *The Friends* (Japanese title: *Natsu no niwa*) is about three twelve-year-old boys who are afraid of death. They decide to stalk an old man in their neighborhood in order to witness what really happens when a person dies, and the story follows the relationship that develops between the boys and the old man. I knew from the outset that school and *juku*, a kind of school after school, were going to be major obstacles to understanding for American readers. Although most of the story takes place outside of these venues, they set the rhythm of the boys' lives and are an essential part of the backdrop. *Elementary school* conjures up similar images in both cultures, but the school year in Japan begins in April, and summer holidays are much shorter, with fairly heavy homework assignments. Without some knowledge of these aspects, many of the things the boys do just would not make sense to target readers. Similarly, although the word *juku* conjures up a common image for Japanese children, there is no real equivalent in North America. To simply translate it as *cram school* and leave it at that would make it impossible for North American readers to appreciate its implications in Japanese children's lives.

These problems were solved through a three-way communication process. I consulted the author, who was very clear that her priority was to make her work accessible to the North American audience, and asked her to describe in more detail how she envisioned school and *juku* in the boys' lives, including how often they attended, the time of day etc. I faxed this information to the American editor at Farrar, and she suggested a few key places in the text where additional description could be naturally woven in as briefly and unobtrusively as possible. For example, the longest addition reads:

> Every day, Monday to Friday, we have cram school after regular school. We're there from six until eight and sometimes even until nine o'clock at night, trying to cram in everything we'll need to know to pass the entrance exams for junior high school next year. By the time we get out, we're exhausted, not to mention starving.

It is short, but it makes a tremendous difference to how readers experience the rest of the book.

You can see from this example the amount of cultural significance that is packed into a single word. Trying to convey those unspoken cultural assumptions without overdoing it is one of the challenges of translation. Similar problems arise because of the different levels of speech in Japanese. Just off the top of my head, I can think of eight ways to say *you*, each with a cultural nuance that reflects the speaker's sex or social status in relationship to the listener: a form only used by male speakers, a polite form for someone of a higher status, a more neutral form for a peer, a more familiar form for someone of lower status, etc. Moreover, the use of *you* is generally avoided because it is too direct, and therefore when it is used the translator has to consider whether it contains information crucial to understanding a character or a relationship. If it does, then an alternative way to reflect that in the dialogue must be found, because the word *you* will of course convey nothing of the above to a North American reader.

The Spring Tone follows the internal journey of Tomomi, a thirteen-year-old girl. She is angry and resentful at having to leave behind her childhood *naïveté* and sense of security and begin the painful process of growing up. We experience her dawning awareness of herself and others, her letting go of anger and judgment, through her changing perception of the world around her and her relationships with her brother, her grandfather, her parents, and a woman who cares for stray cats. At one point in the story, there is a brief encounter between Tomomi and Kinko, a boy from her school, that reveals an internal shift. Being rather timid and fastidious, Kinko is appalled to see Tomomi petting a stray cat. Parrotting his mother, he blames the proliferation of strays on the people who feed them. Tomomi hotly refutes this, demanding to know why he does not blame the people who throw their cats away as if they were garbage. The tone of the encounter is set at the beginning by the following exchange:

'Was that your brother?'
'Yeah, so what?' He said 'your.' Why is he putting on airs, that jerk?

Tomomi's anger seems totally unwarranted in the English. The boy appears to be asking an ordinary question. The word he actually used, however, was *kimi*. When this form is used by a child to his peers, it has a slightly snobbish although not condescending tone. It is an unconscious affectation of someone 'well-brought up' and protected from vulgar society, a member of the upper class. To Tomomi he seems to be putting on airs, and she bristles with indignation. In order to give the reader the same impression, I settled for making his speech sound slightly affected and altered Tomomi's response to correspond, as follows:

'That was your brother, I presume?'
'Yeah, so what?' you presume indeed. You jerk.

Even without the differences in levels of politeness and familiarity in speech, translating conversations often requires more ingenuity than descriptive passages. Having lived in Japan for 20 years, Japanese as a spoken language is very alive for me. I spend much of my time talking to children – my own children's friends and schoolmates, and the many children who approach me on the street because I look so different. Kazumi Yamoto is adept at capturing the tone and easy-flowing banter of children's conversations, yet the actual words sound stilted or strange in English. In a scene in *The Friends*, one of the boys has been trying to convince his friends to spy on the old man. He finally succeeds, and the resultant altercation directly translated would read:

'All right.'
' ... say?' Yamashita is nervous.
'To be more precise,' I avoid Yamashita's accusing eyes. 'It must not cause trouble for the old man.'
'Ehh?'
'Did it! Two against one!' Kawabe dances a little jig.

This does not convey any of the humor or rhythm of their give and take. To maintain a feeling for the way North American children speak and to prevent the Japanese language from dominating, I read American children's books and watch American movies constantly during the translation process. Then, after reading a section like the one above, I close my eyes and visualize English-speaking children and imagine what they would say in the same situation. The result in this case was as follows:

'All right,' I say.
'All right what?' Yamashita asks nervously.
I avoid Yamashita's accusing eyes. 'But only on condition that it doesn't bother the old man.'
'No!' Yamashita explodes.
'Yes! Two against one!' Kawabe shouts gleefully, and he dances a little jig.

The words in English are very different, but they capture the tone of the Japanese more accurately.

Probably one of the trickiest problems I face in translation is humor. More often than not, slapstick and situational humor transcend cultural boundaries. Culture specific jokes and puns, however, usually do not.

There are several ways of dealing with this, ranging from the extreme of deleting the joke entirely to making it a completely different joke. In *The Friends,* there is a very humorous scene in which the main character Kiyama is caught daydreaming in class, a situation also familiar to children in America. The teacher puts him on the spot by asking him a question. Kiyama's friend prompts him, whispering 'round' and 'smooth', which Kiyama parrots. But he hasn't a clue what the subject matter is. The question was actually about the characteristics of pebbles in the earth's stratum, but the teacher traps him by rubbing his head and saying, 'Right, round and smooth. Just like me. And whom do you think we are talking about?' Kiyama panics and blurts out the name of Tokugawa Ieyasu, a famous figure in Japanese history. The whole class, of course, bursts out laughing. The use of this name in the English translation, however, would be meaningless to an American child, and would rob the situation of its humor. An alternative was needed – someone with a round, smooth head who would be readily recognized by Americans but still plausible in a Japanese context. The American editor suggested Buddha, and after consultation with the author, this is what we used. The solution is a compromise: it does not convey the same meaning as the original Japanese, but at the same time it does not detract from the overall humor of the situation.

There are so many facets to translation, so many problems and so many different ways of solving them, that I could go on forever. Instead, I would like to share with you something that was very meaningful for me as a translator. *The Friends* was published in recorded book form in 1997, and I was sent a copy. It is five hours long, and I started playing it for myself during a car trip with my children. My son, then ten, had never read the book, and I thought that he was too young to understand, especially in English. I was surprised therefore to find him laughing at the funny parts and listening intently to the rest. When we reached our destination, he carried the tapes inside and listened non-stop for two more hours until it was finished. He wept, heartbroken, at the old man's death (I still cry there, even now), and at the end, he said with satisfaction (and in Japanese), 'that was a good book, Mom'. It is indeed a good book, and it was a gift to be able to share it with my own child, born of both cultures; to see him experiencing Japanese literature through the medium of the English language. And to know that it still came through.

Note

1. Cathy Hirano's translation of *The Friends* won the 1997 Mildred Batchelder Award for translated children's fiction published in the USA for its publisher Farrar, Straus and Giroux.

Anthea Bell

Translator's Notebook: Delicate Matters

By 'delicate matters', in the context of translation, I mean they are fiddly and may look very minor: choice of tense, use of pronouns, those matters of everyday occurrence in translation work which you would think couldn't possibly make much difference to actual meaning. And yes, translators do take them in their stride every day. Only sometimes one has to stride back again for a second look, and it turns out that quite tiny things can affect meaning a good deal after all.

Take tense; take in particular that interesting tense the historic present. English does not, like the languages from which I chiefly translate, leap nimbly from historic present to past and back again as a narrative method. Once you have committed yourself to the historic present in continuous narrative you are more or less stuck with it, and with getting all other tenses (such as conditionals) into line with it, unless you are going to be experimental, which is no part of a translator's duty unless in reflecting the experimental nature of an author's original work. There are not many differences in approach between translating children's and adult literature, but I do find this is one of them. I am most reluctant to use the historic present in English in a middle-of-the-road kind of children's novel, even if it is the main tense of a French or German original. In English, the historic present seems more of a tense for a stylist than is necessarily the case in other languages. I like it myself; I like its immediacy. But I feel it needs to be approached with caution in translating children's fiction.

The historic present commonly used for the brief narrative parts of a strip cartoon is different, of course; the strip cartoon is in the nature of a dramatic performance unfolding before the reader's eyes, with the occasional explanatory bits in between the actual speech bubbles as the stage directions. But otherwise, it seems to me – in children's fiction – that its place is right at the other end of the spectrum, as an unusual, exciting but quite demanding narrative method, not an everyday one. Thus, unless it's an unusual and intentionally demanding book I am translating for children, my general instinct is to abandon the historic present of a foreign original.

Of course it can't invariably be done: there are bound to be exceptions.

One book, *So Long, Grandpa* by Elfie Donnelly, a moving little story of a boy's relationship with his dying grandfather – saved from over-earnest sociological concern by the freshness of the child's eye view – had to stay in the present because it was so much a stream of consciousness, reflecting the boy's reactions as his grandfather's illness progressed.

And quite recently I resorted to the opposite of my usual practice and turned something into the English historical present when it was in the past in German. Willi Fährmann's prize-winning novel for older children, *The Long Journey of Lukas B.*, is about a gang of carpenters leaving the poverty of their Prussian village in the 1870s to find work and make money in America. Crossing the Atlantic, young Luke has many conversations with the ship's sailmaker, Hendrik, an Ancient Mariner figure who tells good tales, some of which may concern the lad's long-lost father. In the original the sailmaker speaks perfectly ordinary standard German, so that one would expect his speech to present no problems at all, nor did it, except that somehow, once translated into English absolutely straight, it no longer seemed quite right for the character. I therefore worked on creating him a colloquial idiom of vague provenance; I did not want to pin him down with an actual dialect, either English or American (the translation being for both sides of the Atlantic), but aimed for something which might sound like the way a shrewd but uneducated old sailor would tell his tales. I tried to get this effect partly by giving him the historic present for his narratives, along with various elisions, inversions and colloquial tricks of speech. They may not have been present in the German, but I hope that they faithfully reflected the author's intention in the portrayal of his character. As ever, it is the spirit rather than just the letter that the translator pursues.

The sailmaker might have had a German dialect, of course, and that is another problem that does come up from time to time. Again, I am usually in favour of some kind of colloquial idiom rather than the substitution of a recognisably English, Scottish, American, etc., dialect. (I am speaking of dialect passages within a book, in the mouth of a particular character. When a whole story is involved, as with the excellent Scots and Irish versions of some of the Grimms' dialect tales in the *Selected Tales* in the Penguin classics, the method can succeed brilliantly.) But if just some characters in a work of fiction are dialect speakers, you do run the risk of destroying the whole fragile foundation of translation by adopting an equivalent from the English-speaking world. What, thinks the reader, is this man from Cologne (or Marseilles or wherever) doing speaking broad Yorkshire (or deep South or whatever)? Come to that, what are the rest of these people in Central Germany or the south of France doing speaking English at all? And come to that, these are not the author's own words, and what am *I* doing reading anything so artificial as a translation anyway?

This is a train of thought that translators are naturally reluctant to suggest. It explains why no British dialects are used for the various French regional accents of characters from assorted parts of ancient Gaul in the *Astérix* saga. The translation has tried to compensate for the loss of them with different kinds of wordplay instead. In any case, we already have a Scotsman and an Irishman, McAnix and Overoptimistix, in *Astérix in Britain*. It was different, of course, when BBC Radio broadcast a version of *Astérix in Britain*. In the nature of things, everyone had to be heard speaking, and, with visual impact entirely gone, had to be aurally identifiable; the producer made the Gauls Northern, the Romans Cockney spivs, and the druid Welsh, and it worked all right because of the change of medium.

Those tiny parts of speech, pronouns, can be the trickiest of all. English is a language that has lost grammatical gender; French and German have not. Obvious, of course, but therefore, if you must assign 'he', 'she', or 'it' to a noun that has grammatical gender in the original (and automatically takes a pronoun to match) but has no built-in gender in English, you are inevitably loading the whole idea with extra significance.

This is not a problem that arises with very great frequency, but it is more likely to present itself in a children's book than elsewhere, because children's fiction is especially likely to contain personifications or anthropomorphized animals. Animals in particular abound, as anyone who has been reading John Goldthwaite on the anthropomorphic fantasy world in these pages[1] (*Signal*, 47 and 48) will readily understand.

And once an animal fable or fantasy, or a personified natural phenomenon such as sun or moon, has been given human characteristics, or speech, or simply enough identity to make it an important character in the story, it very likely requires (in English) a pronoun more personal than just 'it'. Even 'it' may convey a stronger degree of impersonality in English than in German, where it is simply the pronoun proper to neuter words, including a child of either sex, *das Kind*, and a girl, *das Mädchen* (because she happens to have the diminutive suffix *–chen*, which inevitably makes any noun neuter; *Mädchen*, little maid).

I don't know that it would be accurate to say that grammatical gender has no influence at all on the way in which people using it think; take the sun and the moon. We tend to think of the moon as feminine; our poets have thought of it that way for centuries. The *Concise Oxford* dictionary unhesitatingly defines 'she' as 'The female (or thing personified as female, e.g. the moon ...) previously mentioned'. But when we still had grammatical gender, back in Anglo-Saxon times, moon was masculine and sun feminine, as is still the case in German. When we lost grammatical gender, why did we decide the moon was feminine and the sun masculine? Were we influenced by sun gods and moon goddesses of classical and pagan mythology, or was it some atavistic notion of masculine vigour versus gentle female passivity? (Yes, I know I am approaching deep sexist waters, to which I shall return.) A medievalist friend thinks astrology mingling with classical mythology in the late Middle Ages may have something to do with it. Anyway, there we are: sun masculine, moon feminine. But to the Germans, no less well acquainted with Apollo and Artemis, sun is still feminine in a folk-tale context, and moon masculine, with pronouns to match, so that where Ludwig Bechstein in the 19th century collected one of the glass-mountain tales (of our British 'Black bull of Norroway' type) and the king's daughter must visit the Sun and Moon, who are making chicken soup, to beg the chicken bones from which she can build a ladder to help her up the mountainside, Bechstein's 20th-century illustrator provides a picture of a warmly golden, very female and matronly sun.

However, personifications are not nearly as common in children's books as animals. Animals are far more likely to cross the path of the translator working from languages with grammatical gender, and just because we must choose a pronoun, where choice is automatic in the source language, the matter becomes peculiarly delicate, since the chosen pronoun may make a much more definite statement in the genderless target language.

Sometimes there is no problem because context makes the animal's biological sex quite clear. Both cat and mouse are grammatically feminine in German, one is grammatically masculine and one feminine in French. I mean the basic nouns, of course; there are feline nouns that of themselves make the cat's biological sex perfectly clear, *la chatte, der Kater*. But if you are just talking about any old cat, sex unknown, those words will not be used, and may not even be used if you do know its sex.

A few months ago, I was translating from German a collection of folk and fairy tales all having cats as their central figures. In a couple of the stories, *Kater*, tom cat, was the noun used. In one story at least there was no doubt in context that the cat itself was either really a tom or regarded as masculine by the humans in the tale, but the ordinary noun was used; however, it was clear enough that I should use 'he' as the pronoun. In some of the others there was obviously no problem in determining the cat's feminine sex (and pronoun), supposing she either had kittens, or was under an enchantment and changed into a beautiful young woman when the spell was broken, as in the Swiss/Austrian story behind Mme d'Aulnoy's 'The White Cat', familiar to us from Andrew Lang's *Blue Fairy Book*.

But in at least a third of the stories, there was no such indication, and it was up to the translator to make a choice. Several of these stories were purely animal fable, involving several species of creatures displaying various kinds of typical characteristics and/or, with the shift of emphasis proper to the genre, various kinds of human folly. Take a story (and there was more than one) involving the contrasted conduct of cat and dog. It so happens that English convention goes along with German grammatical gender here; I agreed with the book's English editor that we would automatically make a dog masculine and a cat feminine if a contrast were called for. Outgoing, straightforward masculinity ... sly, unpredictable femininity ... dear me, can that be it? (The sexist waters are definitely beginning to rise, and I shall shortly be obliged to dip at least a toe into them.) Fair enough, anyway: those are the conventions of the language once you have dog and cat in the same story. But cat and mouse are not so clear-cut. And what about cat and lion in one story, or cat and lamb and cockerel?

Perhaps all this seems very trifling, but it can be a delicate matter to try striking the right note where the nature of the target language means that, once struck, that note will sound a little louder than before. 'Bottom, thou art translated,' perhaps, but with these animals it is in the opposite direction – from animal into something with a slightly more human (or with 'it', more inhuman) set of associations than in the original.

I have just had to make a number of such choices for a book in one of those fields where the borders between children's and adult fiction become remarkably blurred: fantasy, science fiction, allegory, those genres which I suppose appeal basically to an appetite for the marvellous, but tend to work best when they don't go right over the top, when one senses some kind of solid framework beneath the fantasy, often calling on our vague feeling that there is still validity in the ancient myths. In the wake of German translations of Tolkien, and especially of the great success of Michael Ende's *The Neverending Story*, a number of publishers in Germany were encouraged to put out vast fantasy novels. Some of these were rather obviously imitations – not of Ende, actually, but of Tolkien; one guesses they had been lying around for some little while until the publishing climate seemed right. The one upon which I was working in 1985, Hans Bemmann's *The Stone and the Flute*, is particularly long, but does not strike me as derivative, though it certainly has that firm underlying foundation of Indo-European myth and legend I mentioned above. As the extremely flawed central character, inheritor of the magic stone and flute of the title, progresses through his life and a number of complex adventures, learning painfully from them, so that (as Sybil Gräfin von Schönfeldt has said in *The Times Literary Supplement*) his story becomes a true *Bildungsroman*, the reader is also offered stories within stories, pictures in depth of various societies (hierarchic, nomadic, agricultural), figures of myth such as shape-changers, water spirits, werewolves – and a great many animals with whom the hero finds he can converse when he himself is changed into a faun. These beasts and birds retain their animal nature, but once they begin to use human speech, they require pronouns beyond 'it'.

Some (as with those cat stories) were obvious; there is a company of brave mice, whose various sexes are made clear by the context in which they feature. Some are not: the blackbird was a problem, *die Amsel*, a feminine noun in German, but was I right in thinking it is generally the male bird that does the singing? And this blackbird's particular function was to sing, communicating thus with the previous owner of the magic flute. I am not much of an ornithologist; I consulted bird books and they did say cautiously that the singer is usually the male bird. Yet the emphasis seemed to shift too strongly if I definitely made that blackbird 'he' throughout; I tried playing this one by ear, avoiding pronouns wherever possible. Then there is a toad, a toad with a caustic tongue. The toad, again, is a noun of the feminine gender, and I did not have much hesitation in keeping her that way in English; she just felt like a female toad to me.

More difficult was the case of the falcon. There had been a good many falcons earlier in the story, since hawking as a pastime plays some part; but the problematical bird is an enchanted girl, a perilous maiden, who, horrified by her bridegroom's appearance (the central character is a hairy man) and by sexuality in general, casts the faun spell on him before she herself is trapped into falcon shape by her own magic. 'Falcon' is a masculine noun in German; we do not know at first when the bird appears to the hero in his dreams, what is to happen, so that 'he' seemed the correct pronoun, and yet later it becomes obvious that these dreams are a foreshadowing of what is to come and bird and girl are the same. In the end, I found it necessary to make it clear once or twice more than in the German that the strange falcon, much discussed by genuine birds and beasts, is a female, so that I could then stick firmly to 'she'.

The mice in that particular book sorted themselves out, with occasional use of the less common noun for a male mouse, and enough contextual clues to biological sex, as when in discussion an elderly female mouse gets up and robustly tells the male mice off for indulging in too much talk and not enough action: just like a man, she says, and is respectfully addressed by the mouse leader as Mother of our council. It was a much less clear-cut issue in a picture book by Erwin Moser, *The Happy Beaver*, in which the beaver (masculine gender in German) is accompanied on his adventures by a friendly mouse. I made the mouse 'she', but there is nothing really in the text to indicate a female. Yet 'she' felt right. I found myself having to justify this, and in the process working out *why* I thought 'she' felt right, I suppose I was partly influenced by the grammatical gender of the original, partly by a wish to have the main characters of different sexes, and – yes, I suppose it was also partly that the main character of the beaver seemed male, the subordinate character of the mouse female...

I know, I know. And indeed, to have to make a choice of pronoun necessarily entailed an emphasis not present in the original. But if that is the feel of the book, it is not really up to the translator to step in. I do sometimes envy the users of language with grammatical gender for this very ability to avoid sexist undertones. There is no need for the Germans to bother about chairpeople; they have only to add the appropriate article and adjectival ending to the word employed. There is no need for them to bother about 'mankind' or to employ a made-up word such as 'humankind', having an unexceptionable word in *Menschheit*, feminine in gender.

Change of attitude, it seems to me, more naturally precedes change in linguistic usage than the other way around: and changes tend to take place at their own rate. Recently I was tracking down the literary roots of Tchaikovsky's ballet *Swan Lake*: they are very tenuous roots, but such as they are, they exist in a complicated pre-Romantic extravaganza by the 18th-century J.K.A. Musäus, featuring a couple of hermits, two swan maidens in successive generations, and a quantity of dreadful remarks uttered by these ladies to the effect that 'life, you know, is over for our sex, once Youth and Beauty are fled' (the swan maiden referred to, or by then ex-swan maiden, as she is the mother of the new youthful model, must be about 35, poor decrepit soul). Obviously no one would now, a couple of centuries later, write in such terms, the accepted commonplaces of their time as imposed by Musäus on his partly traditional sources, but the process whereby such observations became unacceptable was gradual.

However, I had an example not long since of a much more rapid change of attitude affecting one's choice of language, though this was a matter of style rather than words themselves. A couple of years ago, when one of the London Boroughs aroused some controversy (and a fair amount of ridicule) by accusing Tintin and Astérix of racism, I felt rather indignant on Astérix's behalf, since the only possible basis for the attack was in the character of one of the pirates who put in regular guest appearances: a black man, who, in French, uses the colonial French accent known as '*petit-nègre*', pidgin French. This accent was judged unacceptable in English; that surprises French people, to whom I have several times had to explain the point. In the Parisian theatre, said one young woman who had never thought of it that way before, there is a comic whose act depends largely on the *petit-nègre* accent. Anyway, much effort, over the years, has gone into making up new and extra jokes to replace that pirate's accent, where the original could get a simple laugh out of his inability to pronounce the letter '*r*'.

But we began to make that effort *after* publication of the first four titles, when an American edition of the English translations of the saga was on the cards. At the time American sensitivity was rather greater than that in Britain. Thus, in three of those early *Astérix* translations the English equivalent of the French accent had been used, and still stood. (The character didn't appear in the first book at all.) I was brought face to face with it when rereading *Astérix in Britain* for the purposes of the radio show mentioned above. I was absolutely horrified; I reached for the phone to ring our *Astérix* editor at Hodder and say that the London Borough of Brent was perfectly correct about these particular passages, and I thought we'd better do something about it. So, starting with the radio script itself, and proceeding to new wording of the passages concerned for the next reprints of those three titles, we did do something about it, obliterating the accent and providing new allusions in line with subsequent practice. And yet, back at the end of the 1960s, there had seemed nothing wrong, from the translation angle, in just following the French original, though I think we were quite glad to have the excuse of America for abandoning that method and adopting a freer style of translation on this point.

Which I fear goes to show that it is particularly difficult to produce a translation that won't date. At the time of writing or indeed translating, one can't by definition see what *will* date, or one would avoid it. I suspect, however, that forced change to the language is still no good unless, perhaps, in a work intended to be didactic rather than literary. And of course, if one is translating such a work, one must, as always, find a style to parallel what the original author aimed to do in the original language ... but then again, has our *Astérix* translation gone beyond its brief in abandoning that pirate's accent? The arguments become circular.

But I feel (or think that I feel, for this is indeed a delicate and ever-shifting linguistic area) that determinedly saying 'humankind' is different from discovering that a *petit-nègre* accent has come to read badly. However, if to eschew the use of such an accent now seems natural and desirable, will the use of 'humankind' rather than 'mankind' eventually come to seem equally natural and desirable? I believe the difference, in my own mind, resides in the distinction between choice of style and the attempted alteration of words themselves, the actual building blocks of the language. (Just look at the trouble the purist French have in trying to banish *franglais*, once accepted, from their own language.) But give it another hundred years or so, and such a distinction could seem meaningless.

Delicate matters, yes. *Fingerspitzengefühl*, a nice German word, meaning sensitivity, instinct, but literally fingertip feeling, that is what one is after, and supposing the original text is good, the translation never comes out quite as good as one could wish. Perhaps that is only as it should be, and the text that can actually be improved by translation is not worth translating in the first place ...

Note

1. This article first appeared in *Signal*, 49.

Notes on Contributors

Anthea Bell has had a long and distinguished career as a translator, primarily from German and French. She has received a number of translation awards, including the 2002 Schlegel-Tieck Award for translation from German (UK), the Independent Foreign Fiction Prize (UK), and the Helen and Kurt Wolff Prize (USA). For the translation of children's books she has been awarded the Certificate of Honour in the Hans Christian Andersen translators' honour list (three times), the US Mildred L. Batchelder Award, and the UK Marsh Award for Children's Literature in Translation (twice).

David Blamires has recently retired as Professor of German at Manchester University. Children's literature has been a major interest throughout his academic career; he has researched early translations into English of the tales of the Brothers Grimm and the impact of German writing on British Children's Literature 1780–1918.

Mieke Desmet wrote her doctoral thesis on Comparative Children's Literature at University College London; she also holds an MA in Children's Literature from Roehampton University. Her doctoral research investigated the effects of literary status – from popular fiction to classics – on the translation of English-language girls' fiction into Dutch. She is currently lecturing at Feng Chia University, Taiwan.

Marisa Fernández López is a Senior Lecturer in the Faculty of Education of the University of León (Spain). Her research fields include comparative literature and children's literature in translation. She is the author of *Traducción y Literatura Juvenil* (1996) and many research papers in those fields. She is currently involved in an inter-university project: an in-depth study of literary censorship during Franco's dictatorship.

Cathy Hirano is a translator from Japanese to English who specialises in children's books. Her translation of *The Friends* won for her publisher the US 1997 Mildred L. Batchelder Award for the translation of a book originally published in a foreign language.

Nancy K. Jentsch teaches German and Spanish at Northern Kentucky University. She has translated poetry and edited an anthology of poetry written in German by women living in the US, *In Her Mother's Tongue*, 1983.

Gillian Lathey is Reader in Children's Literature at Roehampton University. Combining interests in children, childhood and literature, she now teaches children's literature at undergraduate and Masters levels, supervises PhD students undertaking children's literature projects, and researches the practices and history of translating for children. She also administers the biennial Marsh Award for Children's Literature in Translation.

Eithne O'Connell is Senior Lecturer in Translation Studies at the Centre for Translation and Textual Studies at Dublin City University and the author of *Minority Language Dubbing for Childrn* (Bern: Peter Lang, 2003). She is a founder member of the Irish Translators' and Interpreters' Association and the European Association for Studies in Screen Translation.

Riitta Oittinen teaches translation at the Universities of Helsinki and Tampere in Finland, where she is Senior Lecturer (University of Tampere) and has been senior scientist (2001–2002, Finnish Academy). Riitta is the author and editor of several books on translation, and of over 100 articles, including translating for children and teaching translation. She is also a published author, translator and illustrator of children's books and has produced 40 animated films. Her current interests include multimedia and translation, translating picture books, and translating Finnish children's literature into English.

Emer O'Sullivan graduated from University College Dublin and continued her postgraduate studies at the Freie Universität Berlin where she wrote her doctoral thesis on the aesthetic potential of national stereotypes in children's literature. She has been teaching and researching at the Institut für Jugendbuchforschung at the Johann Wolfgang Goethe-Universität in Frankfurt since 1990, and is now Professor of English at the University of Lüneburg, Germany.

Tiina Puurtinen, PhD, is Lecturer in English at the Savonlinna School of Translation Studies at the University of Joensuu, Finland. In addition to children's literature and translation, her research interests include relations between ideology, language and translation, and both corpus-based and manual comparison of translation vs. non-translated Finnish texts.

Karen Seago is Senior Lecturer in Translation Studies at London Metropolitan University. Her monograph *Transculturations: Making Sleeping Beauty; The Translation of a Grimm Märchen into an English Fairy Tale in the Nineteenth Century* is forthcoming with Wayne State University Press (Detroit). Future research projects focus on proto-feminist translation strategies in 19th century translations of German fairy tales.

Zohar Shavit is full Professor of the Unit for Culture Research, Tel Aviv University and is a world authority in the fields of The Child's Culture, the History of Israeli Culture and relations between the German and Jewish cultures. She has also translated several children's books into Hebrew, including E.B. White's *Charlotte's Web* for which she received the Hans Christian Andersen Medal for distinguished translation.

J.D. Stahl is Associate Professor of English at Virginia Tech, and also teaches at Hollins University. He specialises in comparative studies of German and English-language children's literature and has published widely on the subject.

Birgit Stolt is retired professor of German at the University of Stockholm. She has written on the philology of older texts, particularly those of Martin Luther; on text linguistics, rhetoric, stylistics, translation in theory and practice, and discourse analysis.

References

Primary texts

Ahlberg, J. and A. (1986/1997) *The Jolly Postman or Other People's Letters*. London: Heinemann.

Ahlberg, J. and A. (1987/1997) *De Puike Postbode of: Briefgeheimpjes* (Ernst van Altena, trans.). Bloemendaal: Gottmer.

Ahlberg, J. and A. (1991/1996) *The Jolly Christmas Postman*. London: Heinemann.

Ahlberg, J. and A. (1992) *De Puike Pakket Post* (Ernst van Altena, trans.). Bloemendaal: Gottmer.

Ahlberg, J. and A. (1995) *The Jolly Pocket Postman*. London: Heinemann.

Ahlberg, J. and A. (1996) *De Piepkleine Puike Postbode* (Ernst van Altena, trans.). Bloemendaal: Gottmer.

Baum, L.F. (1982) *The Wizard of Oz*. New York: Galahad Books.

Baum, L.F. (1977) *Ozin velho* (Kersti Juva, trans.). Keuruu: Kustannusosakeyhtiö Otava.

Baum, L.F. (1977) *Oz-maan taikuri* (Marja Helanen-Ahtola, trans.). Hämeenlinna: Arvi A.Karisto Oy.

Bechstein, L. (1967) *Fairy Tales of Ludwig Bechstein* (Anthea Bell, trans.). London: Andersen Press.

Bemmann, Hans (1986) *The Stone and the Flute* (Anthea Bell, trans.). London: Viking.

Bierbaum, O.J. (1905) *Zäpfel Kerns Abenteuer. Eine deutsche Kasperlegeschichte in dreiundvierzig Kapiteln. Frei nach Collodis italienischer Puppenhistorie Pinocchio.* Köln: Hermann Schaffstein.

Blyton, E. (1948/1986) *Five Go off to Camp*. London: Hodder & Stoughton.

Blyton, E. (1950/1990) *Five Fall into Adventure*. London: Hodder & Stoughton.

Blyton, E. (1952/1986) *The O'Sullivan Twins*. London: Dragon.

Blyton, E. (1959/1986) *Five Fall into Adventure*. Hodder and Stoughton.

Blyton, E. (1960/1985) *Las Mellizas O'Sullivan*. Barcelona: Molino.

Blyton, E. (1965/1985) *Los Cinco van de camping*. Barcelona: Juventud.

Blyton, E. (1966/1990) *Los Cinco frente a la aventura*. Barcelona: Juventud.

Blyton, E. (1981) *Five Get into Trouble* (Betty Maxey, illust.). London: Hodder and Stoughton.

Burningham, J. and Korschunow, I. (1984) *Mein Opa und ich*. Zürich, Schwäbisch Hall: Parabel.

Burningham, J. (1984) *Granpa*. London: Jonathan Cape.

Burningham, J. (1988) *Grosspapa*. Aus dem Englischen von Rolf Inhauser. Von John Burningham autorisierte Ausgabe. Aarau, Frankfurt/M, Salzburg: Sauerländer.

Carroll, L. (1865) *Alice's Adventures in Wonderland* (John Tenniel, illust.). London: Macmillan.

Carroll, L. (1949) *Alicens Abenteuer im Wunderland*. Aus dem Englischen übertragen von Franz Sester (Charlotte Strech-Ballot, illust.). Düsseldorf.

244

Carroll, L. (1963) *Alice im Wunderland*. Übersetzt und mit einem Nachwort von Christian Enzensberger (John Tenniel, illust.). Frankfurt: Insel.

Carroll, L.(1981) *Alice's Adventures in Wonderland and Through the Looking Glass* (John Tenniel, illust.). New York: Bantam Books

Carroll, L. (1992) *Alice in Wonderland* (2nd edn) (D. Gray, ed.). Norton Critical Edition. London: W.W. Norton.

Chambers, A. (1982) *Dance on my Grave*. London: Bodley Head.

Collodi, C. (1904) *The Adventures of Pinocchio* (Walter H. Cramp, trans.). Boston: Ginn.

Collodi, C. (1996) *The Adventures of Pinocchio: A New Translation by Ann Lawson Lucas*. The World's Classics. Oxford, New York: Oxford University Press.

Comenius, J.A. (1659) *Orbis Sensualium Pictus* (Charles Hoole, trans.). London: J. Kirton.

Crompton, R. (1922/1984) *Just William*. Newnes. Newnes/London: Macmillan.

Crompton, R. (1931/1985) *William's Crowded Hours*. Newnes/London: Macmillan.

Crompton, R. (1935/1968) *Travesuras de Guillermo*. Barcelona: Molino.

Crompton, R. (1959/1970) *Guillermo el atareado*. Barcelona: Molino.

Dahl, R. (1978/1988) *Charlie y la fábrica de chocolate*. Madrid: Alfaguara.

Dahl, R. (1985) *Charlie and the Chocolate Factory*. Harmondsworth: Puffin.

de Brunhoff, J. (1933) *The Story of Babar the Little Elephant* (Merle S. Haas, trans.). New York: Random House.

de Brunhoff, J. (1934) *The Story of Babar the Little Elephant* (trans. not acknowledged). London: Methuen.

de Brunhoff, J. (1979) *Histoire de Babar le petit elephant*. Paris: Librairie Hachette.

de Brunhoff, J. (1989) *The Story of Babar the Little Elephant*. London: Mammoth.

Donnelly, E. (1980) *So Long, Grandpa* (Anthea Bell, trans.). London: Andersen Press.

Fährmann, Willi (1985) *The Long Journey of Lukas B.* (Anthea Bell, trans.). London: Andersen Press.

Gay. M. (1986) *Papa Vroum*, Paris: L'école des loisirs.

Gay, M. (1987) *Night Ride* (story adapted from the French by Margo Lundell). New York: Morrow.

Grimm, J. and W. (1812, 1815) *Kinder- und Hausmärchen* (2 vols). Berlin: Realschulbuchhandlung.

Hoffmann, H. (1984) *Der Struwwelpeter Polyglott* (W. Sauer, ed.). Munich: Deutscher Taschenbuch Verlag.

Kästner, E. (1929) *Emil und die Detektive. Ein Roman für Kinder* (Walter Trier, illust.). Berlin: Williams & Co.

Kästner, E. (1931) *Emil and the Detectives* (Margaret Goldsmith, trans.). London: Jonathan Cape.

Kästner, E. (1959) *Emil and the Detectives* (Eileen Hall, trans.). London: Penguin.

Lindgren, A. (1945) *Pippi Långstrump* (Ingrid Vang Nyman, illust.). Stockholm: Rabén & Sjögren.

Lindgren, A. (1949/1965) *Pippi Langstrumpf*. Deutsch von Cäcilie Heinig (Walter Scharnweber, illust.). Hamburg: Oetinger.

Lindgren, A. (1972) Om barnböcker. In L. Furuland, Ö. Lindberger and M. Ørvig (eds) *Barnlitteratur I Sverige. Lösnungför barn och barnboksprogram* (pp. 366ff.). Stockholm: Wahlström & Widstrand.

Lofting, H. (1920/1988) *The Story of Doctor Dolittle*. New York: Dell.

Lofting, H. (1967/1989) *La Historia del Doctor Dolittle*. Madrid: Espasa Calpe.

Milne, A.A. (1926) *Winnie-the-Pooh* (with decorations by E.H. Shepard). London: Methuen.

Milne, A.A. (1989) *Pu der Bär*. Gesamtausgabe. Aus dem Englischen von Harry Rowohlt. Zeichnung von E.H. Shepard. Hamburg: Dressler.

Morgenstern, C. (1995) *Lullabies, Lyrics and Gallows Songs* (Lisbeth Zwerger, illust.; Anthea Bell. trans.). New York: North-South Books.

Moser, E. (1983) *The Happy Beaver* (Anthea Bell, trans.). London: Patrick Hardy.

Nesbit, E. (1899) *The Story of the Treasure Seekers. Being the Adventures of the Bastable Children in Search of a Fortune*. London: Fisher Unwin.

Nesbit, E. (1907) *The Enchanted Castle*. London: Fisher Unwin.

Park, B. (1989) *My Mother Got Married (and Other Disasters)*. New York: Knopf.

Park, B. (1991) *Charly und drei Nervensägen*. Aus dem Amerikanischen von Ulla Neckenauer. Würzburg: Arena.

Rowling, J.K. (1997) *Harry Potter and the Philosopher's Stone*. London: Bloomsbury.

Rowling, J.K. (1998) *Harry Potter and the Sorcerer's Stone*. New York: Scholastic.

Rowling, J.K. (1998) *Harry Potter à l'école des sorciers* (Jean-François Ménard, trans.). Paris: Gallimard Jeunesse.

Rowling, J.K (1998) *Harry Potter und der Stein der Weisen* (Klaus Fritz, trans.). Hamburg: Carlsen.

Rowling, J.K. (1998) *Harry Potter and the Chamber of Secrets*. London: Bloomsbury.

Rowling, J.K. (1999) *Harry Potter y la piedra filosofal* (Alicia Dellepiano, trans.). Barcelona: Emecé Editores.

Rowling, J.K. (1999) *Harry Potter et la Chambre des Secrets* (Jean-François Ménard, trans.). Paris: Gallimard Jeunesse.

Rowling, J.K. (1999) *Harry Potter and the Prisoner of Askaban*. London: Bloomsbury.

Rowling, J.K. (1999) *Harry Potter und der Gefangene von Askaban* (Klaus Fritz, trans.). Hamburg: Carlsen.

Rowling, J.K. (2000) *Harry Potter and the Goblet of Fire*. London: Bloomsbury.

Spyri, J. (1912) *Heimatlos: Two Stories for Children and for Those who Love Children* (Emma Stelter Hopkins, trans.). Boston: Ginn and Company.

Spyri J. (1949) *Heidi* (with drawings by Janet and Anne Johnstone). London: The Heirloom Library.

Spyri J. (1955) *Heidi* (a new translation by M. Rosenbaum). Glasgow: Collins Clear-Type Press.

Spyri, J. (1978) *Heidi*. Vollständige und ungekürzte Ausgabe in einem Band (Paul Hey, illust.) (2nd edn). Aufl. Frankfurt: Insel.

Taylor, J.E. (1846) *The Fairy Ring: A New Collection of Tales, Translated from the German of Jacob and Wilhelm Grimm*. London: John Murray.

Twain, M. (1935) *Slovenly Peter [Der Struwwelpeter]: Translated into English Jingles from the Original German of Dr Heinrich Hoffmann*. New York: The Marchbanks Press.

Twain, M. (1977) *A Tramp Abroad* (Charles Neider, ed.). New York: Harper & Row.

Twain, M. (1985) *Adventures of Huckleberry Finn* (Walter Blair and Victor Fischer, eds). Berkeley, CA: University of California Press.

Twain, M. (1993) *The Adventures of Tom Sawyer* (Lee Clark Mitchell, ed.). World's Classics. Oxford: Oxford University Press.

Yumoto, K. (1996) *The Friends* (C. Hirano, trans.). New York: Farrar, Straus and Giroux.

Yumoto, K. (1999) *The Spring Tone* (C. Hirano, trans.). New York: Farrar, Straus and Giroux.

Critical Literature

Anderman, G. and Rogers, M. (eds) (1999) *Word, Text, Translation*. Clevedon: Multilingual Matters.

Applebee, A. (1978) *The Child's Concept of Story*. Chicago: Chicago University Press.

Ashton, S. and Petersen, A. (1995) Fetching the jingle along: Mark Twain's *Slovenly Peter*. *Children's Literature Association Quarterly* 20 (1), 36–41.

Assmann, A. (1983) Schriftliche Folklore. Zur Entstehung und Funktion eines Überlieferungstyps. In A. and J. Assmann and C. Hradmeier (eds) *Schrift und Gedächtnis. Beiträge zur Archäologie der literarischen Kommunikation* (pp.175–193). München: Fink.

Attali, J. (1985) *Noise. A Political Economy of Music* (Brian Massumi, trans.). Minneapolis: University of Minnesota Press.

Auerbach, N. (1982) *Woman and the Demon: The Life of a Victorian Myth*. Cambridge, MA: Harvard University Press.

Bakhtin, M. (1984) *Rabelais and his World*. Bloomington, IN: Indiana University Press.

Bakhtin, M. (1987) *Problems of Dostoevsky's Poetics* (C. Emerson, ed. and trans.). Minneapolis: University of Minnesota Press.

Bakhtin, M. (1990a) Discourse in the novel. In C. Emerson and M. Holquist (eds) *Bakhtin, The Dialogic Imagination: Four Essays*. Austin: University of Texas.

Bakhtin, M. (1990b) *Mikhail Bakhtin. Creation of a Prosaics*. Stanford: Stanford University Press.

Bamberger, R. (1961) Das Bild der Welt in der deutschen Jugendlektüre. In *Jugendbücher bauen Brücken. Berichte über die VI. Mainau-Jugendbuchtagung 1960* (pp. 33–50). Konstanz.

Bamberger, R. (1978) The influence of translation on the development of national children's literature. In G. Klingberg and M. Ørvig (eds) *Children's Books in Translation* (pp. 19–27). Stockholm: Almqvist and Wiksell.

Barrena, P. *et al.* (comps) (1990) *Corrientes Actuales de la Narrativa Infantil y Juvenil Española en Lengua Castellana*. Madrid: Asociación Española de Amigos del Libro Infantil y Juvenil.

Bassnett, S. (1991) *Translation Studies*. New York: Routledge.

Bassnett, S. (1993) *Comparative Literature: A Critical Introduction*. Oxford: Blackwell.

Bassnett, S. and Lefevere, A. (1998) *Constructing Culture: Essays on Literary Translation*. Clevedon: Multilingual Matters.

Bawden, N. (1974) A dead pig and my father. *Children's Literature in Education* 5, 3–13.

Bell, A. (1980) Translator's notebook. In N. Chambers (ed.) *The Signal Approach to Children's Books* (pp.129–139). London: Kestrel.

Bell, A. (1985) Translator's notebook: The naming of names. *Signal* 46, 3–11.

Bell, A. (1986) Translator's notebook: Delicate matters. *Signal* 49, 17–26.

Ben-Ari, N. (1992) Didactic and pedagogic tendencies in the norms dictating the translation of children's literature: The case of postwar German–Hebrew translations. *Poetics Today* 13 (1), 221–230

Bermejo, A. (1999) *La Literatura Infantil en España*. Madrid: Asociación Española de Amigos del Libro Infantil y Juvenil.

Bettelheim, B. (1976) *The Uses of Enchantment*. New York: Knopf.

Bordet, G. (1985) Traduction et littérature pour enfants: Soeurs jumelles ou parentes pauvres? In D. Escarpit (ed.) *Attention! Un livre peut en cacher un autre ... (traduction et adaptation en littérature d'enfance et de jeunesse)* (pp. 27–33). Pessac: Nous voulons lire!

Briggs, J. (1989) Reading children's books. *Essays in Criticism* XXVIX (1), 1–17.

Bromley, H. (1996) Spying on picture books: Exploring intertextuality with young children. In M. Styles and V. Watson (eds) *Talking Pictures: Pictorial Texts and Young Readers* (pp. 101–111). London: Hodder & Stoughton.

Broms, H. (1985) *Alkukuvien jälhillä: Kulttuurin semiotikkaa.* Juva: WSOY.

Brossard, N. (1988) *The Aerial Letter* (M. Wildeman, trans.). Toronto: The Women's Press.

Cadogan, M. (1994) *Just William, Through the Ages.* London: Macmillan.

Caws, M. (1989) *The Art of Interference. Stressed Readings in Verbal and Visual Texts.* Princeton, NJ: Princeton University Press.

Cech, J. (1986) The triumphant transformations of Pinocchio. In F. Butler and R. Rotert (eds) *Triumphs of the Spirit in Children's Literature* (pp. 171–177). Hamden, CT: Lib. Professional Pub.

Chatman, S. (1978) *Story and Discourse: Narrative Structure in Fiction and Film.* Ithaca: Cornell University Press.

Chatman, S. (1990) *Coming to Terms: The Rhetoric of Narrative in Fiction and Film.* Ithaca: Cornell University Press.

Chester, T.R. (1989) *Children's Books Research: A Practical Guide to Techniques and Sources.* South Woodchester: Thimble.

CRW (Children's Rights Workshop) (1976) *Racism and Sexism in Children's Books.* London: Writers and Readers Publishing Cooperative.

Cohn, D. (1978) *Transparent Minds: Narrative Modes for Presenting Consciousness in Fiction.* Princeton: Princeton University Press.

Collinson, R. (1973) The children's author and his readers. *Children's Literature in Education* 4 (19), 37–49.

Colomer, T. (1994) A favor de la niñas: El sexismo en la literatura infantil. *Cuadernos de Literatura Infantil y juvenil (CLIJ)* 57, 7–21.

Colomer, T. (1998) *La Formación del Lector Literario: Narrativa infantil y juvenil actual.* Madrid: Fundación Germán Sánchez Ruipérez.

Company, F. (1993) Enid Blyton: Un fenómeno sociológico. *Cuadernos de Literatura Infantil y juvenil (CLIJ)* 50, 48–54.

Davies, E. (2003) A goblin or a dirty nose? The treatment of culture-specific references in translations of the Harry Potter books. *The Translator: Studies in Intercultural Communication* (9) 1, 65–101.

Demers, P. and Moyles, G. (eds) (1982) *From Instruction to Delight: An Anthology of Children's Literature to 1850.* Toronto: Oxford UP.

Dixon, B. (1977) *Catching them Young 1: Sex, Race and Class in Children's Fiction.* London: Pluto.

Dixon, B. (1977) *Catching them Young 2: Political Ideas in Children's Fiction.* London: Pluto.

Doderer, K. and Müller, H. (eds) (1973) *Das Bilderbuch.* Weinheim: Beltz.

Doderer, K. (1986) Wie sollte ein internationales Netzwerk der Kinder- und Jugendliteratur aussehen? *Mitteilungen des Instituts für Jugendbuchforschung* 3, 10–17.

Dollerup, C. (2003) Translation for reading aloud. *Meta Translators' Journal* 48 (1–2), 81–103.

Dundes, A. (1982) *Cinderella: A Casebook*. Wisconsin: University of Wisconsin Press.

Du-Nour, M. (1995) Retranslation of children's books as evidence of changes of norms. *Target* 7 (2), 327–346.

Dyrenfurth-Graebsch, I. (1942) *Geschichte des deutschen Jugendbuches*. Leipzig: Harrassowitz.

Escarpit, D. (ed.) (1985) *Attention! Un livre peut en cacher un autre ... (traduction et adaptation en littérature d'enfance et de jeunesse)*. Pessac: Nous voulons lire!

Even-Zohar, B. (1992) Translation policy in Hebrew children's literature: The case of Astrid Lindgren. *Poetics Today* 13 (1), 231–45.

Even-Zohar, I. (1978) *Papers in Historical Poetics*. Tel Aviv: Porter Institute for Poetics and Semiotics.

Even-Zohar, I. (1979) Polysystems theory. *Poetics Today* 1, 237–310.

Even-Zohar, I. (1981) Translation theory today. *Poetics Today* 2, 1–7.

Ewers, H.H. (1990) Die Grenzen literarischer Kinder- und Jugendbuchkritik. In B. Scharioth and J. Schmidt (eds) *Zwischen allen Stühlen: zur Situation der Kinder- und Jugenbuchkritik* (pp. 75–91). Tutzing: evang. Akad.

Fernandez, J. (1986) Folklorists as agents of nationalism: Asturian legends and the problem of identity. In R.B. Bottigheimer (ed.) *Fairy Tales and Society, Illusion, Allusion and Paradigm* (pp. 133–48). Philadelphia: University of Pennsylvania Press.

Fernández López, M. (1996) *Traducción y Literatura Juvenil: Narrativa anglosajona contemporánea en España*. León: Universidad de León.

Fleischman, S. (1990) *Tense and Narrativity: From Medieval Performance to Modern Fiction*. London: Routledge.

Fox Weber, N. (1989) *The Art of Babar*. New York: Harry N. Abrams.

Freeman, T. (1977) Heinrich Hoffmann's *Struwwelpeter*: An inquiry into the effects of violence in children's literature. *Journal of Popular Culture* 10 (4), 808–820.

Freese, H. Ludwig (1992) *Lapset ovat filosofeja. Ajatusmatkoja kasvaville ja kasvattajille* (orig. *Kinder sind Philosophen*) (E. Wiegand, ed.). Jyväskylä: Gummerus.

Frey, C. and Griffith, J. (1987): *The Literary Heritage of Childhood: An Appraisal of Children's Classics in the Western Tradition*. Contributions to the Study of World Literature 20. New York: Westport.

Furuland, L. (1978) Sweden and the international children's book market: History and present situation. In G. Klingberg, M. Ørvig and S. Amor (eds) *Children's Books in Translation* (pp. 60–76). Stockholm: Almqvist and Wiksell.

Gadamer, H.G. (1976) *Kleine Schriften I Philosophie Hermeneutik (Sammlung)*. Tübingen: J.C.B. Mohr.

Gárate, A. (1997) Niños, niñas y libros. Las diferencias de género en la LIJ. *Cuadernos de Literatura Infantil y Juvenil (CLIJ)* 95, 7–17.

Garner, J.F. (1995) *Politically Correct Bedtime Stories: Modern Tales for Our Life and Times*. London: Macmillan.

Grumann, A. (1913) *Die Geschichte vom hölzernen Bengele: Lustig und lehrreich für kleine und große Kinder*. Nach C. Collodi deutsch bearbeitet von Anton Grumann. Freiburg: Herder.

Hancock, C.R. (1988) Musical notes to *The Annotated Alice*. *Children's Literature* 16, 1–29.

Hazard, P. (1932) *Les livres, les enfants et les hommes*. Paris: Flammarion.

Hazard, P. (1944) *Books, Children and Men* (Marguerite Mitchell, trans.). Boston: The Horn Book.

Hearne, B. (1991) Research in children's literature in the US and Canada: Problems and possibilities. The International Youth Library (ed.) *Children's Literature Research, International Resources and Exchange*. Munich: K.G. Saur.

Hermans, T. (1985) (ed.) *The Manipulation of Literature. Studies in Literary Translation*. London: Croom Helm.

Hermans, T. (1996) The translator's voice in translated narrative. *Target* 8 (1), 23–48.

Hildick, W. (1974) *Children and Fiction: A Critical Study in Depth of the Artistic and Psychological Factors Involved in Writing Fiction for and about Children* (rev. edn). London: Evans.

Hoffmann, H. (1985) *Lebenserinnnerungen*. Frankfurt: Insel-Verlag.

Hollindale, P. (1997) *Signs of Childness in Children's Books*. Stroud: Thimble Press.

Horne, R.H. (1851) A witch in the nursery. *Household Words* Sept. 20.

House, J. (1977) *A Model for Translation Quality Assessment*. Tübingen: Gunter Narr.

Hunt, P. (1991) *Criticism, Theory and Children's Literature*. Oxford: Blackwell.

Hunt, P. (ed.) (1992) *Literature for Children: Contemporary Criticism*. London: Routledge.

Index Translationum. Fourth Cumulative Edition (1979–1996). On WWW at http://www.unesco.org/culture/xtrans/html-eng/graph18.htm.

Iser, W. (1984) *Der Akt des Lesens. Theorie ästhetischer Wirkung* (2nd, rev. edn). Munich: Fink.

Iser, W. (1990) *The Implied Reader. Patterns of Communication in Prose Fiction from Bunyan to Beckett* (W. Iser, trans.). Baltimore: The Johns Hopkins University Press.

Jakobson, R. (1959) On linguistic aspects of translation. In R. Brower (ed.) *On Translation* (pp. 232–239). New York: Oxford University Press.

Klingberg, G. (1986) *Children's Fiction in the Hands of the Translators*. Malmo: CWK Gleerup.

Klingberg, G. and Ørvig, M. (1978) *Children's Books in Translation*. Stockholm: Almqvist and Wiksell.

M. and Malmkjaer, K. (1996) *Language and Control in Children's Literature*. London: Routledge.

Koller, W. (1972) *Grundprobleme der Übersetzungstheorie, unter besonderer Beruucksichtingung schwedisch-deutscher Übersetzungsfälle*. Bern und München: Peter Lang.

Koppen, E. (1980) Pinocchio im Reich des Simplicissius. Otto Julios Bierbaum als bearbeiter Collodis. In G. Schmidt und M. Tietz (eds) *Stimmen der Romania. Festschrift für W. Theodor Elwert zum 70. Geburtstag* (pp. 225–241). Wiesbaden: Heymann.

Lathey, G. (2005) The travels of Harry: International marketing and the translation of J.K. Rowling's Harry Potter books. *Lion and Unicorn* 29 (2), 141–151.

Lefevere, A. and Bassnett, S. (1998) Where are we in translation studies? In S. Bassnett (ed.) *Constructing Cultures: Essays on Literary Translation* (pp. 1–11). Clevedon: Cromwell.

Levý, J. (1969) *Die literarische Übersetzung. Theorie einer Kunstgattung*. Deutsch von Walter Schamschula. Frankfurt am Main: Athenäum.

Lewis, D. (2001) *Picturing Text: The Contemporary Children's Picturebook*. London: Routledge Falmer.

Liebs, E. (1977) *Die pädagogische Inse: Studien zur Rezeption des 'Robinson Crusoe' in deutschen Jugendbearbeitungen*. Stuttgart: Metzler.

Lindgren, A. (1969) Traduire des livres d'enfant: Est-ce possible? *Babel* 15 (2), 98–100.

de Lotbinière-Harwood, S. (1991) *Re-Belle et Infidèle. La Traduction comme pratique de réécriture au feminine/The Body Bilingual. Translation as Rewriting in the Feminine.* Toronto: The Women's Press.

MacLeod, A.S. (1994) *American Childhood: Essays on Children's Literature of the Nineteenth and Twentieth Centuries.* Athens: University of Georgia Press.

Marx, S. (1990) *Le Avventure tedesche di Pinocchio. Letture d'una storia senza frontiere.* Firenze: La Nuova Italia.

Mathieu-Colas, M. and M. (1983) *Le Dossier ... Club des Cinq (... The Famous Five d'Enid Blyton).* Breteuil-sur-Iton: Magnard/ L'École.

Menzies, J. (1950) *A Complete List of Books: Enid Blyton.* Edinburgh: Menzies.

Meyer, B.J.F. (1975) *The Organization of Prose and its Effects on Memory.* Amsterdam: North-Holland.

Miles, A.H. (1892) Preface to *Fifty-two Fairy Tales, Wonder Stories, Legends, Visions and Fables from German, Italian, Spanish, Swedish, Oriental, Classical, Ancient and Modern Sources, with Illustrations.* London: Hutchinson and Co.

Mohl, B. and Schack, M. (1981) *När barn läser. Litteraturupplevelse och fantasi.* Suodertälje: Gidlunds.

Moss, E. (1990) A certain particularity: An interview with Janet and Allan Ahlberg. *Signal* 61, 20–26.

Müller, G. (1968) *Morphologische Poetik* (Elena Müller, ed.). Tübingen: Niemeyer.

Munday, J. (2001) *Introducing Translation Studies.* London: Routledge.

Nead, L. (1990) *Myths of Sexuality.* Oxford: Blackwell.

Nel, P. (2001) *J.K. Rowling's Harry Potter Novels: A Reader's Guide.* New York: Continuum.

Nel, P. (2002) You say 'jelly', I say 'jell-o'? Harry Potter and the transfiguration of language. In L. Whited (ed.) *The Ivory Tower and Harry Potter* (pp. 261–284). Missouri: University of Missouri Press.

Newmark, P. (1991) *About Translation.* Clevedon: Multilingual Matters.

Nida, E. and Taber, C. (1969) *The Theory and Practice of Translation.* Leiden: Brill.

Nières, I. (1992) Livres d'enfants en Europe. In *Catalogue of the Exhibition at Château des Rohan, Pontivy* (pp. 9–17). Pontivy: Agence de Cooperation des Bibliothèques de Bretagne (COBB).

Nikolajeva, M. (1996) *Children's Literature Comes of Age: Toward a New Aesthetic.* New York and London: Garland.

Nikolajeva, M. and Scott, C. (2001) *How Picturebooks Work.* New York, London: Garland.

Nodelman, P. (1985) Interpretation and apparent sameness of children's novels. *Studies in the Literary Imagination* 18 (2), 5–20.

Nodelman, P. (1988) *Words about Pictures: The Narrative Art of Children's Picture Books.* Athens, GA: University of Georgia Press.

Nord, C. (1991) *Text Analysis in Translation: Theory, Methodology, and Didactic Application of a Model of Translation-Oriented Analysis* (C. Nord and P. Sparrow, trans.). Amsterdam, Atlanta: Rodopi.

Nöstlinger, C. (1988) *Der neue Pinocchio. Die Abenteuer des Pinocchio neu erzählt. Mit farbigen Bildern von Nikolaus Heidelbach.* Weinheim, Basel: Beltz.

O'Connell, E. (1999) Translating for children. In G. Anderman and M. Rogers (eds) *Word, Text, Translation* (pp. 208–216). Clevedon: Multilingual Matters

O'Connell, E. (2003) *Minority Language Dubbing for Children: Screen Translation from German to Irish.* Bern: Peter Lang.

Oittinen, R. (1988) Lastenkirjallisuuden kääntämisestä lapselle kääntämiseen: autoritaarisuudesta dialogisuuteen. Unpublished PhD dissertation, University of Tampere.

Oittinen, R. (1989) On translating for children: A Finnish point of view. *Early Child Development and Care* 48, 29–37.

Oittinen, R. (1990) The dialogic relation between text and illustration: A translatological view. *TEXTconTEXT* 5, 40–53.

Oittinen, R. (1993a) On the dialogics of translating for children. In C. Picken (ed.) *Translation: The Vital Link. XIII FIT World Congress* (pp. 10–16). London: Institute of Linguists.

Oittinen, R. (1993b) *I am Me – I am Other.* Tampere: University of Tampere.

Oittinen, R. (2000) *Translating for Children.* New York: Garland.

Olohan, M. (2004) *Introducing Corpora in Translation Studies.* London and New York: Routledge.

Onega, S. and Landa, G. (1996) *Narratology.* London: Longman.

Ørvig, M. (1981) Some international aspects of children's books. In B. Hearne and M. Kaye (eds) *Celebrating Children's Books: Essays on Children's Literature in Honor of Zena Sutherland* (pp. 218–240). New York: Lothrop Lee & Shepard.

O'Sullivan, E. (1993) The fate of the dual addressee in the translation of children's literature. *New Comparison* 16, 109–119.

O'Sullivan, E. (1998) Losses and gains in translation: Some remarks on the translation of humor in the books of Aidan Chambers (Anthea Bell, trans.). In E.L. Keyser (ed.) *Children's Literature* 26 (pp. 185–204). New Haven: Yale University Press.

O'Sullivan, E. (2000) *Kinderliterarische Komparatistik.* Heidelberg: C.Winter.

O'Sullivan, E. (2001) Alice in different Wonderlands: Varying approaches in the German translations of an English children's classic. In M. Meek (ed.) *Children's Literature and National Identity* (pp. 23–32). London: Trentham.

O'Sullivan, E. (2005) *Comparative Children's Literature* (Anthea Bell, trans.). London and New York: Routledge.

Painter, H.W. (1968) Translations of traditional and modern material. In H. Huus (ed.) *Evaluating Books for Children and Young People.* Newark, DE: International Reading Association.

Paley, V.G. (1981) *Wally's Stories: Conversations in the Kindergarten.* Cambridge, MA: Harvard University Press.

Perkins, J. (1989) *Women and Marriage in Nineteenth-Century England.* London and New York: Routledge.

Perrin, N. (1969) *Dr Bowdler's Legacy: A History of Expurgated Books in England and America.* New York: Atheneum.

Philip, N. (1989) *The Cinderella Story.* Harmondsworth: Penguin.

Piek-van Slooten, M. (ed.) (1990) *Boek en Jeugd '90/'91; Gids voor jeugdlektuur.* Den Haag: NBLC.

Prawer, S.S. (1973) *Comparative Literary Studies. An Introduction.* London: Duckworth.

Pullman, P. (1989) Invisible pictures. *Signal* 60, 156–186.

Puurtinen, T. (1989a) Two translations in comparison: A study on readability. In S. Condit and S. Tirkkonen-Condit (eds) *Empirical Studies in Translation and Lingusitics, Studies in Language.* Savonlinna: University of Joensuu.

Puurtinen, T. (1989b) Assessing acceptability in translated children's books. *Target* 1 (2), 201–213.

Puurtinen, T. (1995) *Linguistic Acceptability in Translated Children's Literature.* Joensuu: University of Joensuu.

Reiss, K. (1971) *Möglichkeiten und Grenzen der Übersetzungskritik.* München: Max Hueber.

Reiss, K. (1982) Zur Übersetzung von Kinder- und Jugendbüchern. *Lebende Sprachen* 1, 7–13.

Reiss, K. and Vermeer, H.J. (1984) *Grundlegung einer allgemeinen Translationstheorie.* Tübingen: Max Niemeyer.

Ricoeur, P. (1984) *Time and Narrative* (Vol. 1) (K. McLaughlin and D. Pellauer, trans.). Chicago: Chicago University Press.

Robyns, C. (ed.) (1994) *Translation and the (Re)production of Culture.* Leuven: CERA.

Rose, J. (1994) *The Case of Peter Pan: Or the Impossibility of Children's Fiction* (rev. edn). London: Macmillan.

Rosenblatt, L. (1978) *The Reader, the Text, the Poem: The Transactional Theory of the Literary Work.* Carbondale and Edwardsville: Southern Illinois University Press.

Rudvin, M. (1994) Translation and 'myth': Norwegian children's literature in English. *Studies in Translatology* 2 (2), 199–211.

Ruzicka, V., Vázquez, C., Garciá, M. and Herreo, E. (1995) *Evolución de la Literatura Infantil y Juvenil Británica y Alemana hasta el Siglo XX.* Vigo: Ediciones Cardeñoso.

Santucci, L. (1964) *Das Kind, sein Mythos und sein Märchen.* Aus dem Italienischen von Hansi Keßler. Berlin: Hermann Schroedel.

Schiavi, G. (1996) There is always a teller in a tale. *Target* 8 (1), 1–21.

Schwarcz, J. (1982) *Ways of the Illustrator: Visual Communication in Children's Literature.* Chicago: American Library Association.

Seitz, G. (1984) *Die Brüder Grimm, Leben, Werk, Zeit.* München: Winkler.

Shavit, Z. (1986) *Poetics of Children's Literature.* Athens: University of Georgia Press.

Shavit, Z. (1992) The study of children's literature: The poor state of the art. Why do we need a theory and why semiotics of culture? *Barnboken* 1, 2–9.

Stephens, J. (1992) *Language and Ideology in Children's Fiction.* London: Longman.

Stolt, B. (1978) How Emil becomes Michel: On the translation of children's books. In G. Klingberg (ed.) *Children's Books in Translation* (pp. 130–146). Stockholm: Almqvist and Wiksell.

Stone, A. Jr. (1961/1970) *The Innocent Eye: Childhood in Mark Twain's Imagination.* New Haven: Archon/Yale University Press.

Störig, H.J. (ed.) (1963) *Das Problem des Übersetzens.* Darmstadt:Wissenschaftliche Buchgesellschaft.

Surmatz, A. (1998) Kannibalen und Pistolen: die übersetzte Pippi Langstrumpf. *Der Rabe* 52, 136–140.

Tabbert, R. (ed.) (1991) *Kinderbuchanalysen II. Wirkung – Kultureller Kontext – Unterricht.* Frankfurt: dipa.

Tabbert, R. (2002) Approaches to the translation of children's literature: A review of critical studies since 1960. *Target 14* (2), 303–51.

Tellegen, S. and Coppejans, L. (1991) Imaginative reading. Research into imagination, reading behaviour and reading pleasure. Summary of report published in The Hague: Dutch Centre for Libraries and Literature.

Thomson-Wohlgemuth, G. (2003) Children's literature and translation under the East German regime. *Meta Translators' Journal* 48 (1–2), 241–249.

Toury, G. (1980) *In Search of a Theory of Translation.* Tel Aviv: Porter Institute for Poetics and Semiotics.

Toury, G. (1985) A rationale for descriptive translation studies. In T. Hermans (ed.) *The Manipulation of Literature. Studies in Literary Translation (pp.116–41).* London: Croom Helm.
Toury, G. (1995) *Descriptive Translation Studies and Beyond.* Amsterdam: John Benjamins.
Trelease, J. (1989) *The New Read-Aloud Handbook.* New York: Penguin Books.
van Altena, E. (1985) De vertaler als blikopener. *Nieuw Wereldtijdschrift II* 2, 51–55.
Vanhalewijn, M. (1997) Warme woorden en zoete inkt. Knisperende verhalen in wonderlijke brieven. *Standaard der Letteren,* 2 January, 10.
Venuti, L. (1995) *The Translator's Invisibility: A History of Translation.* London, New York: Routledge.
Venuti, L. (ed.) (2000) *The Translation Studies Reader* (M. Baker, advisory ed.). London: Routledge.
von Fieandt, K. (1972) *Havaitsemisen maailma.* Porvoo: WSOY.
Wall, B. (1991) *The Narrator's Voice: The Dilemma of Children's Fiction.* London: Macmillan.
Warner, M. (1994) *From the Beast to the Blonde: On Fairy Tales and their Tellers.* London: Chatto and Windus.
Weeks, J. (1990) *Sex, Politics and Society. The Regulation of Sexuality since 1800* (2nd edn). New York: Longman.
Weir, R.H. (1962) *Language in the Crib.* The Hague: Mouton.
Wells, G. (1987) *The Meaning Makers.* London: Hodder.
West, M.I. (1996) Censorship. In P. Hunt (ed.) *Encyclopedia of Children's Literature* (pp. 498–507). London: Routledge.
Whited, L. (2002) *The Ivory Tower and Harry Potter.* Missouri: University of Missouri Press.
Wollstonecraft, M. (1989) Elements of morality for the use of children. In J. Todd and M. Butler (eds) *The Works of Mary Wollstonecraft* (Vol. 5; pp. 1–210). London: William Pickering.
Worton, M. and Still, J. (1993) Introduction. In M. Worton and J. Still (eds) *Intertextuality: Theories and Practices* (pp. 1–44). Manchester: Manchester University Press.
Wunderlich, R. and Morrissey, P. (1982) The desecration of *Pinocchio* in the United States. Proceedings of the Eighth Annual Conference of the Children's Literature Association (pp. 106–18). University of Minnesota March 1981.
Wunderlich, R. (1992) The tribulations of Pinocchio: How social change can wreck a good story. *Poetics Today* 13 (2), 197–219.
Yngve, V.H. (1960) A model and hypothesis for language structure. *Proceedings of the American Philosophical Society* 5, 444–466.
Zipes, J. (1979) *Breaking the Magic Spell.* London: Peregrine.
Zipes, J. (1983a) *The Trials and Tribulations of Little Red Riding Hood. Versions of the Tale in Sociocultural Context.* London: Heinemann.
Zipes, J. (1983b) *Fairy Tales and the Art of Subversion: The Classical Genre for Children and the Process of Civilization.* London: Heinemann.
Zipes, J. (1986) The Grimms and the German obsession with fairy tales. In R.B. Bottigheimer (ed.) *Fairy Tales and Society, Illusion, Allusion and Paradigm* (pp. 133–48). Philadelphia: University of Pennsylvania Press.
Zipes, J. (1988) *The Brothers Grimm: From Enchanted Forests to the Modern World.* New York: Routledge.

Index

n/*ns* indicate endnote/s.

255